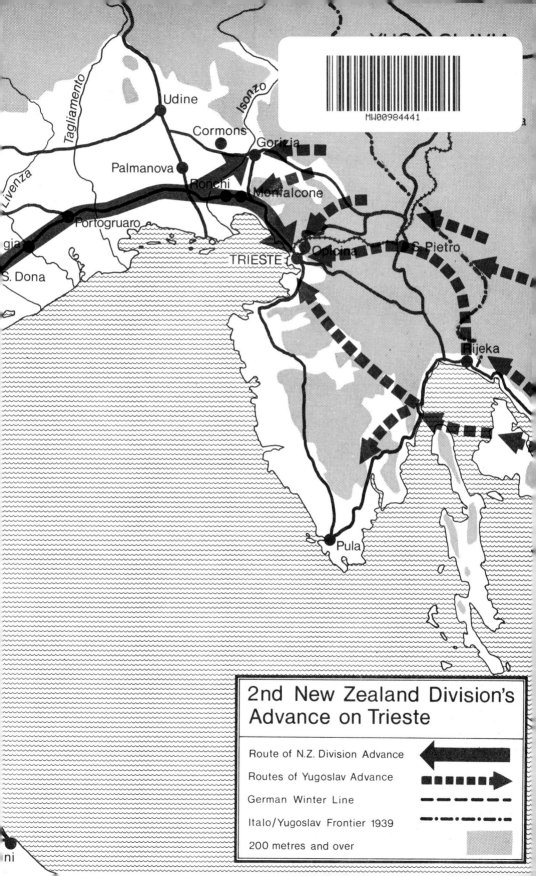

Udine

Tagliamento

Cormons

Isonzo

Gorizia

Palmanova

Ronchi

Montfalcone

Livenza

Portogruaro

S. Dona

gia

TRIESTE

Opicina

S. Pietro

Rijeka

Pula

YUGOSLAVIA

MW00984441

ni

2nd New Zealand Division's Advance on Trieste

Route of N.Z. Division Advance	←
Routes of Yugoslav Advance	▪▪▪▪▪►
German Winter Line	– – –
Italo/Yugoslav Frontier 1939	–·–·–
200 metres and over	▨

THE RACE FOR TRIESTE

THE RACE FOR TRIESTE

Geoffrey Cox

WILLIAM KIMBER · LONDON

First published in 1977 by
WILLIAM KIMBER & CO. LIMITED
Godolphin House, 22a Queen Anne's Gate,
London, SW1H 9AE

© Sir Geoffrey Cox, 1947, 1977

ISBN 0 7183 0375 X

Typeset by Watford Typesetters
and printed and bound in Great Britain by
The Garden City Press Limited,
Letchworth, Hertfordshire, SG6 1JS

Contents

List of Maps

Foreword

As the war drew to its end in the Mediterranean in the spring of 1945, two armies raced for Trieste. From the east the Yugoslav Fourth Army thrust up the Dalmatian coast. From the west the British Eighth Army attacked across the wide curve of the northern Italian coastline. Both were to reach the city almost simultaneously, to come face to face in the one corner of Europe where no demarcation line had been agreed upon in advance by the Allies.

The Yugoslavs were determined to hold Trieste, and its immediate hinterland, and incorporate them immediately into Yugoslavia. Britain and America were equally determined that this should not be done, that the fate of the area should not be settled prior to the peace conference.

This produced a highly dangerous situation. To the troops on the ground, of whom I was one, these dangers were apparent. We were told to prepare to fight, if need be. Indeed I spent VE Day drawing up orders for a possible battle with Tito's forces in Trieste. To the world outside, preoccupied with the end of the war in Europe, with the death of Hitler, with the continuing war with Japan, this Trieste crisis attracted little attention. Only thirty years later when the official documents became available – and in particular the papers of Churchill, of Truman, of the British Foreign Office and of the Mediterranean High Command – did the true dimensions of the crisis emerge. These documents make clear that Trieste was the first major confrontation of the Cold War. It was an exercise in what had not yet been termed brinkmanship, and in brinkmanship at the highest level, and was an exercise all the more remarkable because one central figure, the American President, Harry S. Truman, had been in office barely three weeks.

From the Yugoslav side the official account of their drive on Trieste has now also been published. Many reminiscences have appeared of Allied commanders and diplomats caught up in the crisis. I have drawn on all these sources, and on my own personal memoir which appeared soon after the event (*The Road to Trieste*, Heinemann 1947) for this study of those days in April, May and June 1945 when Trieste was not only one of the last battlegrounds of World War II, but the first battle-field of the Cold War.

The confrontation of which it was the scene ended in a victory for the Western Allies. After five weeks of defiance Tito withdrew. The influence of this experience on the new President of the United States must have been considerable. He had backed his own judgement, and had succeeded. This could have had a major influence in shaping his stance for the subsequent crises of the Berlin blockade and the Korean war. On Marshal Tito, too, the Trieste crisis had its impact. In this first post-war test he found that the Soviet Union was not prepared to stand by him once Truman showed himself to be truly resolute. It was a development which provided one further argument for the breach between Yugoslavia and the Soviet Union which was to follow three years after this moment of high drama in a corner of the Mediterranean in the spring of 1945.

CHAPTER ONE

The Goal

Under clouded skies which belied the date – it was late afternoon on 1st May 1945 – the armoured cars found the long tarmac sweep of Route 14 completely deserted. No road-block, no crater checked them as they raced forward at thirty-five miles an hour, their wireless masts swaying like saplings, their tyres sizzling on the wet road surface, their commanders upright in the turrets, earphones over their soft black berets. Ahead to the east were the skeleton-grey, rock-strewn slopes of the Carso; beyond, climbing into the rain clouds, the mountains of Slovenia. Near at hand, hidden by the trees in the fields, must be the bed of the Isonzo river. Yes, there it was – and there, undamaged, was the great white concrete bridge that carried the road to Trieste, twenty miles farther east. Partisans with rifles and red scarves waved to them from a building near the riverside. The waters in the wide shingle bed gave back the drab grey of the skies.

The bridge was mined. Explosive, packed under the central arch and dug into the roadway, could be seen easily. The cars swung their machine-guns to cover the far bank as the sappers went forward, and removed the detonators. Then the cars moved on again, over the bridge, over the Isonzo, into Venezia Giulia. The roadside houses grew more frequent, until they formed a suburban street, over which the great cranes of the Monfalcone shipyards showed up to the south-east. More partisans, each with some red badge or scrap of red clothing to mark his faith, stared at them and waved. At last, by the roadside, they saw two men in more formal uniform – khaki jackets, Sam Browne belts, fore-and-aft caps. The cars pulled up. The leading troops of the British 12th Lancers, acting as the cavalry screen for the 2nd New Zealand Division of the Eighth Army, had contacted troops of Marshal Tito's National Army of Liberation in Ronchi dei Legionari, just inside the borders of Venezia Giulia. In the Mediterranean Zone the Balkan and the Italian fronts had merged.

It was a meeting with few formalities. The orders of the British cavalry were to reconnoitre the road to Trieste, on to which the 2nd New Zealand Division, under General Sir Bernard Freyberg's command, was directed. The troop leaders were concerned primarily with information about the enemy ahead. Was the coast road held by them? Had the tunnels cut through the rock been blown? The Yugoslavs spoke no English, but with soldier's Italian they indicated that Monfalcone, just ahead, was in the hands of pro-Tito partisans, and that all was well. So the armoured cars started their journey again, their olive drab tank bodies – they were in reality light tanks on wheels – shining now in a shower of rain. They sped on through Monfalcone, where crowds with red banners and red-starred caps turned to cheer, out on to the Trieste road. There, on a stretch which curved over a boulder-strewn slope, beside a memorial to Italian cavalry killed in the carnage of the last war, they were suddenly fired on from the high ground to the east. They signalled back to their headquarters that they had contacted enemy, swung their cars into such cover as offered, and prepared for battle.

Behind them, in a great column of vehicles which covered the road from Monfalcone back over the Isonzo and round the curve of the Italian coast, were advancing the tanks and trucks and guns and carriers and ambulances and supply vehicles of the 2nd New Zealand Division, moving nose to tailboard like some immense railway train. Near the head of the column drove General Freyberg in his jeep. His driver was busy weaving a way in and out of the trucks of the forward brigade, the 9th New Zealand Brigade. The trucks were covered with lilac and with the Italian tricolour flags thrown to them, or torn from the windows and walls of villages through which the column had been passing all day. But there were no flowers in the men's rifles, no flags clustering on the twenty-five-pounder guns or their ammunition limbers. The brigade was ready for battle. When Brigadier Gentry, their commander, reached the far side of Monfalcone and heard fire from the Lancers he ordered his tanks forward and prepared for immediate action. The hopes of open road right through to Trieste were dashed. It was clear that there were still at least pockets of the enemy to be fought.

General Freyberg too heard the firing, and urged his driver anxiously to get ahead. He was afraid, not that it was Germans whom we had contacted, but that it might be Yugoslavs. We might be in conflict not with our enemies but our allies. He drove forward to where the tanks were at that moment opening fire. But before he could call a pause the tank shells were bursting among the rocks, and white flags went up almost immediately from amidst the dust and smoke. Five minutes later, to his relief, he saw that the prisoners being escorted in were indeed in the rough grey of the Wehrmacht.

It was now nearly dusk, and the rain was falling steadily. To go farther that night on the narrow coast road on which the Germans still clearly had positions looked unwise. Freyberg called a halt and went back to the square at Monfalcone. Here the Yugoslav officers who had met the 12th Lancers were waiting. The New Zealand commander had with him a foreign affairs expert from Allied Force Headquarters, Lieutenant-Colonel Wilkinson. He spoke excellent German, and it was through this, the language of their common enemy, that he and the Yugoslavs talked in the open square, with partisans and curious townspeople crowding around. Freyberg had a sense of occasion, and put a touch of formality into the words he asked Colonel Wilkinson to translate. The New Zealand Division, he said, as the forward troops of the British Eighth Army, were glad indeed to link up with Marshal Tito's magnificent troops who had fought so long and so bravely in the common cause. Now that we had linked up we could either push straight on to Trieste and Gorizia, to the north, or we could pause here and discuss future plans with the Yugoslav commanders. The Yugoslavs were emphatically in favour of the second alternative. They would go back to their headquarters and bring over that evening the commander of the Yugoslav forces in the area for a conference. The time was duly fixed at 1930 hours, the place as the town hall at Monfalcone. Thankfully, in the rain which grew heavier every minute, the New Zealand troops turned their vehicles off the roads and sought shelter after a day of constant movement which had brought them eighty miles from the banks of the Piave river.

So it was that, as senior Intelligence officer of the 2nd New Zealand Division, I found myself on this chill May evening waiting in the mayor's office in Monfalcone to notify General Freyberg when the Yugoslav commander should arrive. The Committee of Liberation made us welcome. The mayor was a tall, round-faced Slovene, with a slow manner and slow speech, wearing black knee-boots that he had clearly acquired from an Italian prisoner – the Italians made the best and softest knee-boots we had encountered. Partisans with Sten guns, wearing blue caps with red stars on them, and blue uniform overalls, stood by the door. A tall fair girl, with a blue cap with the same red star, rushed about on everyone's errands. She, it appeared, was the mayor's secretary. Monfalcone, with its huge Adriatic shipyards, had been liberated, they told us, only that morning, though the bridge over the Isonzo had been in the hands of the partisans for four days. The German garrison had surrendered at once, and were now to be seen waiting miserably, under partisan guard, in the yard of a big school. It was

clear that the partisans had had a first class organisation in this town
which was fully functioning. Already a huge red star, lit up with electric
bulbs, was in position outside the town hall, its blazing bulbs a reminder
that the power system too had escaped destruction. Portraits of Tito
on bluish paper were being pasted on every wall, and slogans were being
painted alongside them. From the balcony of the town hall hung an
immense red-and-white Yugoslav flag with a red star on its centre, the
Red Flag of Russia and an ample Stars and Stripes. I asked them if they
had a Union Jack. With some indignation they pointed to a small,
home-made flag, with no white but with the red and blue parts in
correct order, hanging alongside the others. They had made it that
morning when it was found that there was no proper one available.

Half-past seven came, then eight o'clock, then nine, then ten. Still
there was no sign of the Yugoslav commander. It was clear that something had gone wrong. We explained to the committee that we would
go back to our headquarters, but if anyone did arrive he should be
directed to where our trucks and caravans were parked in Ronchi dei
Legionari. Then I went back and slept in the corner of a schoolroom
where the desks were piled against the wall, and placards in Italian –
but not in the banned Slovene tongue, I noticed – urged Fascist virtues
(or vices, according to your view-point) on the pupils.

Freyberg read this situation with what was to prove remarkable
accuracy. Late that evening he sent a message to the Corps Commander,
General Harding, saying that it was obvious that the Yugoslavs had not
expected our arrival for at least a further forty-eight hours, and expressing his doubts as to whether Trieste or Gorizia were held by the
Yugoslavs. 'I am continuing my advance on both places on 2nd May,'
he concluded.[1]

Events the next morning confirmed this view. A messenger from the
Town Hall was at our headquarters early. An officer from the partisans
had arrived there at half past ten the previous evening, bringing word
that the commander would be with us at eight-thirty this morning. Duly,
therefore, at eight-thirty General Freyberg drove to the square, and
waited. No officer arrived, so he went forward to 9th Brigade Headquarters to check the reports on the situation. They indicated that there
were still Germans in Trieste and in the intervening area. Our artillery
spotting planes had been over the city and reported empty streets, no
flags and some signs of fighting. At two places on the coast road to
Monfalcone they had encountered light flak. The general waited no
longer, but ordered Brigadier Gentry to continue his advance along the
road to Trieste.

He added a further instruction. 'Do not hand over any prisoners you may take to the partisans.'

This was the first sign to the British troops that something new was afoot, for in Italy we had thankfully used the local partisans to escort prisoners to the rear. Soon afterwards a messenger arrived from the town hall. A Yugoslav officer, who was described as Commander of the IX Partisan Corps, had arrived. This time there was no hitch. Waiting alongside an ochre-coloured motor-cycle and side-car, still bearing its Wehrmacht lettering, was an officer in his late twenties or early thirties. He wore a neat khaki uniform, with shirt open at the neck, a Sam Browne belt, two broad gold stripes on his cuff, and gold bars on his collar. A metal decoration hung from his left pocket. He introduced himself as General Dusa. He spoke no English, nor did he need any to make at once the impression of being a first-rate commander. Watchful eyes appraising and studying us all, a clear-cut, firm mouth, and a face unmarked by lines of doubt or frustration or indecision told their own story.

There was saluting and handshaking in the square, and then General Freyberg led the way up to the mayor's room. It took only two words from the Yugoslav to clear out the handful of members of the Committee of Liberation. Then the two commanders settled down to communicate through a maze of language difficulties. We had no one with us who could speak Slovene or Croat or Serb, so we conducted the interview at long range. Dusa spoke in his own tongue to his interpreter who put his words into Italian which Heyden, our interrogator, turned into English. At times they used German as the medium instead.

It rapidly became clear that the Yugoslav commander had indeed not expected British forces in the area so soon. It was, after all, only three days before that the foremost elements of the Eighth Army had been on the Adige river, south of Venice, nearly half-way back across Northern Italy. A network of rivers, a mass of German garrisons had lain between them and Venezia Giulia. Nothing in the Italian campaign to date had suggested that such rapid movement was likely. Freyberg announced that his orders were to occupy Gorizia and to press on to Trieste, so as to open up the port as a base for the British Armies which were to move into Austria. The Corps Commander looked concerned. This was clearly not a proposal to his liking. Equally clearly it was a situation which went beyond his authority. He countered with the suggestion that we could move towards Austria along the edge of the Italian plain. When Freyberg insisted that it was of paramount importance that the port of Trieste be opened up, the Yugoslav officer explained that it would be better if we could meet his superior officer, the General of the Fourth Army, which was the chief Yugoslav force in the area, and talk matters over with him.

So it was agreed that he would return to his headquarters and send a signal to the Fourth Army commander to come to Monfalcone at half-past two that afternoon. Was he sure it could be arranged in that time? Yes, two-thirty would be fine. So he saluted, got back into his side-car, and drove off through the lines of curious partisans.

This meeting never took place. At two-thirty that afternoon General Freyberg again drove to the square, which was filling up with column upon column of demonstrators marching in for a liberation ceremony. Now there were red stars in every buttonhole, red and white Yugoslav flags, Italian tricolours with a red star on the white centre panel. There were portraits of Tito, and placards with *Viva Gli Alleati,* and *Viva L'Armata Rossa,* and one proclaiming *'Viva Churchil'.* The columns were carefully marshalled, and the men marched with that slightly embarrassed air which characterises most demonstrations in most countries.

It was extensive, impressive, yet clearly thoroughly organised, very different from the spontaneous uprush of feeling in the Italian towns and villages through which we had raced during the last few days. There was a sense of individualism being directed, if not crushed, of wariness if not fear mixed with the rejoicing. But for all that it was a stirring spectacle, with the great red and white flags, the children in white blouses or white shirts with flowers in their hands, the girls with shining eyes singing as they marched.

'Pretty good,' I commented to Colonel Wilkinson.

He looked at me keenly. 'Yes' he replied. 'But beware. Many a man has had his hand crushed in that grip.'

Though the square was filled to bursting point with these columns, no Yugoslav Army party turned up. So the General abandoned his wait, and set out to follow the advance into Trieste, leaving behind a liaison officer to bring on the Yugoslavs should they arrive. Then events suddenly got into top gear. By two-thirty that afternoon our tanks had reached the outskirts of Trieste. By three o'clock they were in the city centre, and linking up with the infantry and light tanks of the Yugoslav Fourth Army, who had arrived there the day before. The greater part of the city was clear, but the German garrison was holding out in the Castle, the Law Courts, at Villa Opicina on the hills to the north, and in a number of smaller strongholds.

Most of these hastened to surrender to us, to avoid capture by the

Yugoslavs. One which did not – the Law Courts – was stormed jointly by Yugoslav infantry and New Zealand tanks. In another – Villa Opicina – the Yugoslavs managed to enforce a surrender to themselves, rather than to us. By nightfall both the New Zealand and Yugoslav commanders in the city were able to report to their respective High Commands that the city was captured, and that their troops were in occupation of it.

It was an outcome highly unpalatable to both the Yugoslavs and the Western Allies. An area to which both Yugoslavia and Italy had strong claims was now under the control not of one army under one command, but under two armies responsible to two very different sets of powers. Overnight Trieste changed from a meeting place of victors in a shared cause to an arena of potential conflict between powers who were still formally allies in arms. The rest of the embattled world still glowed with the wartime unity against the common foe. But in this corner of the Mediterranean that glow was fading rapidly. In the outside world the crowds who gathered to rejoice in the streets of London, Washington and Moscow felt only the relief and radiance of victory. The thought of new tensions and new conflicts, the knowledge of the harsh words which were already finding their way into the diplomatic telegrams were not in their minds. But for us the transition was immediate. In Trieste we were not only in a new area, but in a new era, the post-war era of the emerging Cold War.

Trieste had inherited this fate because it was the one part of Europe where no clear demarcation line had been agreed in advance between the Western Allies and the Soviet Union. Across the rest of Europe from the Baltic to the southern frontier of Austria the British, American and Soviet governments had agreed on boundary lines for their immediate post-war areas of influence and control. In Germany the exact frontiers of the various Allied zones of occupation had been decided upon in the autumn of 1944. A general pattern for the occupation of Austria had been established.

Only along the seventy miles between Austria and the Adriatic had no line been determined. This was the province of Venezia Giulia, a part of pre-war Italy thrusting itself down into the Adriatic in a mountainous peninsula. It was a region of mixed nationalities, with a Slovene and Croatian hinterland, and with cities which had Italian majorities – Trieste, Gorizia, Monfalcone, Pola – the population of a hinge of Europe where Italy joined the Balkans. The exact figures of the population mix had been debated and challenged over the years, but the basic facts were clear. The countryside was Slav; the cities predominantly Italian, with a dash of Austro-German dating from the days of the Hapsburg Empire. Trieste itself between the wars had about 250,000 inhabitants, of whom 180,000-200,000 were Italians. The province had been Austrian until 1918, but had become Italian after World War I.

It was not these national complexities however which had deterred the Allies from grappling in good time with the problems which would arise as their armies converged onto this narrow strip of territory. The reason was simpler. Each side – first the Americans and British, and then the Yugoslavs with their Soviet backers – thought in turn that it had most to gain by leaving the future of Venezia Giulia vague.

Each in turn had missed the chance of a settlement which might have been to its advantage. In the summer of 1944 Marshal Tito was ready to settle for a demarcation line which would have divided Venezia Giulia in half, giving him the predominantly Slovenian mountainous interior, leaving Trieste and the mainly Italian cities to the West. This made at the time good military and diplomatic sense to him. In Italy the Allies had liberated Rome and were surging northwards. There seemed a good chance that the war in Italy might end that year. The Yugoslav forces were, on the other hand, still held deep in Croatia and Serbia, well to the south of Venezia Giulia, under strong German pressure.

But Churchill, who was on a visit to Italy and talked to Tito in person, would have none of this.[1] He believed the Allies could break through to the River Po by the autumn, and have a chance to strike east through Trieste and Ljubljana towards Austria. He was urging on the Americans that we give the Reich 'a stab in the Adriatic armpit'. The planners spoke of an attack on Trieste by three seaborne and two airborne divisions. So the Yugoslav leader was told that the Allies intended to impose their Allied Military Government, of the type which administered Italy as it was liberated, in all areas which had been under Italian rule at the outbreak of war. This meant over the whole of Venezia Giulia, including those parts which Tito had proposed should come under his control. Nor was this all. The Yugoslavs were notified that the Allies would need to station their troops within the boundaries of pre-war Yugoslavia to protect their lines of communication through Ljubljana to Austria. On this point Tito was informed that the Allied Commander-in-Chief 'looks to the Yugoslav authorities to co-operate with him'.

This was too much not only for Tito, but for the Royalist Yugoslav

Ministers who formed part of the coalition Government of the time. The Yugoslavs refused Churchill's terms, and there the matter rested.

But the basis for the calculations of the Western Allies soon proved far too optimistic. By the year's end the British and American armies were bogged down in winter snows in the Apennines and at the entrance to the Po valley. Trieste suddenly seemed to the British to be dangerously far away. Anthony Eden, the Foreign Secretary, therefore came forward at Yalta with a proposal for a dividing line very similar to that which Tito had advocated.[2] But the Yalta Conference shelved the issue. It was now Tito's turn to show himself unwilling. He was now sitting in the former Royal Palace in liberated Belgrade, and had good grounds to hope that his forthcoming spring offensive, for which the Western Allies had made available substantial equipment and supplies, would bring him into Trieste well ahead of anyone from the West.

For the Yugoslavs possession of Venezia Giulia was understandably of the highest priority. It would round off their frontier at the Isonzo, give them control of a long contested region, wipe out memories of the Italian seizure of the fort of Fiume (the Yugoslav Rijeka) after World War I, and help reconcile the Slovenes to the Communist-led regime of Tito.

The Western Allies were however to enter the final campaign in Italy with no such clear objectives. Field Marshal Alexander, the Allied Supreme Commander in the Mediterranean, had been given no instructions about any advance towards the contentious area of Trieste, even though the Yugoslav Fourth Army was known to be directed onto it. The Field Marshal himself knew very clearly the reason why this part of his task had been left obscured. He and Mr Harold Macmillan, the British Minister Resident at Caserta, had both been present at a meeting called in the British Embassy in Athens on 15th February by Mr Anthony Eden, then on his way back from the Yalta Conference.[3] Eden had reported his failure to secure agreement on demarcation lines which would have split Venezia Giulia in half, with Trieste and Gorizia in the hands of the Western Allies. The best way forward seemed to lie in getting agreement between Alexander and Tito on a soldier-to-soldier basis. Alexander was due to visit Tito in Belgrade within the next fortnight. It was agreed that he should stress to Tito the British need to control the railway lines from Trieste northwards to Austria, and would propose therefore that the most practicable way to do this was for all of Venezia Giulia to come under Alexander's control up to a line ten miles east of the railway – pending a peace settlement.

This amounted to re-stating Eden's Yalta line in military rather than political terms, and Tito quickly showed that such a deal had no attractions for him. He replied in careful terms, for he still had need of Allied supplies for the offensive he was about to launch towards Trieste. Field Marshal Alexander could of course have access to the lines of communication towards Austria. He could institute Allied Military Government within these zones – with one proviso. Yugoslav civil administration installed in these zones should be retained.

This left the issue dangerously vague and Field Marshal Alexander hastened to communicate his anxieties to the Combined Chiefs of Staff. On 2nd March he warned them that the Yugoslav partisan forces were already in occupation of large areas of Venezia Giulia, and that Tito's forces would 'probably be in a position to extend their hold over the whole country before other Allied forces can arrive'. The best course therefore was to make a virtue of a necessity, and invite the Yugoslavs to participate, as an ally, in the Allied Military Government of Venezia Giulia. Any Yugoslav forces in the area would come under the Allied Commander but the new Military Government 'be associated with such existing civil authority as may be found functioning in the territory'.[4]

This message alarmed Mr Macmillan. He quickly commented to the Foreign Office that this was 'not a very clear document', and proceeded to clarify it in the direction he thought events should be guided. 'Marshal Tito,' he wrote 'intends by hook or crook to obtain Pola, Fiume and, if possible, Trieste in any final settlement.' Tito was 'anxious therefore to obtain a de facto situation by survival of his so-called civil organisation in Istria in some form or another'. Macmillan was against any idea of dividing the area into separate zones, one under Alexander and the other under Tito as likely to produce a 'premature· judgment of Solomon'. He equally rejected a plan the Americans had had to impose rule of the Western Allies over the whole of Venezia Giulia. This he saw as 'quite impracticable' and in any event the Americans 'would certainly back out of such a scheme when it came to blows'.

These telegrams reached London at a time when Churchill had many other matters on his mind. The final battles to clear the path for the Rhine crossing were under way. Above all the Russians were steadily making plain that the democratic Government of Poland agreed on at Yalta meant for them a communist dominated Government. In these circumstances Churchill had no difficulty in making up his mind on Trieste. On 11th March he minuted, 'My feeling is that henceforth our inclination should be to back Italy against Tito'.

This went too far for Eden, who replied at once that however much one might sympathise with the Italian claims, 'the fact is that Tito at present controls most of the disputed territory, and on the withdrawal of the Germans might well control all of it before our armies can get there'. For good measure he added, 'I do not much relish the idea of being drawn into armed conflict with Tito on this issue'.[5]

In a paper circulated to the War Cabinet Eden developed this point.

Except perhaps for the towns such as Trieste, Pola and Gorizia, the major portion of the province will, with the withdrawal of the Germans, be occupied and indeed administered by Yugoslav Partisans. And even if under extreme pressure Tito was forced to accept Allied Military Government in the province, his Partisans would remain in arms and it would be a miracle if sooner or later they did not obstruct our military administration. We should then have to take forceful measures to assert our authority, and fighting would begin.

But the key to it all was American support. The British made clear to Washington that they would go along with any plan which the Americans were prepared to back with American military force. The Americans hesitated. The future of this tiny corner of the Mediterranean had to take its place on an agenda crowded with the problems of the closing stages of the war in Europe. The war with Japan had still to be won. The American President was ailing, and all decision making had slowed down. Trieste could wait. All the Americans did was to notify the Russians on 19th March of their claims to administer all Venezia Giulia. The Russians did not bother to reply. They were prepared to await the outcome of a campaign which seemed to be moving in Tito's favour.

So the war entered its final phase without any agreement about the region which Eden had described at Yalta, with force if not with originality, as a 'potential powderkeg'.[6] Both sides had left the question to the arbitrament of events. Neither had contemplated that the arbitrament might be dangerously indecisive.

CHAPTER TWO

Start Lines

It is a long way from Trieste to the former Papal States of Central Italy which lie in the valleys rising inland from Ancona towards the lower Apennines. Yet there, in small towns whose squares bear plaques commemorating their liberation last century from 'Tyranno theologico', had begun the road which ultimately brought us to Trieste in these opening days of May. The valleys of the Papal Marches had been selected by the Eighth Army as a training area, and in them we prepared, in the sunshine of March, for the battles which had still to be fought. For at that time there still lay, between the Allied Armies in Italy and the roads to Austria and Trieste, the formidable and strongly-manned mountain and river defence lines of the Wehrmacht. The lines had to be broken, and the forces holding them smashed and destroyed, before the end could come in Italy.

This was the old, old situation which had faced the Allied Armies again and again during the long, disappointing months of the Italian campaign. It seemed this spring much more than a year and a half since the desert divisions, hardened by victory and the North African sun, had stormed confidently ashore in the south to knock Italy out of the war. That same confidence had run high as Montgomery and the Eighth Army had swept up the Adriatic Coast to take the Foggia air-fields and to poise for the drive across the Sangro towards the lateral road to Rome. It had kept the Fifth Army going in the battle through the squalid outskirts of Naples and Capua, across the brown Volterno, up the slopes of Million Dollar Hill, and to the edge of Cassino. The Sherman tanks of the Americans had moved down the valley of the Rapido towards the northern outskirts of Cassino town with the same surety that they had moved on Tunisia. Six months later their rusted carcasses were still there in the mud and ruins, symbolising the hopes which had halted and dwindled as autumn ran on into winter, that hard black winter of Cassino which our own men still mentioned with hatred in their voices. Hope had risen again when the landing came at Anzio in February 1944, and fallen as abruptly when the Germans had stabilised this beachhead line, as they were to stabilise so many others.

20

Then had come the battles in the poppy-strewn cornfields in May, the rush to Rome, the surge forward to the foothills covering Florence, the cracking of the Gothic Line in August 1944 on the Adriatic Coast by the audacious Canadians. The end seemed at hand. In the Apennines the Fifth Army with great losses but great determination was driving through the mountain passes towards Bologna.

The Eighth Army levered open yard by yard the door guarding the eastern edge of the Po plain. We grouped ourselves in the fading September sunshine into mobile columns to dash to Venice. Yet once again the Germans held. Once again the dust turned into mud, and the battle bogged down, and another harsh winter came in amongst the mountains and along the rivers.

It was harder than the other because by now Italy was not only a disappointing front but also a forgotten front. We slipped from the front pages and from the radio headlines. Soldiers complained that their girls at home called them 'D-Day Dodgers', and they chalked the name in derisive self-justification on their trucks and jeeps. In the *Eighth Army News* the favourite cartoons were of the Two Types – two bewhiskered, foppishly-dressed officers with fly whisks, spotted scarves and desert boots, looking back sadly from the Italian mud to the good old days of flies and sand and wadis. The whole Eighth Army, it seemed, looked back, not only to the days of sunshine and fast, open fighting, but also to the days when the Eighth had been the pride of the Western Allies, when it lived on its present, not its past.

So it was too with the American troops of the Fifth Army. In 1943 and 1944 they had been the only American formation of any size in action in Europe. They had had all that blinding glare of the American publicity machine concentrated on their landing at Salerno, their conquest of Naples, their advance to Cassino and Anzio. General Mark Clark, who commanded the Fifth in those days, and who now commanded the Fifteenth Army Group, in which the Eighth and Fifth Armies were linked, had been more in the American public eye than any other general except Eisenhower, MacArthur, and Patton. But now the Americans in Italy had slipped too from the headlines, which wrote largely of the Ardennes and the Rhine, and very scantily of the Apennines and the Po.

In Italy we seemed to be fated to finish our war plugging away at the rugged underbelly of Europe, while other men tasted the rich wine of swift victorious advance. With resignation therefore rather than eagerness we prepared that spring for one more assault against one more range of mountains, one more series of rivers. We were not to know that action as rapid and exciting as anything in the desert lay ahead.

The drive which was ultimately to bring us into Venezia Giulia, and to the junction with Tito's forces, began for the 2nd New Zealand Division (if any military operation can be said to have an exact beginning) in the mayor's office in the small town of San Severino on the morning of 18th March. San Severino is not a town of either importance or great beauty. It does not sit, as do most mountain towns in Italy, compactly on a hill-top, surrounded by a wall above which rise red and grey roof-tops. Instead it straggles up the side of a valley, albeit a valley fresh then with young poplars and willows. But it has a peculiarly charming oval-shaped piazza, reminiscent of a Regency terrace, with arches and pale gold stone buildings. We used the piazza for parades and inspections, while the mayor's office had this morning been turned into a conference room. Our military police, not red-capped like the British, but marked only by their red-and-blue arm-bands, guarded the doorways and the staff cars which were parked in the square outside.

The senior officers of the division (this was what was known technically as a 'lieutenant-colonels and above' conference) packed the old, square, high-ceilinged room, like an audience at a theatre. But no theatre audience ever gave more concentrated attention than did these men to General Freyberg on that spring morning. They sat on rows of chairs facing a small dais, where stood the high-backed carved chair of the mayor, and his desk, between two tall windows whose shutters had been pulled together to keep out the blinding sunshine. Behind the dais hung three big diagrams. It was of these that the General was speaking, and it was on these that the eyes of every man in the room was fixed with that intensity which fighting, or the planning of fighting, gives to those whose lives are directly affected.

'The division,' the General was saying, 'will attack as part of a large-scale offensive on a very broad front. The object of the general offensive, in which the whole Eighth Army will take part, will be to take Bologna and exploit to the Po, destroying the enemy. The object of the immediate operation to be carried out by this division is to obtain and exploit a bridgehead over the Senio river and subsequently the Santerno.'*

This was not, of course, the whole plan; it was only that part of it which concerned us directly. The Eighth Army plan was however to fit in with an assault northwards by Fifth Army, who were to take Bologna and hit northward to the Alps and westward to Milan and Turin. We were to plug on steadily across the five river lines which lay between us and Bologna – the Senio, the Santerno, the Sillaro, the Gaiana and the

* See the map on page 85.

Idice, tying down the enemy's forces there, and, if possible, his reserves, while the Fifth Army broke out and finished him off. But for the moment the Senio alone concerned us.

We knew the Senio well, and did not like it. It was one of the many rivers which ran from the steep slopes of the Northern Apennines northward to the Po, cutting across the plains of the Po valley like veins across a leaf. The Eighth Army had pushed the Germans back to it in December, and after that had for two and a half months probed towards the river-banks, waiting for fine weather and enough ammunition for the general offensive to be launched. The more we had probed, the more unpleasant an attack against this line seemed.

It was not the river itself which was formidable. The Senio is a nondescript enough stream, one which the traveller in peace-time would scarcely notice as he crossed it on the long straight Route 9 from Bologna to Faenza and Rimini. Ten to fourteen yards wide at the most, and narrower still in places, its brown waters swirl along in a muddy channel cut through the black silt of the Po valley. Had there been just the water barrier to contend with, the problem would have been straightforward enough, even though all bridges across it had been blown long since. There was however much more. On both banks of the Senio, as on every one of these rivers in the Po valley, the peasants had built centuries ago great flood-banks as formidable as the dykes of Holland. They were designed to keep in check the waters which could flood overnight with heavy rain or a sudden thaw in the mountains. These dykes were ramparts of earth that looked like the old type of fortification you see still on the outskirts of Paris or Brussels. They were thirty or forty feet high, as high as the roof of a suburban house, and about as steep, sloping up from the water's edge towards a flat top wide enough to make a pathway for a cart or a truck. The outer face then slanted down towards the farmlands below, towards the thick rows of trees and vines and the frequent white houses and winding white roads.

Into the flood-banks the Germans had dug defensive positions. Our air photographs showed the dark earth scarred with the white marks of machine-gun posts, slit trenches and dug-outs, which stood out under the stereoscopes like bacteria. There were weapons enough there too. Our patrols, moving forward in the dark and the snow towards the line, had been met with machine- and Tommy-gun fire from both the near and the far stop-banks; and there had been enough leg wounds and amputations to prove that the forward slopes of the banks, and the fields in front of them were heavily mined. Barbed wire, too, stretched along the sides of the banks and amid the vines and trees in front. It was the minefields, however, which made this a particularly ugly obstacle to face in cold blood. For minefields were, in the closing stage of this war, the dread of all infantry. The commanders of our units, many of them still in their twenties and early thirties, who sat now in this room in San Severino in the peace of a Sunday morning, had had experience enough of them. They had known them before Florence and before Cassino, on the Sangro and in Tunisia, along the long road that had led from Alamein to Tripolitania, and at Alamein itself. Sitting in the foremost row at this very conference was Major General Kippenberger who on a hillside overlooking Cassino exactly a year before had lost both feet on German S mines. The black crosses which marked the minefields on the diagrams of the Senio stood out like an ugly fence between the division and the hopes of the war's end. The Senio, too, was only the first of many such fields, many such lines in the Po plain.

The General turned now to these diagrams on the wall behind him. One showed the Senio in cross section, as if the draughtsman had stood in mid stream and with a gigantic knife sliced down through the banks and the stream exposing it to the bottom of its bed. Blue shading marked the stream; strong purple lines carried the banks out, and then branched upwards on either side to show how the stop-bank or flood-wall rose. With its clear colours and firm lines on a sheet of stiff white paper, it was a pretty enough picture of an ugly reality. Our draughtsmen were first class. The General glanced at the notes which he had written out in his confident, fully rounded hand. Then he went on :

'This will be a very difficult operation. Roughly the tactics will be as follows. We shall first of all knock him off the near stop-bank, so that we can dominate the river itself by our patrols and fire night and day. Then, some days later, the attack will go in after a very heavy air and artillery bombardment. We shall do all we can to smash trip-wires, explode mines, and shake his defence.'

He dealt with facet after facet of the plan which was contemplated – width of front on which the attack would go in, number of battalions to be employed, the way the artillery would be used, and the bombers, the flame-throwing tanks, the bridges which would have to be built, and the approach roads. Steadily the whole complicated mechanism which man has devised for killing his fellows was discussed, co-ordinated, and explained. And then, as the sun swung round to the windows at the far end of the room, and the voices of the San Severini coming from church rose up from the piazza below, we adjourned to the next room. There, in rum cocktails which the batmen had somehow procured for this occasion, we pledged General Kippenberger's health – and our own hopes for success (and personal survival).

Outside in the square the men from the three battalions of the 6th Brigade chattered in the sun at the street corners as they would have done in their home towns in New Zealand, and watched sardonically the cars drive away after the conference. Conferences meant only one thing – future action – and were as such no very good omen to these infantrymen. For to them the stickiest part of the job would fall. They had to tackle the stop-banks.

There was, for instance, my friend Milne, to whose billet I walked over that afternoon. Milne summed up in his person the potential human cost of these final stages of the war. He was an essentially decent, responsible man in his early thirties, married, with one curly-headed son whose photo stood by his bed alongside his revolver, holster and belt. It was taken in the garden of a neat, white-walled wooden villa, a typical home in the typical provincial New Zealand town where he had lived contentedly, and would undoubtedly go back to live con-tentedly after this campaign – if he did not get knocked. But it was a considerable enough 'if'. Milne would go over the Senio stop-bank commanding a company, as exposed and unprotected as he strode for-ward with his wireless operator and runner as any man in the assault. He had only just gone back to a battalion job, too, after several months at divisional headquarters, and his nervous system was still adjusting itself to the strain. He knew well enough what battle meant, for he had served for six weeks inside Cassino, six weeks during every hour of which he saw or knew of men hit around him, and during every hour of which he knew that he too might be hit. He had come into warfare too late to have the suppleness a younger man can get. He must have been thirty at least before he first went into action. In him one could sense the underlying tenseness at what lay ahead. It was a tenseness which found its outlet in occasional dark bitterness about people who had not come to the war, or who, even though here in uniform, were qualifying energetically, but well behind the lines, for Returned Soldier's Association badges.

He took me to tea with the doctor's family with whom he was billeted, in a cool, dark-panelled flat at the top of an old building overlooking the square. The scene was so unrelated to war that it was unreal – the doctor's wife speaking in French, and telling of her pre-war visits to Milan; the two daughters playing the piano or, with a charming lack of self-consciousness, turning out tune after tune from two shiny, elaborate piano-accordions; the paper-thin cakes, and the olives and jam and the weak Italian tea. San Severino had slipped untouched through the prongs of what Churchill had called the 'fiery rake of war', and this family had passed through unscathed. The Senio stop-bank, the minefields, all the hazards ahead through which Milne must march with his men had no contact with this room and this life.

San Severino was one of a group of small towns in which the division was stationed. The Fifth Brigade were around Camerino, the hill-top university town which blocked the eastern end of the main valley like a fortress. The Ninth Brigade were in Fabriano, where the famous paper mills were already working again. The artillery were around the characterless crossroads village of Castelraimondo; and divisional head-quarters were in the city of Matelica, with our command vehicles and trucks parked behind barbed wire in the central square.

Matelica called itself a city because it had a cathedral, dating from the Papal days, though its people numbered only 5,000. It lay, compact as a medieval town, at the bottom of a narrow valley, the towers of its many churches and monasteries rising above the high grey walls which enclosed it. It reminded me frequently of Oxford. Here again were many church bells and narrow, stone-walled streets and the moonlight bright on the house-tops at night. We had been stationed there in the autumn, when we prepared for the dark harsh winter campaign around Faenza, so that it had become one of the places we knew best in all Italy. Training in Matelica for this new campaign was like training at home, particularly in this sunshine which beat with New Zealand intensity down on to the white roads and the fields green with spring crops and the rivers where women did their washing in the noisy mountain waters. By noon each day this sunshine would strike into the piazza, and lie pleasantly across the tailboard of the wooden office truck in which Martin, my fellow Intelligence officer, and I worked at our part of the planning operations.

Just before lunch we would take the *Eighth Army News,* which had just come in, sit on the pile of empty grenade boxes and for half an hour watch the life of Matelica go by. For here, as in every Italian town, there was a ritual period before lunch when the people strolled through the streets. They strolled against a background that fitted together like a stage set. The square, red-and-grey watch tower, with its castellated top leaning slightly off plumb, puzzling the eye and precipitating innumerable arguments as to whether it or the cathedral tower beyond was out of line, the seven brick arches which formed a colonnade, the small fountain which sent up a single squirt, the water shining in the sunshine and falling back into a basin, edged with green slime, and with tiny sculptured nudes, battered and blackened on its side; these all fitted perfectly into one picture. Behind them the March sky was such a sharp blue that it looked as if it were only a foot or two beyond the buildings, fastened to the back of them by some stage manager's craft.

It was very quiet in Matelica, so that you could hear at this time of day the footsteps of the people walking over the cobbles and the roar of the pressure cookers from the men's mess at the back of the town hall. Big ox wagons, drawn by two white oxen with wide high horns, and red bobbins falling on their foreheads to keep away the flies, came slowly down the streets with loads of brushwood, giving way reluctantly to the occasional three-ton lorry which would roar through, breaking the peace for the moment, and causing the strollers to draw back against the walls of the houses.

Over by the sunniest corner a group of men would be discussing politics. In their midst I could pick out the leader of Matelica's nineteen communists, a heavy, square baker who had been one of the leading partisans in the mountains throughout the winter of 1943-44. They looked up with some contempt as a man in black boots and leggings walked past alongside a girl in a fur coat. That I knew, was the local lawyer who was the Conservative candidate for mayor. He had led a rival partisan band in the hills – a band at which the main body of patriots scoffed. On the other side of the square, under the colonnade outside the mayor's office, the refugees from Leghorn waited for their midday soup. They were all women and children, chattering and laughing with panniers or army ration tins in their hands. The Sindaco (the mayor), a short plump figure with a khaki army shirt and a blue beret, his jowl unshaven, hurried up the steps to his office. He was a Social Democrat, a refugee who had escaped from house arrest after being deported back to Italy from Belgium by the Germans in 1940. His mind was still full of nostalgia for the fuller life he had known in Liége – and full of anxiety about the Communists with whom he maintained now an uneasy united front.

He was something of an athlete, the Sindaco. We would pass him in the evenings, on our way back from route marches, playing the local bowling game in lanes on the hillsides out of the town. This game was played with iron bowls like small cannon-balls, and was a mixture of bowls and golf. You tried to see how far you could send your ball bouncing along the curving lane, cannoning off the earthern banks on either side. It required a strong arm and wrist, and a considerable knowledge of every curve and bank along the road.

Now the clock in the town square struck the half-hour. Half a dozen batmen pushed their way through towards the rear of the tower where a big notice, chalked on the ancient wall, informed them that there was 'Two Up To-day – 1300 hours' – and where they might get half an hour's skill and gambling before the provost took too close an interest. A woman with waved blonde hair, whose tailored brown costume and high-heeled shoes struck a note of sophistication which to anyone but Italians would have seemed out of place, came by. The Italian men as well as the soldiers eyed her hungrily as she headed for the Field Security office on her daily quest to see if she could get a lift back to her home in Florence. Then came the girl who had married the Canadian sergeant, and the girl who clearly ought to have married a Canadian. The Canadians had preceded us in their area before they took ship for France.

A small boy detached himself from a group of peasants and came towards us, a note in his hand. It was a plea from the mayor 'Please can our hospital the medicine for the itch have?' We sent him on to the chief medical officer and returned to study the lazy Matelicani.

Matelica felt that it could hold up its head and saunter amid this foreign soldiery. It too had fought. It had worked its passage. It had produced a useful partisan movement, and its boast was that it had liberated itself in the German retreat of July 1944. In this very square the Germans had shot fourteen hostages and partisans only a year before. The Germans had had to classify this as a *Zona Infetta dai Rebelli,* and had had to guard convoys coming up the narrow passes from Ancona. The Matelicani had hidden many Allied prisoners who had escaped from the barracks which were being built as a prisoner-of-war camp farther up the valley – barracks which we had completed, and now occupied. The town walls still bore notices in huge black type telling people to remember 'the martyr Pedro Matellio' or 'the martyr Inez Barturo'.

Against this background we worked during those March days. The date at which we were to go back to 'the sharp end' had not yet been told us, and few put their minds forward to consider it. We lived where we were, in Matelica, and in the present. There was no use anticipating trouble. The division had digested the knowledge that a hard campaign lay ahead before the war could end, and concentrated on the tasks of preparation. So during the day we worked and at night we drank with the Matelicani, and particularly with the family on whom we were billeted.

We had by chance the star billet of the area. It was the home of a wealthy ex-gendarme who had now become the owner of sixteen small farms. He was a 'warm' man, as Soames Forsyte would have said, and he lived on the first floor of a big stone building which was half a baronial hall, half a modern flat. At one end was a big dining hall with lofty oak ceiling and stone floor, a private chapel, a salon hung with innumerable indifferent paintings in gilt frames, walls frescoed with scrolls and dignified colours. At the other end were new bedrooms, bathrooms which would have seemed modern in Hollywood, a sitting-room with modern steel furniture. I slept in this modern part. My bed, with a deep soft mattress, fine sheets, and an elaborate bed-warming apparatus that looked as if some fat guest had preceded me under the blankets, was one of the sights of the division. Visitors used to come and gaze at it as a sign of unbelievable luxury.

The family used neither the new nor the old parts of the house. They spent all day, and all evening, in one back room, which was almost completely filled by a big table, a sideboard, a stove and a couch. Here they sat during the mornings, playing 'Lili Marlene' and 'O Sole Mio' on the piano-accordion. Here they made enormous lunches of spaghetti, garlic, meat and salads; here at night they sat around the table drinking, talking and laughing with us.

Evening in 9 Via Umberto was an experience as appetising and distinct as Italian food. At the table would sit Momma, her hair grey, her hands folded, watching all of us, following part of our bad Italian and none of our English. My fellow-guests had both the same Christian name, Brian, so they had called themselves Bruno Primo and Bruno Secundo to simplify matters. Both captains, both in their early twenties, they were essentially carefree boys carrying the responsibilities of men and carrying them easily. They had both had ample fighting experience with their units, so that their minds were at ease in a way which comes to few people in the world. They had the gaiety of certain courage, and a full gusty enjoyment of life. Momma mothered them, and had long since adopted them, along with the fourth billettee, Stephano. She watched them with satisfied maternity on her face throughout the evening, her eyes smiling, though she kept at the same time a careful check on Stephano's flirting with Maria, her dark haired, thin daughter. In addition to Maria, the family consisted of the son, in his thirties, who surprised me one evening by claiming to be a communist, and his pretty young wife and baby son. The wife was the daughter, we were told, of the city butcher, and was something of a local belle, but was thought to have married above herself by entering into this family. Be that as it may, she was certainly among the best looking girls in Matelica, and one of the sweetest.

While we talked around the table, drinking white wine and laughing out of all proportion to the merit of the wit, in that way which army life, and only army life, seems to produce, Poppa, the ex-gendarme, would sit in an arm-chair in the corner, his hat on his head, emerging only occasionally to insist on more wine being poured out. He had attained fame, and started his fortune, back in the eighteen-nineties, by capturing a notorious brigand in Sicily. Under pressure – not very great pressure either – he would bring out the yellowed papers with the story of his deed and his photographs, with side whiskers and moustaches, against Sicilian hillsides.

The other inhabitants of the room were two black poodles, Stephano's setter, and noise. The noise was fantastic. From a murmur of conversation it could rise suddenly until it was a fully orchestrated mixture of talk, yells, barks, music and the radio. We would all be arguing in soldier's Italian when the baby would be brought in after his evening meal, and start to cry. That would rouse Poppa to loud remonstrance. The dogs would start to bark. The baby's mother would play on the accordion to soothe him. The radio would be shouting the news in, as often as not, some incomprehensible Balkan tongue. If by any chance the dogs failed to join in, we could rouse them to fury by a series of low whistles. In short everyone would be having the time of his life, not the least Stephano and Maria flirting in the heart of it all, with the two Brunos crying encouragement to Stephano in English which seldom bore translation. Yes, the evenings were not dull in the Via Umberto.

When we left Poppa produced his best Orvieto and we drank a round for luck and another for victory, and Momma wept as she kissed us good-bye. It was in truth good-bye. There was little chance that the road of war would lie again for us through the narrow streets of this remote Italian city.

With the banal irony of war, we began our move forward from Matelica to the Po Valley on Good Friday. We moved in conditions of secrecy, with the white fernleaf sign painted out from our trucks and jeeps, and with our cap badges removed. To the Matelicani we spread the rumour that we were off to France, for it was quite impossible to hide the fact that we were moving somewhere. It was just a quarter-past six in the evening, when the crowds were filling the streets, and the women were coming away from church with black and coloured scarves in their hands, that our trucks moved one by one out of the square, swung into line, negotiated the detour by the blown bridge on the north-western edge of the town, and started off on the road down the pass towards the coast.

Ah, those roads to war! How clearly they were to be graven into the memories of all who travelled them. Who of the Desert Army would be likely to forget the tarmac winding through the sandhills beyond Mena, past the pyramids and out towards Alexandria, branching west-wards at the big black and white notice – 'Western Desert – Beware of Enemy Air Attack', and then along the ridge through Alamein to Matruh and Halfaya? Who would forget Route 6 north of Naples, winding up from Caserta, with its squalid streets and shouting, ragged children, and its great palace which Nelson and Emma had known, until it crossed the Volturno where Garibaldi had fought, on towards the mountains of Cassino? Or Route 6 again, entering Rome, through its dusty outer streets, past white gaunt workers' flats? Or Route 2 below Florence, where the black fernleaves stencilled on white crosses by the roadside showed where our summer battles had gone. And now Route 16, following the line of the Adriatic Coast northwards, towards one more front. Here was Pesaro, with its outskirts levelled and blown, and the tangled minefields and wire and severed trees to mark the Gothic Line, rushed in an afternoon by the Canadians last summer; Rimini, with on its outskirts the cemetery of the Greek Brigade, and the luxury hotels along the coast battered and windowless; then the Rubicon, with half a dozen streams to make your choice from in arguments about where Caesar had crossed; then the plain suddenly opening out ahead, so that you knew Northern Italy for what it really was, another land from the south, a country as different from Naples and Sicily as England is from France, Cisalpine Gaul rather than Italy proper.

We drove all night, in the dark, to avoid the German agents picking up our move. The rear area was crammed with agents, the Frontlaufer who ran the gauntlet of the two lines to provide the Germans with information. So that it was daylight when we came out on to the open country beyond Rimini, and linked up again with the familiar road names and signs which the Eighth Army had used ever since they guided the convoys forward at Alamein – Sun, Hat, Bottle, Boat.

The countryside that morning was itself a good omen. During the month we had been in the south, spring had transformed these plains, dreary and harsh in the extreme in the winter, into places of supreme beauty. The lines of osiers and mulberries, and the bare vines which had thrust brown, hard arms into the frosty December air, had dis-appeared now under soft greenery and blossom. The mud had gone, changing overnight to the white powder which is the dust of Italy, finer and more irritating and filthier than any dust the desert ever saw. There were purple irises in the fields, and violets and primroses, as we drove forward along narrowing roads, until we reached our own sign of a 50 and a fernleaf. Finally we were at our new location. Divisional head-quarters swung off into the farm-yard which was to harbour our vehicles. Here the division spread itself, a community of 17,000 men, over the countryside, into farms and houses, under hedgerows, along fields. And here in the dining-room of what had been the home of a wealthy Bolognese landowner, with an orchard in full bloom outside the window, we settled down to the final stages of preparation for the battle of the Senio.

Most of this planning work was done at small conferences, presided over by the General, and attended by his senior commanders – the three infantry brigadiers, the artillery brigadier, the commanders of the divisional engineers and signallers, the heads of the supply services and medical services and the senior members of the General's staff. They were conferences which were to continue daily, morning after morning, and often evening after evening as well, until we had broken the back of the German resistance and had the way to the Isonzo and Trieste open to us. At them the course of the battle for the past day and night was reviewed, and at them the main lines of attack for the next twenty-four hours were settled. They were, so to speak, meetings of the Cabinet of the 2nd New Zealand Division, meetings where the past course of the battle was mirrored, and where its future course was shaped. They had as a result all the fascination of any conference which exercises power, and whose shifts of opinion and of decision can mould and affect the lives of many men.

It so happened too that the battle which developed during this April in Northern Italy was to be very largely affected by the actions of our division. After the initial attack we became the leading formation, whose moves and policy affected fundamentally the whole course of the campaign. To a large extent we were to set the pace of the battle, and it became a battle where pace was all important.

This divisional policy was made largely by five men – the two senior infantry brigadiers, the artillery brigadier, the commander of the engineers, and by Freyberg himself. Of these, four were professional soldiers, the only peace-time civilian being the engineer colonel. General Freyberg – or to give his full name and title – Lieutenant-General Sir Bernard Cyril Freyberg, VC, GCMG, KCB, KBE, DSO, and two bars (the third was to be added in this campaign) was planning what he knew was almost certainly his final campaign. I do not think he was sorry. He was in his eleventh year of fighting service in the field, which is enough for even the most vigorous. He had spent four and a half years on Gallipoli and in the trenches of Flanders in the last war, and five and a half in Greece, Crete, the desert and the Italian mountains in this war, a period of active duty which few other officers have known. With most commanders the passage of time carries them back from the fighting formations to posts with a corps, an army or an army group. The field soldiers of one war become the higher command of the next, directing the fighting from the headquarters zones instead of conducting it in forward areas, with all that that involves in physical danger and arduous living. Alexander and Macarthur were, for instance, both brigadiers in World War I. Wavell and Montgomery were colonels. Freyberg, by accepting command of the Second New Zealand Expeditionary Force in 1939, had assumed the obligation of commanding in the field the division which, except for brief periods, was the largest force which New Zealand maintained in the European theatre.

He had, it is true, commanded all the British forces in Crete, and had commanded Ten Corps at the close of the African campaign, and a specially formed formation, New Zealand Corps, at Cassino. Throughout the bulk of the Mediterranean campaigns, however – in Greece, in the desert from 1941 to the closing stages of 1943, and in Italy from the Sangro onwards, with the exception of Cassino – he had remained a divisional commander. He could no doubt have had higher posts permanently, but he preferred this New Zealand command. For he had rediscovered himself in this war as a New Zealander (he had been in the British Army during and after the last war), and it was with this New Zealand force that he was determined to see it through to the end.

Freyberg looked the commander. Though he had put on some weight after an aeroplane accident which, in September 1944, had gashed his stomach muscles, his big frame and powerful swimmer's shoulders carried it easily. Driving forward in his jeep, his red hat-band showing up through the dust, or standing by the cross-roads directing movements in a crisis, he was unmistakably the man in control. It was the same in these planning conferences. His expression, which could be almost that of a boy when he relaxed, would settle into quite another pattern when decisions were required. His mouth would shut so tightly that the lips almost disappeared, and his eyes would stare from under their deep-set brows, bright and intense as he watched speaker after speaker.

Freyberg's honours and decorations covered a great expanse of his battledress jacket with bars of ribbons, and filled about as many lines in

the Army Gradation List. Columns of newspapers and magazines have
been filled with accounts of his exploits in the last war, and in this. Any
reader of these articles knows probably more, accurately or inaccurately,
about Freyberg's life in the last war than those of us who served with
him in this. For very, very rarely did he ever reminisce about the past.
He would always turn aside any questions referring to it with great
skill. He was antagonistic to those war correspondents who wrote him
up personally as an heroic figure, and extremely reticent in conversation
about his own life. Indeed one of the few stories which Freyberg ever
told concerning his battle experiences was one which reflected on them
with mild satire.

It was set during the present war, at the time of Alamein. The
division was hurrying down from Syria to help hold the line at Alamein.
Freyberg, en route, called at the New Zealand Club in Cairo. Outside
the door were a group of New Zealanders and two Australians who had
drunk deeply of the good New Zealand beer which in those luxurious
days was still shipped over to us. The Australians studied with interest
the tall figure with a General's badge on his hat whose appearance was
arousing the Kiwis to an unwonted degree of saluting. Then one
Australian swayed forward: 'I know who you are,' he said with
triumph, 'you're that bastard who swam ashore at Gallipoli.'

There was more in this reticence than modesty – there was boredom
and judgment. Instinctively brave, with an aggressiveness and a
belligerency which carried him right through fear, he found nothing
to discuss in individual courage. It was of interest to him, as to any
genuine commander, primarily as an element in the morale of a unit,
as a symptom that a force was well led and in good shape. Discussion
of individual cases of it he avoided, above all if they were incidents
affecting himself. Freyberg too, so far as I could judge, believed that,
important as courage may be, judgment and the capacity for swift
decision in the shifting currents of the day's battle are equally important.
He valued clarity and training of mind immensely, both for warfare and
for the ordinary business of living.

This led General Freyberg to a genuine respect for learning and
intelligence. He had read widely and talked widely, with an appetite for
information which was stimulating to anyone around him. He could
quote copiously from Jane Austen's writings and Winston Churchill's
talk. This intellectual interest arose, I believe, largely as a result of his
experiences in the last war, when chance threw him, in the Hood
Battalion of the Royal Naval Division, among some of the liveliest
intellects and most truly cultured men of the time. Rupert Brooke,

Arthur Asquith, Denys Brown, Patrick Shaw Stewart, A. P. Herbert, Julian Grenfell were all among his fellow officers. There were many others of this type, drawn into the Royal Naval Division when it was first formed by Winston Churchill. It is not difficult to envisage the impact which these men had on the open, curious and vigorous mind of the young New Zealander who sat with them around mess tables on Mediterranean troopships, in caves on the shores of Gallipoli, in dugouts in Flanders. His immense strength, the legacy of long hours of swimming in Wellington Harbour and his military instinct and experience – for Freyberg came to the Hood Battalion after fighting in 1913 in the Mexican civil war – had carried him to leadership over these men of talent and culture. There was nothing in the educational system of New Zealand at that time which could have given him similar intellectual development, for he had grown up in the robust but Philistine atmosphere from which his contemporary Katherine Mansfield had fled to Bloomsbury. But he had the intelligence and interest enough to appreciate their gifts.

In these later years, in his occasional periods of reminiscence, he would recall the Latin tags which they flung at each other under bombardments, the stir in the lounge of the troopship at Malta when Rupert Brooke, handsome and laughing, had come aboard, the letters which poured in from all over the world after Brooke had been buried on Skiros and his fellow officers had heaped his grave with rough white marble. Rupert Brooke, Freyberg said, incidentally, spoke very little throughout this last voyage, and kept to himself, apart though not aloof, as if he already knew the fate that awaited him.

It is not surprising, therefore, that when the last war ended one finds that one of General Freyberg's closest friends was not another soldier but James Barrie, who was to pay eloquent tribute to him in his address on 'Courage'. Freyberg tried, too, to get permission to go up to Balliol and read history, which he considered would be of value to him in the career as a British regular officer on which he had embarked. But the War Office thought otherwise, and packed him off to St Cyr to take a French Staff Course, along with two other officers who were to become, in time, Field Marshal Lord Wavell and Field Marshal Sir John Dill – and with whom he was in World War II to have some mighty disputes about strategy in the Middle East.

Under these influences, Freyberg developed the hallmarks of the sanely educated man. He spoke well, and wrote a good robust clear prose. His campaign reports were essentially his own work, and they read well – particularly the one describing the final battle at the Mareth

Line. Even at this stage of his life he retained too a willingness to observe and acquire further views and information.

On to Freyberg, the expatriate New Zealander whose ways had been shaped by life in a cultivated and still wealthy England in the twenties and thirties, there fell in the forties another profound influence. He returned, in commanding the Second New Zealand Expeditionary Force, to the atmosphere of his own country. For this Force remained throughout the war a segment of New Zealand transplanted overseas. And if Freyberg exercised a profound influence on the men who served under him, they in their turn exercised a great influence on him. For Freyberg encountered here, among these New Zealanders abroad, many of the qualities which he had found lacking in the British society of the past twenty years. Here was no officer caste drawn largely from the ranks of wealth, separated by a wide gulf from troops of poorer physique and inadequate education. Here was an army which, owing to the physical and educational opportunities which New Zealand affords, literally showed no gap, except in duties and responsibilities (and therefore in rank and prestige) between the officer and the man. The General felt at home among these stocky men in grey New Zealand jerseys who watched him appraisingly, sceptically, quizzically, as they stood up from around their gun pits, or as his jeep passed them trudging forward on roads that were now dusty, now muddy, month after month. The ordinary New Zealand soldier was not only physically as tough as Freyberg himself, but mentally as independent and critical. Here were officers, from brigadiers down to second lieutenants, with minds of their own, which they were prepared to express, and who paid a very high respect to efficiency and responsibility. As the years went by, and as the General became more and more of a New Zealander again, and his troops became, by their long years abroad, more Europeanised, this division developed a personality entirely its own. It acquired a corporate sense as strong as that of a great university, so that those who served with it, whether they realised it or not, would to the end of their days carry its impact in their minds and their personalities.

Whatever its internal feelings, however, the task of the division was to fight, and now on the Senio it prepared to fight once again. Grouped around the table in the dining-room of this farm-house in the Romagna were senior officers who had been with the General throughout these years. The New Zealand Army was too small, and its tradition of anonymity too strong, for these men to have caught the spotlight of publicity during the war. But they are worthy of attention, because they were typical of the men of a dozen armies who brought the war to success, men who had to make their chief decisions not at long range in the calm of planning offices and conference rooms, but in forward command posts often under fire, when a decision one way or the other could spell victory or disaster.

Two of these men represented something fundamental in New Zealand life as well as in the New Zealand Division – the belief that what counts in a man is, above all, how well he does his job. They were Brigadier Gentry, who commanded now the 9th Infantry Brigade, and Brigadier Queree, who commanded the artillery. Each had been in his turn chief of staff to the General (or in Army jargon, each had been GI on the divisional headquarters staff). Gentry, short, with spectacles, and a quick thrusting manner, Queree lean, critical, quiet until called on and then suddenly slashingly assertive, were both regular soldiers. They were both members of the New Zealand Staff Corps, that small body of officers who had built up this war-time fighting machine. For if Freyberg led this army, it was the staff corps who had built the bones of it. Life for both Gentry and Queree turned, and had turned now since 1939, completely on the division. They saw the war in the terms of its development. Their task had been to build up this force to a peak of fighting ability and to that end they had spared the energies of neither themselves nor the officers under them.

Gentry had been GI from Crete to Alamein, where he had gone off to command a brigade. Queree had remained GI from the desert until the summer of 1944. With an almost puritanical zeal (in itself another New Zealand characteristic) he had carried on this labour of building up the division so that it should be, above all else, efficient. With the inefficient, or those who he felt had not the interests of the division foremost in their minds, he was prepared to be ruthless, abrupt and unforgiving. His was the very reverse of 'I say, old boy, jolly good show what? worth a pound a minute' attitude of the staff officer who was then common on the stage (and often enough in life). The result was reflected now in the smooth functioning of the division.

These men had, too, a further qualification which they imparted to their successors – the ability to work in well with the General. They knew how to take his broad orders to attack here or probe there, and translate them into terms of rounds-per-gun and starting-times and starting-lines and rate-of-advance and the countless other interlocking elements which make up a military plan. They were both, also, very skilful at opposing the General when they thought it necessary. Their method, I observed, was to oppose always on a basis of fact. They would not just pit opinion against opinion, military instinct against military instinct, but would argue with details and figures and ranges and timings to prove that their view was more likely to bring success. They would brief themselves for their case more thoroughly than any advocate at law, and fight it skilfully.

Now they had both passed from the role of staff officer to that of commander. Gentry had under his hand the new weapon which had been forged that winter – the 9th Infantry Brigade, about to fight its first series of battles. Queree had under his hand the greatest weapon of all those we possessed – the guns. It was not his first battle as a commander, but it was to be the first time he had exercised command of the artillery in a fast moving battle.

The other dominant brigadier was also a professional soldier, Brigadier Parkinson. He was another type altogether. Leaning forward on his chair, his head thrust out of the collar of his furlined leather jacket, pipe in mouth, walking-stick tracing designs on the floor, there was something shaggy and leonine about this stocky aggressive man. You felt that here was a commander who would if need be go forward and with his own shoulders burst open the barriers in his way. He was indeed, just that – a hard-fighting, burly soldier, full of soldierly craft and shrewdness, well aware that war is an ugly business, won by taking ugly decisions, disliking the cost of them but prepared to pay it. He too demanded a high standard of fighting ability from his men and his officers. When an officer came up before him as a possible candidate for a staff course, 'Parky' would look him over carefully and then suddenly demand 'Ever killed a German?' Heaven help the man who tried to bluff in reply, for Parky knew that in fact few men in modern war see or contact their enemy at close range.

Very like him in many ways was the engineer commander, Colonel Hanson. Hanson was a solid block of a man with greying, crinkled hair and a lined, open face. He looked for all the world like the Red Army commanders of wartime propaganda pictures. Here was the same solidity, the same determination, which you saw in the faces of photographs of Red Army officers, grouped around a tank in some snow-covered forest. Hanson was in private life one of the leading civil engineers in New Zealand, and one of the foremost experts in the world on road making. He had turned down a high post in the New Zealand Public Works Department to come back to the Army after leave in 1944, because he felt he should see the thing through. And see it through he did, with great thoroughness. He had already made of the New Zealand Engineers one of the finest bodies of specialists in this war. In the desert they had developed much of the minelifting technique which had been used at Alamein, and which later became standard throughout the British Army. They had bulldozed roads through remote areas of the desert to pass the division through 'impassable' country in the left hooks at Agheila and Mareth.

Here in Italy they had had even dirtier work to do. For the war in Italy was an engineers' war, a war of lifting minefields, building approach roads, filling craters, clearing demolitions, and above all of building bridges. The Germans' most valuable weapon in Italy was not the field-gun or the 'plane or the machine-gun, but the demolition charge which could block a ravine or blow a bridge and hold up an entire army until the new Bailey was in position.

'Bull' Hanson and his hard-faced, hard-bitten sappers, who handled dynamite as another man would handle a packet of cigarettes, were in the end the people who set the pace of all our advances. Every battle we had fought in the past, except for the summer fight south of Florence, and every battle we were to fight now was for a bridgehead across a river or canal, tenable only if we could build bridges quickly enough and big enough to get our tanks over. No plan could be drawn up, no battle could go in, until the CRE – for in technical parlance, Hanson's rank was Commander of the Royal Engineers – had decided when and where he could build his bridges.

Hanson and Parkinson were so alike in temperament that they were bound to clash. When they would open out into an argument at a planning conference it was like two tanks charging each other head on. But each knew his own strength so that they clashed only rarely, and with caution. But they were noteworthy encounters.

These were the stars of these conferences. But there were others of major calibre too. There was Brigadier Bonifant, the peace-time stock auctioneer who had risen from a troop leader in the Divisional Cavalry to command the Fifth Brigade, a warrior by instinct. I always think of him as I saw him one morning on Sidi Rezegh in 1941, when he commanded a troop of the ridiculous jam-tin Mark VI light tanks of those days. He was summoned to the General.

'Bonifant,' the General had said, 'we aren't sure who those chaps are' – and he pointed to a skyline covered with what looked suspiciously like the tanks of the Italian Ariete Armoured Division. 'I want you to find out.'

And off Bonifant went in his tin-can, straight towards the Italians, who were fools enough to fire on him and give him the knowledge he sought. So, its engine boiling like mad, the Mark VI came down the escarpment again in a cloud of dust, bringing back Bonifant and the information. No cutter of Drake's facing up to the Spanish Armada ever did a job with more verve.

There was too Colonel Campbell, the peace-time civil servant, who commanded the Armoured Brigade, Colmore Williams, the liaison officer with the Air Force, Colonel Cook, still in his twenties, a quiet-voiced lawyer who controlled all questions of supplies and reinforcements in his job as adjutant and quartermaster-general of the division, Elliott, the chief medical officer, Foubister, the signaller, Gilbert, the GI, another officer still in his twenties, who spoke good German, and who carried, as did all of these young officers, a burden of responsibility which in any other circumstances might have staggered them.

This then was the divisional 'Cabinet', the officers who attended the General's 'Orders Group' or conference. There was nothing peculiar to the New Zealand Division about these conferences. They are part of the drill laid down for the planning of any military operation, and they were held by other formations as well. The only difference we could claim – and I think it was an important difference – was in procedure. These were never formal 'Orders Group' conferences, to use the technical term, in which the divisional commander called in his immediate subordinate commanders and issued his orders. They were meetings at which each senior officer reported on events on his particular front or in his particular sphere, and at which any officer could – and did – put forward his own views about what should be done. It was only after there had been a full discussion that the General would announce the main outlines of the plan, which would be confirmed later – if there was time – in writing. This had great advantages. It meant, that, although the final decision lay with the General, all those who would have to carry out his orders knew that their own view had been considered and examined. They also knew the whole plan, as it affected all branches of the Division – artillery, armour, signals, infantry and all the others – so that risks of a misunderstanding or breakdown between the different arms was reduced to a minimum. This was a lesson we had learnt in the desert. There, when we were raw ourselves, and had had often to work with other units who were raw too, we had seen how essential it is before an action that everything should be properly 'tee'd up' or 'buttoned up'.

I have said that the final decision lay with the General. This was of course also the accepted military method. His was the final responsibility for success or failure; on him therefore rested the final act of choice which would send the division in at this place, at that time, in these ways. He had to measure up to the one fundamental criterion of generalship – did he win battles? Therefore he kept the final control. It was the same principle on which Abraham Lincoln ran his Cabinet. Lincoln's first Cabinet was, as is well known, not all of his own choosing. Many men opposed to his policy had been packed into it for Party reasons. At its opening meeting the crucial question of sending reinforcements and supplies to Fort Sumpter had to be decided. To send them meant risking war with the South; not to send them meant appeasement. Lincoln asked each member of the Cabinet his view. The other six members each said: 'My view is "No". We should not take the risk.' It came to Lincoln's own turn. 'Gentlemen,' he said, 'my opinion is just the contrary. I say "Aye" to the question. The Ayes have it.'

I do not remember many cases in which the General carried his own view through against a mass of contrary opinion, but he was able to do so if he chose. That was possible both under military procedure and under the terms of his own personality. But before he did so he took careful stock of the views of these other officers whose sunburnt faces watched his around the conference table, who had each an element of expert knowledge to contribute to the final decision.

CHAPTER THREE

Planning for Battle

As senior Intelligence officer of the division (technically, G2 I) I had a corner of my own at these discussions. It was the almost invariable practice for the conference to be opened by a statement made by the G2 I on the enemy's situation – what strength the Germans were estimated to have opposite, what positions they were holding, what indications there were as to their likely policy, what the ground was like, what the weather and the moonlight might be. These facts posed the problem which the conference then went on to consider. There was the enemy. How was he to be best 'sought out and destroyed'?

So that when the first conference was called on our return to the line I went to it clutching my notes about enemy strength and dispositions, and lugging a big diagram showing the Senio stop-bank and the general layout of the enemy forces in Italy. For good measure, Martin had taken care to listen in to and brief me about the latest BBC bulletin on the Russians, and to summarise the latest Eighth Army report about progress on the Western front and on the Russian front. It was well to be prepared on such points. Some brigadier was sure to ask about them. I had been long enough in the game to know that a wise intelligence officer, like a good lecturer, keeps at least one jump ahead of his listeners.

The situation which faced us this spring was essentially the same which the Allies had met since the first winter in Italy. A strong German force was spread across from the western to the eastern coast of Italy, prepared to fight stubbornly in the naturally strong defensive ground which the peninsula affords at practically every turn. Against these enemy lines we as a division had taken part already in six major Italian offensives, six of the blows which had been delivered again and again ever since the Eighth and Fifth Allied Armies had first squared up against the Germans around Salerno. Sometimes the Germans had held us; more often we had pushed them back steadily, but always their line had reformed on still another mountain or another river. Never yet had we succeeded either in destroying the bulk of their forces on the ground, or in securing the break-through which might have given us a chance to roll them up from the rear, though around Rome in May-June 1944, this had seemed a possibility.

This time the chances for a complete victory looked much better. The enemy was on a far wider front than ever before. As the leg of Italy widened out towards the north, so the German commanders had had to keep extending their line. It now ran in a curve, like a wooden long-bow, pressed towards us. One tip rested on the Ligurian coast just north of Viareggio, off the area where Shelley had been drowned. From there the curve ran across the great range of the Apennines just south of Bologna, meeting the plains of the Po where the Senio wriggled its way through the foothills between Imola and Faenza, and then ran across to the Adriatic at Lake Commachio. Its farthest tip met the sea near the haunts of yet another English poet – Byron's Ravenna.

This was a long front, on which the Germans had twenty three divisions, The German formations were fully up to strength in men and in armament. But the ground they had to cover was extensive. They were stretched very thin between Viareggio and the valleys below Bologna, where miles of mountains were held on our side by the 92nd Negro Division and the Brazilian Expeditionary Force. The bulk of the German divisions in the mountains held the heights and passes leading to Bologna, with the Allied Fifth Army facing them. Opposite the Eighth Army on the Po plain were six German divisions. On the coast by the Adriatic were the 42nd Jaeger Division, and the 162 Turcoman Division, both indifferent formations; to their right was the 362nd Infantry Division; to their right again, opposite the area in which we had moved, was 98th Division, a seasoned infantry force. Opposite the two Polish Divisions to our left stood the Germans only armoured division in Italy, 26th Panzer. With it, guarding Route 9, the great road running as if drawn with a ruler from Rimini to Piacenza along the foot of the Apennines, was 4th Parachute Division, certainly one of the best fighting forces left in the German Army anywhere in Europe.[1]

The line which these enemy troops held was one which we had not been able to break in the winter; but now our chances were more favourable. For the German bow was stretched very tight. Most of their troops were forward in the line, and had been there throughout the hard, fiercely cold winter. Vietinghoff, who had taken over in Italy when Kesselring was summoned to command on the Western Front, had only three divisions in immediate reserve to meet a break-through in the mountains or on the plain. These were the 155th Infantry Division, and two motorised formations, 29th Panzer Grenadier Division, and 90th

Panzer Grenadier Division. 90th Panzer Grenadier Division was a re-constructed version of the famous 90th Light Division which had pro-vided the elite infantry for Rommel's Afrika Korps. We had fought 90th Light across the face of Africa. They recognised themselves as old foes of the 2nd New Zealand Division, and had insisted on surrendering to us, and to no one else, when the end came in Tunisia in 1943. 29th Panzer Grenadier Division was well away from the battle front at this stage. Skilfully planted false reports of an Allied plan to land on the North Adriatic coast had lured it to the area east of Venice.

The enemy had therefore enough forces forward to make it possible for us to break him if he were hit hard enough. This was one point which argued for a spring offensive. The second was that these Wehr-macht troops could no longer be expected to fight as doggedly this spring of 1945 as they had done in the past. The Rhine was crossed; the Russians were close to Berlin. Even though the German propaganda service might din into the ears of the Sudfront fighters that they were holding the southern flank of the bastion into which the whole Reich forces would ultimately retreat, they were not likely to have much heart for a long hard fight. Their morale was likely to be brittle, though only a fool would expect it to be soft.

Such, then, was the enemy against whom Field Marshal Alexander and under him General Mark Clark were preparing to strike with both the Fifth and Eighth Armies. For strike we must. However tightly stretched the Germans might be, however apprehensively they might be looking over their shoulders towards the Reich, it was impossible to count on collapse in Italy without a further Allied offensive. Indeed the know-ledge that this offensive was coming was already influencing the minds of the German High Command in Italy. Though we were not to know it, envoys from the German Command in Italy were already on their way to talk surrender in Switzerland when we moved back into the Po valley. Yet this surrender was unlikely unless the fronts were broken in. The German willingness to stop fighting would certainly depend on the pro-gress which we made in breaking in their front. Only if we were winning in the field were the generals who favoured surrender likely to carry the day in their own inner councils.

The German front-line soldier would, we knew, fight on till he was told to quit. We knew the German as a good soldier, even in retreat, and this Wehrmacht force in Italy had been formed by Kesselring into a superb defensive machine. The German Tenth and Fifteenth Armies, however filthy the cause in which they fought – and the massacred civil-ians and the burnt buildings up and down their path were evidence enough of this – knew their business as soldiers. Their defensive battles in Italy will be studied by the commanders of the future, if war is ever again a matter of army against army, and not just of bomb against bomb, or bomb against civilians. We knew that the battalion officers would keep their men forward for the fight, and knew too that the higher officers were under Hitler's specific order not to retreat until they were forced back. This was the Führer's own decision. We had captured copies of it in Faenza in the winter. The penalty for retreat, except in the face of overwhelming pressure, was death, and had already been imposed. The German Commander, Colonel-General Heinrich von Vietinghoff-Scheel, was an outstanding field general who had commanded the Germans at Cassino. Military logic dictated that he should give up north-western Italy, with its big troublesome cities of Milan and Turin, and pull back to the formidable and shorter line of the Adige River. But no such logic got a hearing in the Führer's bunker in Berlin. The enemy records were later to show that Vietinghoff had sought some room for manoeuvre. But he was told that his mission was to 'defend every inch of the North Italian areas entrusted to your command'.

Everything in these circumstances suggested that the quickest way for the Allies to secure the end in Italy was to strike the enemy very hard, with everything we had, so as to break these brittle lines and – we hoped – brittle hearts, and open up the roads north, west and east. This Field Marshal Alexander and the Fifteenth Army Group Commander, General Mark Clark, now decided to try. On the ground we had by no means the margin of superiority which military science deemed necessary for an offensive against a strongly entrenched enemy. The two armies were remarkably evenly balanced. But in the air we had a margin of superiority which was to prove decisive.

In the air we had a thirty to one advantage, an advantage which enabled our troops to go about their business confident that the hazy blue Italian sky above them was secure in the hands of the Allied air forces, but which made those same skies to the Germans the source of a constant, paralysing threat of danger which never left them throughout daylight hours. We had experienced this in Crete, and we knew what a nightmarish extra dimension it gave to the other problems of the battle field. The Germans were strong in anti-aircraft guns, and skilled in building and camouflaging their defences. But they fought this final battle, as so many others in Italy, under a degree of harassment from the air which was worth to us the equivalent of several extra divisions on the ground.

The Allied High Command decided that the first phase of the attack would be two-fold – a right punch by the Eighth Army on the Po plain; a left punch by the Fifth Army in the mountains. The Eighth Army attack would go in first, in the hope that the troops on its right flank could push swiftly northwards to the Po. This would enable the bulk of the enemy forces to be trapped against this wide, unfordable river by the pressure from the Fifth Army, striking northwards from the Apennines. The goal of the battle was set clearly as the destruction of the enemy armies, not the capture of territory or of cities. That could follow once the enemy was defeated.

These two Armies, the Fifth and the Eighth, faced up to the job with mutual confidence. We were a polyglot lot. Churchill was to comment later that never had so many nations advanced and manoeuvred in one line victoriously.[2] British, Americans, Indians, Poles, Brazilians, South Africans, New Zealanders, a Jewish Brigade, and the newly formed free Italian Army were ranged together for this assault.

The Americans were all in the Fifth Army. Their divisions had by now been weathered in the same hard Italian school as we had known. The rivalries and tensions which arose between them and the other Allies in other theatres had been burned away here by experience of a long, common hardship. Though there was surprisingly little personal mingling between the Americans and the British, or the Americans and the Dominion troops in any theatre of war, there was in Italy little of that stiffness and indeed suspicion which were to be in due course reported from the Western Front. We knew that these US infantry and armoured divisions would pull no punches in this battle which lay ahead, however close the end of the war might seem. Like all American units they had that willingness to accept big casualties which is the characteristic of a country with a big population. They were now truly battle-worthy troops, too, whom we had watched grow leaner and harder and more efficient every week in Italy, so that in these GIs you could see the plump, curved-cheek city man of the twentieth century disappear and the lean, rangy backwoodsman and pioneer of the earlier days come out again.

They, too, knew how to use the vast mechanised implements of modern war. We had noticed this particularly the last summer near Florence, when the American division which had taken over from us had moved in overnight with an immense mass of great vehicles which raced along the roads, turned, backed and fitted themselves and their equipment into the area with a swiftness at which even our own experienced drivers wondered. They were an army which would go well if they ever got open country ahead of them.

The information about the armies was marked in red and blue chinagraph (red for our troops, blue for the enemy) on the transparent talc, which, like a windscreen, covered the big map along one wall of our Intelligence truck. I had only to turn my head to see the square flags, each with a segment cut out of its side, and looking like birds with ever open mouths, which indicated the German divisions. They stood in single line along the Senio and then clustered in groups amid the brown contour lines that marked the mountains, thinning out again towards the west coast. For conferences we could unhook the map and carry it across the farm-yard, past the reeking cow byres and through the yard where the mess cookers roared, into the conference room. But it was not this coast to coast map which really drew attention from the conference. Its information was generalised and distant. The map on which we worked when it came down to the actual problem confronting our division – how to cross the Senio – was in much greater detail. It was formed by two sheets – 88 11 Italy 1/25,000, and sheet 88 11 SE – which showed every curve and bend in the river, every farmhouse, road, track and canal.

We had sat opposite that map, pored over it, written about the places on it ever since the previous December. For months afterwards I could close my eyes and recapture much of the detail of it. At first glance it looked as if a check design had been printed diagonally on the sheets, so regularly and squarely did the roads lie at right-angles one to another; a great natural grid based on the long straight red line of Route 9.

These were Italian Army maps, reprinted by the British, and with the light tracing of our own reference grid superimposed on them. The Germans used precisely the same map, but with different reference squares of their own on it. The original maps were not coloured, but our draughtsmen had worked on them so that the country stood out almost as on a photograph. Three blue snakes wriggled roughly parallel courses across the sheets, marking the Lamone River, just under the spider web of streets which was Faenza, then the Senio and beyond that, the Santerno. Between the brown and green masses which were the foothills, the Senio's course came down in great curves which sometimes threatened to intersect, forming strange tongues and segments of land like the pieces of a fretwork puzzle. It wound its way steadily in a north-west direction until about two-thirds of the way across the sheet, and then flowed almost due west for three miles, straightening out as it did so. It was along this relatively straight stretch that we were now taking over from 78th (English) Division, and across it that we were to attack.

The map showed, with delicate hatching, the flood-banks of the river. It was studded with tiny marks to show trees and orchards, and with the black dots which were farmhouses and even outbuildings. Yet even this detail failed to give a true idea of how thick was the vegetation and foliage of this country. You could see it stretching away below the window as we worked, dead flat for mile upon mile, with vines slung on wires, like green washing on a line, between mulberry-trees and stunted osiers. These, and the poplars and the young willows, turned the whole area into one dense orchard, green now and lovely with blossom, but making vision impossible for more than a quarter of a mile in any one direction. Even the blue tracing with which the draughtsmen had marked in the streams and canals hardly brought home the endless network of these minor water obstacles, across which a man or a tank could pass easily, but which required bridging or bulldozing before trucks could get over them. And without its supply trucks the army could not live or advance.

We had not been on this particular stretch of the Senio before. All winter we had held the sector to the south, astride Route 9, where the Poles now were. We knew that area well, but this we had to learn afresh. So on the ground the forward infantry began their careful patrolling; in the air the photo recce planes flew daily along the river, giving us a record which would stand up under the stereoscope like a model; and from prisoners and other sources we built up our picture of the enemy who were opposite us.

First signs were encouraging. Our predecessors, the 78th (British) Division, whose yellow battle-axe shoulder flash had been known to us from Cassino days, were one of the best British infantry divisions, and they had not rested inert during their time in the line. They had done half of our preliminary task of getting a substantial foothold on the near stop-bank, the complete control of which was laid down by the General as an essential forerunner to the main attack. Only nine enemy posts remained on our side of the river in the sector. It was clear that we should be able to get the enemy off with local actions, fought without heavy artillery support. This increased greatly our chance that the main attack would be a surprise.

Nor were we dissatisfied with our opponents. The enemy troops in this sector were the German 98th Infantry Division. Though it bore one of the low numbers which indicated early formation, and usually a high standing, in the German Army, it had never recovered from the hammering it had got in the Russian campaign of 1943-44. The remnants of 98th Division had been evacuated from the Crimea in 1944, and had been sent to the not over-healthy area of Zagreb to reform. Its reorganisation there had been hammered, not only by the Tito partisans, but by the inter-unit banditry, reminiscent of competing Chinese Armies, which was by this time being indulged in by German formations. Men from 98th Division who were on leave in France on D-Day were press-ganged as reinforcements for the Normandy front. The 98th Division replied by taking men off reinforcement trains heading for other units deeper in the Balkans. By such methods it attained some sort of strength again for the campaign in Italy, into which it had been called in 1944.

The 98th Division was commanded by a forty-eight-year-old Wurttemberger called General-lieutenant Alfred Reinhardt. He had fought in the 1914-18 war, had commanded a regiment at Kiev, and commanded a division in the Kuban bridgehead. He was known well to our troops, even though we had not come up against his division before, because a prisoner had reported that he kept three Russian girls as 'laundresses' at his tactical headquarters – one of those minor items which stay in the soldier's mind long after the more significant details of intelligence summaries have faded. His divisional sign was a cat, and we were to capture plenty of copies in the next few days of his divisional newspaper *Die Katze.*

As far as we could discover, almost all of the infantry of 98th Division were forward in the line. Only one battalion, with an estimated strength of 200 men, was held as a divisional reserve. This gave the Germans a strength of one man to every five yards in the holes along the Senio stopbanks and in the shell-torn ground behind. One could hear the cliché experts already trundling forward the expression beloved of military planners of the day about the enemy 'having all his goods in the shop window'.

Through this window we were now preparing to heave a very considerable brick. Lined up along the Senio was the main striking force of the Eighth Army. Astride the Via Emilia – Route 9 – was the 2nd Polish Corps. Then came our own division. To our right was 78th Division, then 8th Indian Division, then the 2nd and 9th Armoured Brigades, 56th London Division, and a number of independent brigades – 2nd Parachute Brigade, 2nd Commando Brigade, and the Italian Cromona Combat Group. 21st Tank Brigade provided further armoured support. We were to hit the enemy right along the line, and in particular to break through if possible on the right, along the edge of the big marshy stretch of Lake Commachio towards Argenta, the key to the River Po.

This was the first phase of the Allied plan – a break-through of the river line defences by the Eighth Army, accompanied by a break-out from the Apennines by the Fifth Army. In the second phase both Armies were to do a massive right wheel, and advance across the River Po and on to the German reserve position along the River Adige. This Adige Line guarded the open Friuli plain and the road to Venice and Trieste. The third phase was to capture Padua and Venice, whilst the Fifth Army swung left to liberate the great industrial cities of Milan and Turin. With Padua and Venice in our hands the way would be clear to Trieste. But at this stage no mention of Trieste as a goal had reached us.

The role of the New Zealand Division was defined as going bang at the Senio with everything we had. That sounds simple enough, as I write it now. But on the Senio line were enemy with machine-guns, Tommy-guns, rifles, grenades; in front of it was wire, and many mines. Behind were the German guns, and tanks. These included the heavy and formidable German Tiger and Panther tanks. Even Mr Churchill's most eloquent arguments in the House of Commons, where tank quality had recently been debated, had failed to convince our tank crews that their Shermans, despite their new seventeen-pounder guns and ammunition, were a match for a Tiger. How was this crowded shop window to be smashed?

General Freyberg's answer was one which the New Zealand Division had used as its orthodox form of set attack ever since Alamein. This was an attack by night under a very heavy artillery barrage. There was of course nothing new about such a method. It was the last war policy, as used on the Somme. Indeed the battle of Alamein had simply been the battle of the Somme over again, but fought on ground which was hard enough to stand up to the bombardment, and allow for manoeuvre and pursuit. There were no muddy morasses, torn up by months of previous shellings, no sunken roads and endless trench systems in the Western Desert to make the scheme unworkable. On the Senio we proposed to use the same technique. Massed artillery – our own and all we could borrow from Corps, Army and other divisions – would pound the enemy front and would then move ahead of our advancing infantry, raining splintered steel from the skies on to all the enemy who might otherwise resist. We would attack with two brigades forward, on a front of 4,500 yards, and go 4,000 yards into the enemy lines before we halted. Such was the formula.

The barrage formed a line of shell-fire which was marked on the gunners' maps in pencil and on the ground in flame, dust and smoke. This line could be pushed back steadily by gradually raising the range of the guns, so that the barrage crept forward. This provided a moving screen of fire behind which infantry could attack, as under the bombardment it was impossible for the enemy to do anything but crouch at the bottom of his dug-out or behind the wall of his house. For him to put his head up and open fire was to stand a very good chance of death. Few men, experience has shown, have the courage, the nervous resistance or the foolhardiness to do this, though they will pop up again quickly enough once the barrage has passed.

Provided the infantry follow right up under the barrage – in practice the safe distance to keep behind the shell-bursts is 200 yards – they can be on top of the enemy before he surfaces for a fight. Instead, then, of having to do battle with machine-guns posts and strong-points, the attackers can spend most of their time rounding up stunned and alarmed prisoners. Particularly is this true if the attack is put in at night, the time which we chose whenever possible.

This is obviously a most effective way of attack. But it is also a difficult one. In the first place it can be carried out, particularly at night, only by very well trained troops. Your gunners must be able to shoot with absolute accuracy, or otherwise their shells will fall among their own troops. Your infantry must know how to keep up under the barrage, a far more difficult thing than one might think. It involves walking forward with the air above your head torn and shrieking with passing shells, and with the knowledge that one faulty turn of a gunner's wrist, one error in timing, can bring all of this down on you. It involves obeying orders swiftly, keeping contact and direction amidst incredible noise, dust and confusion. It is also difficult to use a barrage in a moving battle. It is expensive in ammunition, for unless the barrage is heavy enough it will defeat its own purpose.

This is, perhaps, the cardinal factor. Attacks under a barrage involve great problems of supply and of transport. The tens of thousands of shells must be brought up and dumped near the guns before each attack goes in. As the campaign moves forward and new attacks are mounted, fresh supplies must be dumped, fresh gun positions surveyed and pre-pared, fresh plans drawn up. It is straightforward enough to prepare one barrage : to prepare a series, day after day, night after night, is another matter. Artillery was, in this war at least, still the boss of the battlefield, as Stalin had commented after Stalingrad. But it is a boss who needs great skill and training. It was our pride as a division that we had learnt how to do this. For such skill and training could pay their dividend not only in victories but in casualties avoided, in lives saved.

We were not, of course, going to use only artillery on the Senio. Into the pattern of the fire of the guns two other threads were to be woven – bombing and flame-throwing. The first had nothing new about it for us. We had now had fighter-bombers working closely with us – ever since the desert. But the flame-throwing was new. During the winter we had had our first demonstrations of Crocodiles, Churchill tanks which could hurl jets of flaming fuel, red on the top, black below, over 100 yards.

Eight of these tanks, each with its trailer filled with liquid, were already now moving forward to their positions close behind the front. Thirty-two flame-throwing Bren carriers, carrying fuel containers on the back and christened Wasps, were also ready.

And the minefields? How was this problem to be dealt with? It would have been very desirable to have sent forward sappers with mine detectors, as was done at Alamein and in ten thousand places since, to sweep paths through the fields on the slopes of the stop-bank. Yet it was impossible, for the Germans in their trenches along the bank could have picked them off with ease. The infantry brigadiers therefore came to the conclusion that there was nothing else for it but to knock the bank about as much as possible with the bombardment, and then send the infantry smack at it. The risk was calculated, and reckoned as unavoidable. The fields were more patchy here than those the infantry had probed around Route 9. The bombardment would damage them. The remaining mines would have to be left to fate.

So finally the plan was drawn up. 'We are going,' the General said, with some relish, 'to hit him a hell of a crack. We are going to hit him with everything we have got, so as to smash him on the stop-bank as much as possible.'

Out in the green countryside the means for this crack were assembled. The guns were in position, each troop surveyed in carefully so that its shooting could be absolutely accurate. The pits were dug, the camouflage nets spread, the yellow-banded shells stacked neatly alongside. On the airfields to the rear, along the coast at Rimini and farther south, the fighter-bombers waited in rows, the Spitfires with their curved wings, the Thunderbolts, the Kittyhawks. Aussies in hats with turned-up brims, Tommy pilots with blue, crushed RAF caps, came forward to see the troops and the ground before the attack went in. As far afield as Sardinia the four-engine Liberators and Fortresses were getting ready to drench the area ahead of us with anti-personnel bombs. Steadily, all along the front, the engineers were establishing their dumps of bridging material, and at night the bulldozers were moving up to hiding-places behind farmhouses close to the stop-bank. And on to paper, on to pages and pages of typed words and figures, and diagrams drawn as carefully as any architect's plan, all these things were being linked together into the final operation order.

'Operation Buckland' was the dull name which had been given to the offensive. It was dull intentionally, so as to give the enemy, should he hear of it, no clue as to our intention. Not for us the risk of spectacular names such as Round Up or Eclipse or Overlord.

The final plan read, item after item, like the events at a race meeting. The show was to start at ten minutes to two – 1350 hours – in the afternoon of D-Day. The strategic bombers – the Fortresses and Liberators – would then paste the area of the Santerno, and the rear of the Senio. They would use only small bombs to prevent the ground being so cratered as to hold up our tanks. The fighter-bombers would go at targets between the two rivers. At twenty minutes past three the artillery would open up.

There would be five main periods of shelling, spread over the afternoon until twenty minutes past seven, with ten-minute intervals after each of the first four. They would pound the Senio stop-bank and the area immediately to the rear, lifting from time to time to encourage the enemy infantry to pop their heads up, and coming down again to hit them when they did. After each of the first four shelling periods the guns would stop for ten minutes – but not the bombardment. For the fighter-bombers would then take up the job.

Just before dusk, the main infantry attack was to go in. This was H-hour – 1920 hours. The flame-throwers were to go first. The infantry would during the morning have withdrawn silently from the near stop-bank, and would be waiting 400 yards farther back, in slit trenches already prepared. When H-hour came the flame-throwers would roar forward along tracks already prepared, mount up ramps dug into the stop-bank, and flame the far bank. The infantry would follow them. The moment the flaming ceased they would climb up the near stop-bank, down its forward slope, place into position light bridges made of small canvas-covered kapok pontoons, cross over, up the far bank, and attack. Meanwhile the artillery would be pounding a region four hundred yards further on. Twenty-seven minutes later the barrage would begin to go forward and a second wave of infantry would follow it through to final objective just over two miles farther ahead.

The list of weapons we were to employ was heartening. We had under our divisional command, firing on our divisional front, as many guns as had been used to support the entire Eighth Army at Alamein. 470 fighter-bombers were available for use on the corps front, forty-eight medium bombers, and 500 heavy bombers. Once the infantry had cleared the enemy from the Senio area, the engineers were to build six bridges. Three of these would be down at the level of the bottom of the stop-bank, after holes had been blown through the banks by dynamite; two were to be built across the top of the bank; and one was a scissors bridge – a tank wedged into the stream with a special bridge fixed to its superstructure.

A quarter of a million shells were available for the first attack. A whole zoo of vehicles of war stood ready. There were Kangaroos, the hollowed-out Sherman tanks used for carrying troops; Fantails, which were armoured amphibious tracked vehicles, which for some strange reason were known in other theatres of war as Buffaloes; Ducks, or more strictly, Dukws, buoyant six-wheeled lorries which would be driven through water by a propeller; Wasps, the flame-throwing Bren carriers; Crocodiles, the flame-throwing tanks; and Dingo scout cars.

The main lines of this plan could be – and were – reduced to eight pages of foolscap – four for the operation instruction, four for the final operation order. This made it look very straightforward. Indeed, like all good military plans, it was essentially simple, just as a straight left is a very simple blow in boxing. All depends on the delivery of it. As Napoleon said of war : 'It is essentially a simple art – all lies in the execution.'

But it was the artillery plan which really gave an idea of the detail which was involved. For the guns were what mattered. Their plan consisted of fifty-six pages of typing, most of them long lists of eight-figure map references, in any one of which an error of one figure might mean bringing the barrage down on our own troops. There were nine pages of diagrams, each drawn to a very delicate scale. There were thirty appendices, giving further diagrams and other details, each carrying a letter, so that the alphabet had to be used a second time, the last appendix being AD. The plan provided for three separate barrages, for enfilade fire from the flanks, so that the stop-bank should be hit not only from the front but from the sides, for harassing fire tasks, which would bring down shelling on roads up which the enemy might bring reinforcements, or try to retreat. A smoke screen was also laid on, and a series of defensive fire tasks was prepared. These were marked on the map with diagrams like boxes, each with its name, so that the infantry commander who found himself held up or counter-attacked could, with one word given over his portable wireless, call down fire on to a particular area. There were special tasks assigned to some guns to attack the enemy batteries which would shell our advancing troops – counter battery tasks. Heavy and medium guns were told to stand by for anti-tank duties, for we knew that nothing discouraged a Tiger tank so much as a few 4.5-inch shells directed into his path. Each of these tasks had to be laid down in detail, with the time, the target, the type of ammunition to be used, the rate of fire. There was provision for 'Murders' – one kind of heavily concentrated fire – 'Linear' fire, 'Stonks'.

This plan was impressive enough when Brigadier Queree, on the eve of the attack, laid it finally on the planning table. Artillery draughtsmen, clerks, intelligence officers, survey troops and the other great range of specialists throughout that corps had been working for days on it. Yet harder jobs lay ahead for them. This plan had been worked out in relative quiet, with plenty of time for consideration, rechecking, preparing. Not so the other plans which were to follow. They were to be drawn up, checked, typed, and cyclostyled by men who were to spend half each day jolting forward, perhaps under fire, along narrow, dust choked roads; whose vehicles would be hastily parked in some new headquarters area, where the gear had to be unpacked and the work done right through the night, and the next day – day after day, night after night. Yet always there would exist the same need for absolute precision, speed and clarity, always the same knowledge that a slip in figures, read over by one weary clerk to another, might mean disaster, casualties to our own troops. So too it was with the gunners themselves – guns that had to be surveyed in, and the pits dug, under fire; ammunition convoys that must find their way forward in the dark along roads the edges of which were still mined, where a swerve could mean at the least a wheel blown off, to dump the shells by the guns and go back for more. Is it any wonder that artillery, in a moving battle, is a very difficult weapon to use on an ample scale? Indeed one of the biggest difficulties about having superiority of material in warfare is deploying it and using it.

Here, anyway, were the opening plans. Blocks of solid green colour marked with fine lines showed where the barrage would fall; blocks of solid blue showed where the heavy bombers would do their carpeting. The bridge sites were named, after New Zealand towns – Raglan, Seymour, Woodville. The roads were marked 'Red' forward, 'White' back, 'Blue' forward – all one way traffic. Provost detachments with wireless sets would control traffic at them. Searchlights were ready to provide artificial moonlight, Bofors guns to fire coloured tracer as a guide to the advancing infantry. On either side of us, to right and to left, the Indians and the Poles squared up as well. These three forces, which could hardly have been drawn, even by deliberate choice, from more disparate backgrounds, and which could hardly have carried in their minds more varied concepts of what they fought for, made their final preparations. Man is, in truth, a strange creature – and never stranger than when he is devoting his energies to killing his fellows.

CHAPTER FOUR

The Intelligence War

The preliminary thrusts to push the Germans off the near stop-bank went in without delay. By the morning of 4th April we had the banks clear, except for one troublesome post on our right flank. The action had been patchy, requiring hard fighting in some places, whilst in others the enemy had given up easily.

Our patrols had already had a good look at the banks. On the first day we were in the line a German had been wounded in an early morning exchange of fire. Four enemy stretcher-bearers were sent out, under a white flag. They came across the river on one of their many small foot-bridges, formed by roof beams covered with planks, and on to the far slope of the near bank. One of our corporals was a man of initiative. He at once got up out of his slit trench and moved down with three or four companions to the stretcher-bearers, exchanged smokes with them, talked to them in soldier's Italian, and urged them to desert. This they refused to do, but the discussion gave the corporal time enough to observe that the wire on the far stop-bank was already badly cut about by our shell and mortar fire, that there was no wire in the river itself at this point, nor on the far slopes of the near stop-bank, and that at one or two places the river was so low that it might be fordable. He came back and reported this in detail.

We began to get a few deserters, but no more than the average, and we were immensely aided by capturing a trace of the enemy minefields. This we worked up into a full picture of his mine defences, fitting into it information from patrol reports, from other captured documents, and from stray civilians who still permeated through the lines.

It was on the night 3rd/4th April that the real fight to get the near bank went in. In the centre the going was easy, and our patrols even got right across the river without arousing fire from the German sentries. At both extremities of our front, however, there was ugly fighting, with grenades and Tommy-guns, and when morning came the Germans brought down heavy mortar fire on our new footholds. But we had what we wanted – the near stop-bank. Our preparations for the attack could go ahead now as set out in the plan.

56

Then abruptly, three days before the offensive was due, the worries began. One of these was essentially an Intelligence problem. Was it not possible that the Germans had drawn back from the Senio, leaving only light forces forward? Did the enemy commander not appreciate that our attack was coming in, and that if he pulled back from the river with all but a few troops, he could make us expend our main onslaught on empty trenches? With the 5th Corps Intelligence officers behind us and with the brigade and battalion Intelligence staffs ahead of us, we discussed the evidence. What was there in favour of withdrawal? In the first place there was the extraordinary bombardment on the night of 6th/7th April. At five minutes to eleven that night, along the whole Eighth Army front from just below Commachio to Route 9, the enemy guns had suddenly opened up. They had shelled our own gun areas, and forward positions where troops might be expected to concentrate ready for an offensive. It was a beautiful clear night, and hour after hour the shelling went on, the flashes lighting the western sky, seeming to rip and tear it apart, and the shells wailing and whistling in towards us. The house we were in too seemed to expand and contract its thin walls under the return blasts of our own guns. It was months since the enemy had given us such a doing over. And it was good shelling. Gun positions, even those which had been silent till now, were shot up, and casualties and damage caused. The areas in which the attacking battalions were waiting got a thorough pasting.

This could mean one of two things. The enemy was preparing to withdraw, and was firing off his dumps before he went. Or he expected us to attack, and was shelling us first.

There was plenty of reason to think that he expected an offensive. His Intelligence system at this stage was first class. The prisoners we took had all been cautioned to stand on the alert. During the day he had twice had photograph reconnaissance planes over, chalking their paths across the dark blue April sky. However carefully our camouflage was carried out, he must have picked up many of our new gun positions and dumps. He had, too, much to our concern, got some prisoners from us. The night before a local attack had been put in on one of the new posts we had established on the stop-bank, the area had been nearly bracketed by belts of mortar fire, and four men had been seized. It was inevitable that they would be recognised as New Zealanders. Our return to the line would certainly be taken as a good clue to imminent action, for we were known as a shock division.

The Maoris, too, were behaving in a disconcerting manner. Night after night they were getting patrols down into the bed of the river in the centre of our section without drawing the enemy's fire. Were these stop-banks, so carefully watched, already empty? Was all this immense bom-bardment going to fall on empty ground, this quarter of a million shells to be wasted? One's mind quailed before the prospect. There were how-ever balancing considerations. There had been none of the usual sounds connected with withdrawal – the transport heard at night, minor dumps being blown up. There existed too, the iron order from Hitler that no withdrawals were to take place except under attack. So deeply did he by this time distrust his commanders that he had been forced to deny them even a limited freedom of manoeuvre. He literally held a pistol to their backs, and ordered them to stay, even when their professional skill told them it meant disaster. In different times one could have allowed for the possibility of the generals arguing Hitler over, particularly in a case like this, when there existed an even better line, the Santerno, immediately behind. The execution of the officers concerned in the July attempt on Hitler's life had, however, discouraged even the most zealous from expressing unpopular views. Few would now risk counselling withdrawal. It seemed to me that in the face of all this we must assume the enemy to be still on the Senio until he was definitely proved to be gone. He had to be presumed innocent of any intention to withdraw until we had un-shakable proof of his guilt. So, finally, we came to the conclusion that 98th Division was still holding the Senio in strength, and that the attack would hit him all right.

I put this opinion forward – together with a warning of the existence of the Tigers and Panthers in the area beyond the Senio across the river – at a meeting which the General called on the morning of 7th April. It was a meeting of the type which the public has come to associate with the name of Field Marshal Montgomery (though they existed in our divi-sion, and in some other units, before Monty reached the desert) at which the plan is explained in detail to the men who must carry it out. Into a field, bordered by fruit-trees and vines behind our farm-house, there arrived, on this sunny morning, officers of our own division, and of the other units (chiefly British artillery) who were under our command. There were indeed so many officers present that the General expressed doubts, in unusually testy tones, about the security arrangements. Were all these people entitled to be there? It was a hint of nervousness which I had not often seen in him. Something of the same strain showed in his explanation of the plan. He was more discursive than I remembered him on any similar occasion, and it was 11.30 (we had begun at 10 o'clock) before the conference adjourned.

He expressed his confidence in success, however, and to add an element of luck to the show, had worn a new suit of battledress, which he described as his victory uniform. When the conference was over he called me into his caravan and went over once again the arguments for and against the enemy having gone. 'Don't forget – we won't get those quarter of a million shells back if we fire them into an empty bank.' He then rang the brigadiers, and told them to keep probing hard. I was relieved, though, to hear him say on the phone to the corps commander : 'We think he's still there, though he may have thinned out a bit.'

All prisoners and deserters we captured got a thorough grilling, but none were ever done over so carefully as the three deserters whom we brought in the next day – the last but one before D-Day. They, to our relief, confirmed that everything looked normal on the far side. They had been sent forward on a forty-eight-hour spell of duty, an action hardly likely if a withdrawal was on. There were also enemy troops to be seen working on defences on the far bank, groups which had to be severely shelled before they gave up their job. To our right some enthusiasts even thought they saw parachutists. So that it was with a relatively easy mind that night that I wrote in the Divisional Intelligence Summary : 'It appears therefore that, on the evidence available up to the present, the enemy is still on the Senio line.'

One of my visitors on the afternoon of 8th April was Moana Raureti, the Intelligence officer of the Fifth Brigade. He sat on the low, blanket-covered box that served as a seat in the Intelligence truck, and argued with the lieutenant from the Psychological Warfare Branch. Moana's Maori skin was only a shade duskier, though much smoother, than the tanned faces of the other visitors. He talked in a slow, unhurried tone.

'But the Maori boys believe it would be much better if you sent a speaker forward with a microphone, to shout a few insults at the Germans. They reckon that would be better than these canned talks and music. Something to stir the Teds up a bit.'

The PWB expert differed politely. The loudspeaker with which he had supplied us, and which the Maoris had installed right under their side of the stop-bank, was not meant to inflame the enemy, but to weaken their will to fight. Honied words were the diet on which the Germans were to be fed, until they became restive with their own hard lot and deserted. So we broadcast to them, not taunts, but records of news about the bombing of Germany, and the Allied advances, interspersed with 'The Blue Danube' and other tunes calculated to rouse their nostalgia. The Maoris thought this poor stuff.

'Say something that will get the Hun mad. Then out he comes for a fight, and we shoot him down,' their colonel had said, and so Moana, in his capacity of Intelligence officer of the Fifth Brigade, under which the Maoris were grouped, had come to argue their case.

PWB won, for it was too late in the day for any changes. The next day the attack would go in. The brigade Intelligence officers were paying a visit to get any final information we might have. There was a goodly stream of other visitors, among them my brother, who was adjutant of the 26th Battalion, and his colonel. Theirs, I had been relieved to see by the operation order, was not to be one of the assaulting battalions, on this first objective. They were to pass through later in support. John Crawley, who was the head of the Intelligence staff of 5th Corps, had also come forward to look us over. The Political Warfare Bureau man had come with him to get back his loudspeaker machine before the attack went in.

The Intelligence truck was always like this. It was about as peaceful as the news room of a Fleet Street paper just before edition time. There was always someone coming in, or the phone would be ringing, or a conference was at hand and we would be working madly with the draughtsmen to get the maps up to date, or, bang, there would be a thump on the tail-board, and a liaison officer's voice would call: 'Don't know what you make of this – the battalion says it might be a new booby-trap but the engineer thinks it's just an outsize mortar bomb,' and you would look out to see some great projectile or unexploded shell or bomb resting there for examination.

The resemblance to a news desk went deeper than surface impressions, for much of the work of a divisional Intelligence officer was a form of military news gathering and news spreading. In the words of the *Field Service Pocket Book*, you were required to execute the 'Collection, colla-tion, interpretation and dissemination of all information about the enemy'. In practice this meant that throughout the day, while the division was in action, you ran a high pressure telephone news service, taking in information from a whole range of sources, working out as rapidly as the time allowed what this information meant, and then handing on the news and the interpretation to anyone who might be affected – the infantry brigades in the line, the artillery, the engineers, your own com-mander, the corps Intelligence officers above you. Once a day, in addi-tion, you wrote and published what was in effect a secret daily newspaper containing all the main information gathered about the enemy during the past twenty-four hours on your own front, and in the sectors immediately affecting it. You added to this mixture your opinion – or, to use the military term, your 'appreciation' – of what the Germans would do next.

This Intelligence Summary was then cyclo-styled by clerks working in a canvas-covered office truck, freezing in the winter and sweltering in the summer, and delivered the next morning by despatch rider to the brigades, battalions, ambulances and other units of the division.

It was fascinating work. You not only felt the constant throb of events under your hand, but you knew that your diagnosis of them, your recognition of what was significant and what was not, your linking of this fact to that, your note of this move of transport here and that deserter's story there, could affect major decisions, and through them the course of the battle. It required both intellectual discipline and judgment. You had to be as critical, as cautious, and as curious in your examination of new information as any scholar approaching a newly discovered classical text. For here there was no margin for what might or might not be true. Events unfolded themselves at such speed that you would be proved right or wrong in your judgment within twenty-four hours. If you said that there were Tiger tanks across the river, that fact was going to be investigated within the near future by people whose lives depended on its truth or falsity – and you were going to hear very bluntly about their discoveries. Nor was there any margin for the slightest degree of error. A slip of one figure in your map references in these summaries, or in a description dictated over the telephone, could mean at the least wastage of ammunition, at the worst accidents and disasters. It was the best mental training that I have known.

This application of the standards of good scholarship to the work of military Intelligence was, I believe, one major reason for the efficiency of this branch of British military work. And let no one have any doubt that it was efficient. The Intelligence work of the British Army in this war was first class – far superior to the German or the American. The tradition of T. E. Lawrence (whom they had forced out of Intelligence work in the last war) existed here strongly, the tradition of the mind trained in intellectual honesty, courageous enough to have confidence in the deductions from the evidence it had before it, and prepared above all to examine every item of information, poke it about, turn it over, hold it up, tear it to bits, before being satisfied of its truth.

The Eighth Army's knowledge of the enemy was helped greatly by the work of Enigma, the interception and decoding work which gave Britain a swift and intimate knowledge of the German plans and German thinking. Though we knew that use was made of intercepts of enemy wireless messages, we had no knowledge of how full this was until, thirty years later, the fact was revealed that the Poles had secured and passed to us before the war a specimen of the German Enigma encoding machine.

But the high level information this provided – code-named Ultra – had to be applied to the constantly changing pattern of events on the ground, and for an infantry division had to be supplemented by detailed knowledge and analysis of the activities and defences of the enemy on its front. It was important that the higher command should follow, through Ultra, the main pattern of the enemy's strategy. What we had to learn, for ourselves, was what no Enigma machine could tell us – which farmhouse was held, which track was mined, which clump of trees concealed a tank. All this had to come from our own resources, and from those of Corps and Army above us.

The New Zealand Army had many complaints to make, and made them, about the functioning of many things in the British Army, but I never heard, from 1941 onwards, any solid complaint against the quality of the Intelligence which was supplied to us, as a fighting division, by the Corps and Army headquarters above us. Nor did we have any complaint about the uses to which they put the material we supplied to them.

It may well be that the British capacity for losing every battle but the last accounts partly for this. For it is the weaker, the losing army which above all needs sound information about its enemy. You must know exactly how strong the enemy is, and where he is going to strike, and what his plan is going to be, if you have only a few divisions which you can dispose to meet him, and if the displacement of even a few units can spell victory or defeat. David has always been the one who needed to carry out careful reconnaissance, to find out exactly where the best pebbles lay and which was the least armoured spot on Goliath's person. In the American Civil War it was Robert E. Lee, whose Southern Armies were constantly outnumbered and out-gunned, who developed a first-class Intelligence service, and not the North. It was Wellington, not Napoleon, whose spy service became excellent in the closing stages of the Napoleonic wars.

The German Intelligence, in the same way, improved considerably as the war went from bad to worse for them. Towards the end in Italy they knew as much about us as we did about them, if one can judge from the documents we captured in this Italian battle. Yet in the earlier stages, at any rate in Africa, their information was often patchy and inaccurate. The Italian was much better. But that again is understandable enough, they had more reason to be wary. The Germans disposed in 1940-41 of such overwhelming force that they did not need to know exactly where the enemy was, or how strong he was. It did not matter much to them how the French Army and the BEF were disposed in May, 1940. They could smash them wherever they were. But later they had so little strength to spare that they had to think hard.

The same was true at that time of American methods. Ever since the days of Grant, with the massed factories and the massed battalions of the North on his side, their policy had been to accumulate so much force that, whatever the enemy puts against you, you can smash him. Why worry about working out what the foe's moves are going to be, whether he is going to man this line or that, if you have ammunition enough to saturate every possible line with fire? Don't pin-point the target; blot out the whole area. Grant's Cold Harbour policy: 'I am going to fight it out on this line if it takes me all summer' does not require a constantly observant Intelligence service.

The British Army, however, from the first days of the war onwards had had every inducement to sharpen its wits. There were to be, for many months, few other weapons to sharpen. This was particularly true in the North African desert. If you were far out in your estimate of Rommel's tank strength, if you thought he would come along the coast road when his attack was really aimed inland, you could lose a battle which might lose North Africa.

Intelligence became there, in this mobile war between two very evenly balanced forces, one of the major weapons, and it is Field Marshal Montgomery's strength that he rapidly realised this. He gave his own Intelligence officers the chance to overhaul their machine to the full, and he took them, with their knowledge of the German Army and its methods, with him all the way from Alamein to the North German plain. It was in North Africa that much of the main work of studying the German Army in action was done, for from Dunkirk until the North African landings of November 1942 this was the main battlefield on which the British Army fought. The desert, with its fast moving battles, moreover yielded abundant information. Each side was constantly over-running and capturing headquarters of the other, crammed with documents of all types. These documents, and other material, examined with a scholarly eye, yielded a mine of information. It was in building up a detailed picture of the new German Army from such sources that Brigadier Williams, the Oxford don who was to become Montgomery's chief Intelligence officer in Europe, rose from his original post as an armoured car troop leader and then regimental IO with the King's Dragoon Guards.

Our own division had early enough become very I-minded. The General himself was a great consumer of information about the enemy, whether on our own immediate front, or on the corps, army, or army group front or in any other zone of the war. He was particularly interested in every item we could glean from the Russian front. There he followed not only the German but the Russian movements with avid attention, for he regarded the Red Army strategy as first class. It was always an important day when we got a new AFHQ or Eighth Army summary with a study of the latest moves on the Russian front, and when the spring attack went in from the Vistula in 1945 the General had us all in to his caravan to drink success. His particular favourite was a general whom he persisted in calling affectionately Ross-o-kovsky, and the only flaw in the final campaign for him was that it was Zukhov and not Rokosovsky who took Berlin.

Our divisional Intelligence organisation was the normal one for any infantry division. We ran to no frills. Each infantry battalion, artillery regiment, tank regiment had its Intelligence officers who sent back to their brigade headquarters any information which came their way – patrol reports, details of enemy attacks or patrols, prisoners, papers from the dead. The brigade Intelligence officers reported back to us at division. There we had two officers, Martin and myself, working in one office truck. Attached to us we had two specialist groups, both provided by the British Army – an interrogator, Mickey Heyden and two aerial photograph interpreters.

The photo interpreters were known generally as Mae West from direction signs outside their caravan saying 'MAIU (West)'. It stood for Mediterranean Air Interpretation Unit – Western Section. Those who mounted the wooden steps at the back of their caravan, giving voice to, or biting back, according to their natures, the inevitable crack about coming up to see me sometime, found Mae West to be, not one, but two persons – burly Fred Kersh and his mate. Kersh was in peace-time a furniture dealer from Cumberland, with horn-rimmed spectacles, and black unruly hair. His mate at this time was a small, sardonic, virile and equally bespectacled ex-member of the Milk Marketing Board, Alan Primmer. Here, in a caravan painted pale green and cream, they pored over their photographs, annotating machine-gun pits, slit trenches, dumps, vehicle tracks and all the other evidence which gave itself up to the aerial camera.

They were good interpreters. Hanson of the engineers trusted them completely, taking their estimates of river widths as the basic for the planning of his bridges. And if a man could pass Hanson's tests he could hold his head high in the New Zealand Division.

Kersh had also another great gift. He always got us more than our share of air photos. The supply of these was inevitably limited by the quantity of printing paper available, the staff for developing and printing, and the planes. Thousands were after all produced every week. But Kersh was determined that in his adopted division no platoon commander was ever going to go blind into new country simply because not enough photos were available. So he argued constantly for more. I used to curse him when these arguments went on and on, on our phone – we shared a party line – but they did the trick. On what Fred delighted to call the Old Boy basis he would secure for us extra supplies. He ran, as it were, a black market in air photos for our benefit.

All of this information – the battalion and brigade reports, the interrogation of prisoners, the air interpretation, found their way into our I truck, along with the documents and phoned information which came to us from Corps and Army.

The I truck deserves a word on its own. It had its own atmosphere. It had a long tradition of hospitality – so much so that on many evenings it resembled not so much a newspaper office as a blend of a newspaper office and a small Paris bistro. Mess life, at any rate while we were in action, had never developed much in New Zealand divisional headquarters (outside of course, the General's own mess). The canvas lean-to alongside the cooking truck of C mess was all right for meals, but it was difficult to blackout at night, it was cold, and the cooks were apt to be having their own relatively noisy party in the truck next door, or else to be pointing out in no measured terms that the noise in the mess was keeping them awake and if you wanted any breakfast in the morning. . . . So the I truck came, in time, to assume the role of mess anteroom. It was well-lit; it was warm. We could pack eight or nine people in at a pinch and half a dozen with ease. It had established a strong tradition of Bohemian hospitality and wit under my predecessors, Paddy Costello, who had gone to the New Zealand Legation in Moscow, and Dan Davin, the novelist, who was then planning the Germans' downfall in flying-bombed London. Here, too, the liaison officer or the operations officer off-duty came to keep an ear open for what was going on, to read some of the fascinating literature – the geography of the Philippines or new German anti-tank methods in the Ardennes – which the War Office persisted in sending us, to scan the *Eighth Army News* or look up his Italian girl friend's pedigree in the *Libro d'Oro,* Italy's Debrett.

Here, too, there was a welcome attitude of irreverence towards life and events – Davin had long since established this by christening the necessarily formal operations vehicle 'The Chapel', and the I truck 'the café'. What therefore was more natural than that any officer who was lonely, bored, or had some time to spare – three things which, out of action, were constantly occurring – should look over to the I truck, see if there was any vino in the bottle box kept carefully under the shelf, and get a preview of the evening's I summary?

All of this produced an atmosphere which, to say the least, was unorthodox by army standards. I am sure no Field Service Pocket Book lays down that the divisional Intelligence staff should keep open house for anyone who cares to drop in, any time. But it paid us dividends. These visitors may have cluttered up the truck, they maya have filled the atmosphere with smoke so intense that we would have to open the blackout curtain and flap it about until the sentry threatened again and again to put a bullet through it, but at the same time they brought us gallons of information which we would not otherwise have had. The battalion commander who had been called down to see the General, and who thought he'd look in and see what was doing with the I blokes, the man from army headquarters who thought he would go forward and see what the New Zealanders were up to today, the war correspondents who had been poking around in the front or the rear, who might have just come from Rome or just come from the front line area, they all brought us extra information, which we would never have had time to get otherwise.

There steadily, hour by hour, our picture of the enemy was filled out. The little oblongs and squares, denoting the enemy minefields, were marked out more and more exactly on the traces of the enemy's mine defences which Martin and the enginer Intelligence officer kept. The big 1/25,000 map on our wall, used for noting enemy defences, became covered with a blue tattoo of machine-gun posts, headquarters, supply dumps, trench systems, as documents were captured, deserters babbled, prisoners had their information prised from them. On the other 1/25,000 map on the wall in front of my bench the dotted boundaries and the blue figures which marked the layout of the enemy units were re-drawn day after day.

'Here's a PW puts his company mortars at Casa Tampieri – let's see, that's square 330334.'

'Fine. Let the arty have them, and the air.'

'And Headquarters 7 Company 290th Regiment are given now at Casa Bentini. What's the policy about headquarters? Are they going to be bombed now, or do we wait till the show goes in?'

'We wait till the day, so that they won't have time to mend their phone lines.'

'Mines on the banks of the railway embankment. Mines on the far stop-bank at 35 83. Two footbridges at 3335 – they won't survive the bombardment, but we may as well note them. 198th Arty Regiment has an observation post in the church tower at Massa Lombarda. Colmore

might like to get a Spitfire to knock that down. Enemy ration point at
Casa Savini. Ration parties arrive usually at twenty-hundred hours.
That's something for the arty. They want harassing targets for tonight.
Deserter from 14 Company, 289th Grenadier Regiment say that 3 Com-
pany has an approximate strength of forty-five men. 1 Company and 2
Company are weaker. What the hell does 14 Company know about 3
Company? Ah yes, of course. He's one of the anti-tank boys, attached to
them. What's he got? A bazooka. That shouldn't make much trouble. Ah,
I see this new deserter says he saw what he thinks is a Tiger tank
sheltering at house 267415. And another, a definite Tiger, at 341346.
Better get Maiu West to see if they can see any tracks there. What's the
time? Nearly four o'clock. Switch the wireless on quickly, or we'll miss
the four o'clock news, and the Russians will probably have taken Berlin
or something. War may be over.'

So day after day we formed our ever shifting reflection of the ever
shifting picture of the enemy. 'Topographic and Going Report Between
the Senio and Santerno Rivers' – 'Strength Estimate 504 Heavy (Tiger)
Tank Battalion' – 'New large type of Schu Mine, in wooden box 9″ by 4″
by 4″. Thin nail as a shear pin is used for increased firing pressure'. 'Shell
fragment on 20th March at 369371 indicates 21 cm How (Morser 18)
firing in enfilade on to the river. That must have been the big bastard we
heard on Tuesday night. The air people say that a jet-propelled Messer-
schmitt has been seen in the Udine area. Have we got any jet-propelled
planes out here? Just like the Hun to concentrate his latest fighter types
here and try to get local air superiority. That sooner we get this battle
under way the better.'

'There's a good thing in the latest Eighth Army Summary – first impressions of Cologne. I think we'll print that. It's time we had a round-
up on the Eastern front too. We'd better have something about Tolbukin's
offensive from Lake Balaton. Rokossovsky has got Danzig, too. See the
draughtsmen about a map.'

For not all the information we put into the Intelligence Summaries
came from our own front. Much came from 5th Corps behind us, and
from the Intelligence staffs at Army, who watched the entire front from
the mountains to the sea. From all these sources we built up our final
estimate of the enemy, for this final battle into which we now entered.

We went forward to it in company of which we were truly proud. The
Eighth Army, for all the lean lot which it had endured throughout this
Italian campaign, was still a formation with magic in its name. The gold
and blue crusader's cross, on a white shield, which was worn by army
troops on their sleeves, and which marked the army road signs, was as

familiar with us as was our own fernleaf. We had been with Eighth Army ever since their first days under the meagre palm trees of the Baagush Oasis. It was fitting we should be with it at the end.

In the fighting which was to follow we were of course only one part of that Army. The battles which lay ahead were to be battles of British, Indian, Polish, Italian and Jewish troops as well as of New Zealanders. It would take a different type of account, written from a wider perspective, to give the full picture of this final campaign of the Eighth Army. My experience of it was that of a divisional soldier, absorbed by the action on our own front, with the narrower, but perhaps sharper view which such a stance affords.

CHAPTER FIVE

The Final Offensive

April 9th dawned fine and clear, its weather perfectly 'according to plan'. When the morning mist rose the sky was blue beyond the pear blossoms, and white dust lay above the roadways where the supply trucks and jeeps were already going about their business. There was even a bit of wind, blowing towards us from the German positions, and so calculated to keep down the haze.

In the early morning I checked with the brigades. No change reported from foremost positions during the night. Just enough enemy fire, just enough signs of movement on the far bank to show that he was there. He had better be there, anyway. Nothing now could stop the show. Already the final order was out from Colonel Gilbert – 'Topsec. Operation Buckland. Subject to last minute changes timing as follows. D-Day, 9th April, H-Hour 1920 hours. All infm. Ack.'

There was nothing, therefore, but to wait for the curtain to go up and the bombardment to come down. In the meantime we proceeded to cope with the inevitable flood of extra visitors. For a battle attracts, at least as far ahead as divisional headquarters, an unbelievable stream of overseers and sightseers. You would not believe that there were so many strange units, so many extra officers in the world as find it urgently necessary to 'slip forward and see the chaps at div.' when an attack is pending. There are extra liaison officers from army and army group headquarters, other officers representing mysterious forces with alphabetical names like cattle brands – X force and the T force and Y force. There are correspondents and photographers. And hosts of others. The first of these to check in was a film and broadcasting unit from the US Ninth Air Force. They wanted to make a detailed report on the progress of the bombing by the heavies. Where could they get a view? Where, indeed, in this flat country? We shipped them off to the one 'grand-stand' which was available, a half-destroyed sugar factory about half a mile short of Senio. The General had already established a tactical headquarters there, from which to watch the bombardment, and war correspondents had been staking out claims to corners of it. The Americans could force their way in as well.

69

Then the runner arrived with the usual orders of the day – one from Field Marshal Alexander, one from General Mark Clark, and one from General Richard McCreery, who was now commander of the Eighth Army. Each was characteristically different, though all said the same thing – that we were starting what should be the final campaign. Alex used similes, drawn from sport, as Monty ('we'll hit them for six out of Egypt') had done. 'The German forces are now very groggy, and only need one mighty punch to knock them out for good. The moment has now come for us to take the field for the last battle which will end the war in Europe.'

General Mark Clark's message had that Latinate rotundity which the Americans employ on solemn and official occasions. It had too that characteristic shared, in this war chiefly by Mr Churchill and American leaders, of invoking the aid of the Almighty : 'Hit them with all you've got and with God's help we will have a decisive and perhaps a final victory.'

General McCreery, known to the Eighth Army as 'Roaring Dick' because his Irish voice hardly rose above a whisper, evoked the past glories of the Eighth Army. His message reminded us of Alamein and Tobruk. He alone however of the three commanders made reference to the Italians on our side – the Cremona Division, the other forces in the hills, and the waiting partisans.

'The Eighth Army recognises and appreciates the part the gallant Italian forces are taking in this struggle.'

We were going to appreciate them better than we realised.

The morning slipped away quietly enough. There were a few fighter-bomber sorties – not many, but enough to keep up the appearance of normality. One o'clock came, half-past one, and then, a quarter to two. In five minutes more the heavies were due. Surely enough there, distantly as if the sky were a vast metal sheet being shaken till it vibrated, came the hum of four-engined planes in mass.

From the roof of our farm-house we could see intermittently the green line of the stop-bank, above the fruit- and mulberry-trees. Through the trees ahead suddenly broke three orange spurts of flame. The anti-aircraft guns on our side were firing bursts into the air to show the bombers their position. There, through the haze which now spread over the sky, we could see briefly the silver shape of the bombers as they went on their way, like a shoal of silver fishes, moving on steadily, steadily in line. A minute or two later we heard the rumble as the bombs from the first forty-eight of them let drop their burden on the line of the Santerno.

Smithy, one of the headquarters runners, was standing outside our truck, staring reflectively up into the sky. 'I'll be glad when those blokes are finished,' he said. 'I don't like these hundred-bomber raids just over my head.'

The other clerks, standing at the mouth of their truck, agreed. 'Remember Cassino?'

Everyone proceeded to remember Cassino, with elaborate details. There had been a goodly enough percentage of navigational errors there for every soldier in the Eighth and Fifth Armies to have grown wary of close support by strategic bombers. One flight had dropped their load on Venafro, a town ten miles from Cassino. Another had pranged Eighth Army headquarters and destroyed the Army commander's caravan.

The corporal took up the story. 'I got into the best fight of my life just a week after that, with a couple of Yank airmen, all because of their feelings.'

'How was that?'

'We were just having a drink in a bar in Naples, and these two Yanks came in. As soon as I saw their Air Force wings I said: 'Bombs Away,' and everyone in the bar dived under the tables. You'd hardly think a joker would take offence at that. But they did.'

The sky overhead was vibrating again. More specks like silver fish were moving over, hard to pick out now against a sky that was becoming glazed and steely. On the enemy side of the line the blue had disappeared completely in the dust haze, through which rose the black smoke of buildings set alight by the fighter-bombers. The growl and rumble of the bombs came back towards us, rising to a peak as they passed over the level countryside, and then fading away, like a train in a London tube, like the rumblings of some gargantuan gorged stomach.

Like all things in war – except those which bring you into direct danger, the unusual was soon accepted as the usual. It soon became tiring to crane your neck up at yet another flight, and we went back to our own jobs. Only the sudden tuft of a white parachute, swaying down rapidly behind a flight of bombers, aroused attention.

'Somebody's had it. Here comes one bloke,' called the cooks, while they dried the lunch plates. But there was no plane to be seen dropping, even though the sky above the German lines was covered now with the muddy thumb marks of our own anti-aircraft fire.

Even the ugly rip and slither of bombs falling close at hand about three o'clock caused no more than a temporary excitement. We moved smartly into the shelter of the barn, as its wall would keep out anything but the direct impact of these anti-personnel bombs, which burst at ground level and sprayed shapnel far and wide.

'Only one plane, by the sound of it,' said Martin, as the explosions thumped and thundered just down the road behind us.

'Yes, I hope he's not the pathfinder. Forty-eight doses of that will do us no good. I expect he's mistaken the Lamone for the Senio. Nothing would be easier in this haze. All these bloody rivers must look alike.'

The dust from the explosion rose from the trees behind us. It looked very close. Steadily the rest of the flight droned over. Only one bomb-aimer had apparently been trigger happy. We went thankfully back into the open.

As it happened the bombs, though they fell right in our dumping area, caused no casualties, and did very little damage. Our luck was still in. A few minutes later another throaty rumble told us that the remainder of the planes had waited till they were a decent distance across the Senio.

The Poles were less lucky. One of their battalions was hit by a badly aimed pattern of bombs, Forty Polish troops, formed up ready for their attack, were killed, and 120 wounded.

This strategic bombing had been a great feature of the fighting in Normandy, and the offensive had been timed so that it could be used here. The air people talked of "saturating' areas, and 'carpeting' them, and the date had been fixed so that they should have the right weather for bombing from 12,000 feet. The area to be bombed looked impressive on the plans, but in the event the enemy suffered few casualties. The Santerno line, onto which the main bombing was directed, was empty at this time of all but a few working parties. They had taken cover in their dug-outs, where they were comparatively safe. The chief effect of the bombing was to cut telephone cables and damage communications, and to shake the morale of the enemy.

The American broadcasters and cameramen on the sugar factory top floor had however no such doubts about the effectiveness of strategic bombing. A uniformed commentator was busy recording a running commentary on the action. His voice had the urgency of a man covering a football match.

'The sky is just full of these big ships. I can see them clearly from here, silver and shining up there in the haze. Here is another wave coming in now.'

An audience of New Zealanders crowded around him, listening with varying degrees of interest and scepticism. The commentator decided to add some natural sound to the broadcast.

'I'm going to hold the microphone in the open and let you hear the roar of those engines,' he announced into the microphone, before he let it dangle down from the window.

It swayed outside the open window of the floor below. The temptation was too great for John Shirley, the second-in-command of our Divisional Signals. He put his mouth close to the microphone, and intoned in a very good imitation of the American's accent, 'Goddamn, if that isn't another of our ships shot down – and there goes another – and another.'

The delighted audience noticed that the microphone stayed dangling as the planes went serenely on their unharmed way.

Now it was 1515 hours. The last of the big planes were moving out of the sky, leaving behind them on our side of the Senio a relieved army, its ranks increased by one strange recruit – a tail-gunner who had literally fallen out of his aircraft in mid-air. The fastenings of his rear turret had come loose, and he had found himself, to his unquestioned horror, suddenly falling through space. He managed to get his parachute open at the third tug, and duly landed in our lines. He lay now, exhausted and shocked, on the I truck seat.

The curtain raiser was over. At 1520 hours the barrage, our own battle, was to begin. The line of the stop-bank showed through the trees, green with turf in some places, black with earth in others. 1516 hours. 1517 hours, 1518. There was stillness over all our area but for the droning of the cab ranks of fighter aircraft above, and our own air ops. 1519, 1520.

We prepared our ears for the guns, but before we heard them the patch of the stop-bank ahead seemed to be lifted in the air. Black earth, grey smoke, yellow dust, red and ochre flames suddenly rose along its edge. Then, and then only, came the sound of the guns, roaring and baying and clamouring one after another, until the whole eastern horizon was solid sound. Overhead shells raced, with all their multitudinous sounds – twenty-five-pounders slithering, or tearing past like a long curtain being ripped in two; the 4.5 and 5.5 churning their way through the air, as if they were whole trains being driven at speed, invisibly above our heads and hurtling down on the bank. Sometimes the noise would seem to get harsher, as if the sky were a vast steel shutter, being hauled down on to the enemy as a shopkeeper hauls his down to cover his shop door before he goes home. It seemed impossible that all this noise could come from something invisible, and you looked up as if expecting to see the hazed sky streaked and torn by passing shells, as artists show them in comic cartoons. But there was nothing

there but the haze and the circling planes, far up, coming round to
dive.

It sounded spectacular, and by all the visual standards of modern
war it was spectacular. The sections of the bank which we could see
through the trees had disappeared now completely in smoke and dust.
The same thing, you knew, was going on for miles on either side. But
in all honesty it was not nearly as vivid a sight as most descriptions of
war would have you believe.

For the truth is that though this war was one of the most spectacular
ever fought, and this was certainly a vivid enough action, the true
picture is always less dramatic than one would think, when one hears
of hundreds of guns and planes, vast tonnages of bombs, tens of
thousands of men. The impression these figures give is that you see
them all going off, or all in action, whereas you see at best a small part
only. One of the conditions of full-scale action is that you are either
far away or too close up to comprehend the whole thing. No doubt
the fighter pilots circling in 'cab rank' above the Senio saw the bombardment falling on the whole length of the river. But from the height they
had to keep, to be clear of the trajectory of the shells, it looked like no
more than a line of grey and white woollen tufts stretched thinly across
the landscape. To us, who were close at hand, and to the infantry, who
were even closer, only small portions of the bank could be seen. Terrible
as was the action in that area, it was still visible only to the restricted
field of vision of normal men standing in closely wooded country. Moreover even in this same limited field the Senio stop-bank did not take
up the whole of one's vision. There were trees and fields in front, and
to either side – quiet, green and unscarred, which blocked in even more
of the mind's eye than one admitted to oneself at the time. The truth
is that nobody sees the so-called 'big picture' of a battle. Unconsciously,
many watching the bombardment this afternoon felt they did. They
knew hundreds of guns were bombarding the bank on either side of the
limited stretch which they saw (there was plenty of dust and noise to
prove it) they knew that the fighter-bombers were carrying out a record
number of sorties in the rear. Every now and then they would see a
formation dive down and peel off to carry out some such mission; and
in their own minds they formed this bigger picture. But immediately
under their eyes they saw a much more limited canvas – many green
trees, many green fields, farm-houses, and beyond that patches of bank
being smashed and torn.

This is why photographs of fighting are usually so disappointing. The
bombardment which filled your mind and your ears is only a line of

flame or of smoke, and a thin line at that, midway up the film. The infantry attack which sent thousands of men into action is indicated only by an occasional figure darting here, a tank lurching round a corner there, the line of shells again in the front. Only rarely in this war did you get the truly spectacular. You had it in the great air bombardment of Cassino, for there the hills and the monastery and the ruined castle provided a truly theatrical back-drop, and there the bombing put up smoke and flame in unusual quantities. Bombing is by far the most spectacular thing in modern warfare. But descriptions of field attack, even with the mass of artillery which we had on the Senio, would have seemed grossly exaggerated to anyone who had read descriptions of similar battles and who now saw one for the first time.

Even the infantry, waiting in their trenches now for the bombardment to stop, did not see much more, though they saw it with greater intensity. They saw mud, flame, smoke. That night they would see these things made more terrible by the darkness. Yet to them too it would be an individual picture, partly objective, partly the subjective reaction to their fears, excitements, angers, tensions, something too big and close and shapeless to be easy to describe.

I've no doubt, however, that it felt like the end of the world to the Germans crouching in the stop-bank. It did not take much imagination to picture them there in their holes, sweating, smoking when they could get the chance, crouching and bent, with the wounded being helped out one by one, and the dead lying crumpled and bent like the living, at the bottom of their slit trenches. You had to search in your mind, and remember the concentration camps and the gas chambers, and above all remember that if it wasn't them it would have been us, to stifle in your soul the knowledge of this line of murder being drawn across the sunny green plains on an April afternoon. We had studied this division, and its regiments, well enough to feel that we knew them almost personally. That sector just ahead, for instance, would be where the 2nd Battalion, 289th Grenadier Regiment would be entrenched. That should be just about the position of 7 Company, and over there, through that other gap in the trees, would be where 5 Company were in line.

'If they still are in line,' said Martin, wryly.

'They'd better be.' The quarter of million shells were going into the bank, whether the Germans were holding it or not.

I thought of a remark the General had made during the planning conferences. 'If we can catch them often enough on a set line, and pound them like hell, they will break. There is not a unit in the world that can be caught three times under a proper barrage and stay battle-worthy.'

He spoke with the voice, not of this war, but of the last, the voice of Passchendaele and the Somme. For in this war, however much we suffered from the enemy's air superiority at the start, our infantry at no time had to sit under the concentrated and repeated fire of artillery as did troops in the worst years of the last war. The Germans were under it now, however; the 98th Division was this afternoon certainly atoning for its share of Germany's sins.

The shelling lifted suddenly from the bank, and the dust and smoke slowly cleared from the far bank. 'This is the start of Dragnet,' said the artillery observer, cryptically. 'We step it back six lifts to the rear of the bank, just to give them time to get their heads up, and hop out for a leak, and then . . .'

Slowly the dust settled. There was the outline of the bank again, scarred now with black craters, but still as solid as ever. The machine-guns were playing on it, sending up spurts of dirt. You could imagine these German officers and NCOs in their dug-outs working out that this onward move of the bombardment was probably the signal for an assault. Better look around before the British infantry were on top of them. Pop out for just one moment.

Crash. The black earthen geysers were erupting along the bank again. It was the seventh lift, and the barrage was back, on to the holes and slit trenches again.

At last the guns stopped. The first period of bombardment was complete. One by one a few laggards fired off their final round, and there was silence for a moment. In the trees the birds gave a few half-hearted chirps. No doubt in their holes the infantry gave their chirps too. But with less justification. For this time it was the turn of the fighter-bombers and the rocket-firing Thunderbolts. Slowly they would circle above, leisurely, as the fight commander picked out his target. Then steadily they would come down into their dive, until the yellow bombs would break away, and you would hear the machine-guns in the Spitfires and Kittyhawks tear off a sudden strip of sound, unique and unmistakable. I know only one sound in the world like it – the noise small boys in New Zealand make when they drag sticks across fences of corrugated iron.

It seemed a long afternoon to us. It must have seemed an age to the men of the assaulting battalions, waiting in their slit trenches, smoking, making such talk as they could behind battered farm-houses and ditch walls. But now at least it was getting close to 1900 hours. The sun went down slowly into the dust and haze of the enemy lines. The pale yellows and greens of the sunset mixed with the smoke of burning houses and the dust from the stop-bank. In the forward area the infantry were now formed up with their assault boats and their kapok bridges, with their shovels and rifles and packs and all the gear which a man carries into action. The Crocodiles and Wasps, their engines unheard under the guns, must by now be on their rough roadways leading towards the bank.

Martin and I clambered to the top of a tall shaky haystack. Again we looked at our watches. 1919 hours. The barrage was still in full voice, while above it moved a line of fighter planes. 1920 hours. This was it. More clearly than the striking of any clock, the sudden silence marked H-hour. The final rounds of the bombardment struck on to the bank, and around us, where there had been flame and noise among the orchards, there was now only silence, and green trees. You were suddenly conscious that this was indeed beautiful country. For a minute or two the silence persisted. The infantry must be moving forward now, stumbling, sweating towards the bank. The flame-throwers must be nearly there.

And then, quick and red and evil, came the first streak of flame, like a whip-lash between the trees, a streak of red marked in abruptly on a green canvas. The first Crocodile was hosing the stop-bank. The black smoke of burning oil rose straight up against the pale sky. Then another to the right, and others, and others – brief as the spurt of a match but even at this distance, full of awe. One by one, like funeral pyres, the smoke rolled up. Then the orchards shook again, and the noise of the guns came back. The protective barrage was going down four hundred yards farther back, falling in a fence of fire that followed exactly parallel to the bends of the stream. It marked the start of the infantry assault. So far this had been a struggle of machines; now it was over to men.

Now the platoon commanders were calling in flat, urgent New Zealand voices: 'Go – Now,' and the dark shapes of men in the half light were moving up the bank, some grouped around the folding boats and the kapok bridges, already assembled, carrying them as if they were wounded men in blankets; others, weapons in hand, were swarming up the stop-banks, so that the very bank seemed to move, up to the top and down the black slope to the stream and the far bank. They were into it now, Milne and Johnson, Maclean and Murray and their fellows, boys just out of their teens, men into their forties, two thousand five hundred New Zealanders on our sector alone.

'Operation Buckland' was no longer a matter of typed words and

figures, of diagrams and charts and calculations; it was now a matter
of men enforcing on other men the final sanction of war.

Twenty minutes later the phone was ringing. It was Moana.

'The Maoris are across and are mopping the bank. Twenty-one
Battalion are finding things a bit sticky but the Maoris have struck little
opposition.'

Ten minutes later it was the 6th Brigade. 'Twenty-four Battalion
across the bank and forming up under the barrage for the advance.
Twenty-five level with them.'

Twenty-five Battalion was Milne's. Somewhere under that barrage
he was now getting his platoons straightened out for the advance.

'Any prisoners?'

'About forty to date – all 98th Division so far.'

Fifth Brigade had prisoners too. Slowly the total mounted. I knew
that once we had a hundred prisoners we could be sure that the bulk of
the German forces had been there, for that, with the dead and wounded,
would be a reasonable proportion of the division at this hour

By eight o'clock it was clear that the Senio was crossed throughout
our sector, and that all four of our battalions were ready to move forward as the barrages started its march ahead of them, through the
houses and olive groves, at five minutes past eight. It was dark now,
but for the guns glaring and flashing like summer lightning, and the
searchlights meeting, covering, forming great bell tents of light to
provide the artificial moonlight by which the engineers would build
the bridges. Every few minutes the Bofors, firing tracer to guide the
advancing infantry, strung its red, gold and green beads across the
darkness.

I stood for a moment at the back of the truck watching it. Then the
phone went again, and for three hours I never left it. Over it, incessantly, we now fought the Intelligence side of the battle. Counter-attack
forming up on the right, against 21st Battalion. Germans are moving
two tanks down the road at Casa Savini. Get the arty on to Casa
Savini. Tanks reported on the other side too. 24th Battalion have struck
them on their left flank. Could it be 26th Panzer Division moving
across? Are we going to get a major counter-attack from our left flank?
Possible, but not likely. They are busy enough there with the Poles.
How are the Poles doing? Not much yet. They've been knocked back
around Route 9, and are getting a bad time on our left flank in general.
Not surprising. That's the dirtiest bit of the river. All curves and high
banks and stiff with mines. How about the Indians to the right? They

are across all along the way, but they are being heavily counter-attacked. All infantry battalions reporting tanks. Must be the Tigers of 504 Heavy Tank Battalion all right. Another counter-attack towards 21st Battalion. That's for the arty again.

Heyden's driver was waiting with the first list of identifications. All four companies of 1st Battalion 289th Regiment identified. Both battalions 290th Regiment identified. And I Bn. 117, and 98th Fusilier Battalion. What's the P.W. total now – over 200. That settles it. The whole division was there. They were on the bank all right. What's that? More tanks opposite the 6th Brigade? How are the bridges going? Any chance of our own tanks getting up? Bridge approaches being steadily shelled. Enemy defensive fire fairly steady on all roads leading forward.

Steadily, with the barrage roaring, that orderly chaos which characterises a major action was taking shape. In the darkness lit only by the pale artificial moonlight the engineers were pushing on with the bridges, their trucks lurching forward on narrow roads which were being shelled, dropping off their loads of bridging material, backing, turning. The bulldozers were working on the edge of the ten-foot drop into the river, clearing away the gap blown in the stop-bank for the approaches. The enemy shells tore in their turn now into the river bed.

Ahead, into the mangled country beyond the Senio the infantry moved, stalking in the darkness by compass across the fields, unable to follow the roads and tracks, for these ran in most cases across the line of attack. In the darkness they caught up the enemy troops. Through the clamour of the barrage came the sound of tracked vehicles. It could only be the enemy tanks. In the dark the infantry joined battle with them. A Tiger tank and two self-propelled guns, clanking forward on a roadway in the dust and the darkness went right past a group of New Zealanders crouching on a side road. One infantryman chased after the Tiger with a Piat, the compact weapon which fired an anti-tank projectile at close range, and hit the tank from the rear. It blew up. The Piat proved a very handy weapon that night. A Panther and another Tiger were claimed as its victims in the darkness. On another of the narrow roads running through the orchards and vineyards an enemy tank suddenly loomed up, with four Germans riding on its top. A Kiwi corporal jumped out of the roadside ditch, pointed his Sten gun, and called on the Germans to surrender. They climbed down, put up their hands, and the tank went on its way unawares.

By midnight both brigades had reached their final objective, 4,000 yards deep from the river. Work on the bridges was going forward. The

counter-attacks had died down. Only our flanks were a worry. Neither
the Poles nor the Indians were up level with us. As soon as the left-hand
bridges were up the Poles were to use them to pass through and attack
out from our bridgehead.

By midnight the skeleton shape of the new situation was clear. The
Senio line was broken clean open in our sector. By two o'clock the next
morning three bridges were open, and our own tanks and supporting
weapons were across. The Poles had got a tiny bridgehead to our left.
To protect our flank the reserve battalion of 6th Brigade had moved
across and was formed up facing south-west. All was in order. We fell
into bed with the guns still setting the windows rattling and shaking
the walls and floors of the farm-house.

It took some days to collect enough information from documents,
from prisoners, and from our own troops to put flesh on the bones of
this situation. The resulting specimen was interesting. The enemy had
known that an offensive was coming in, and he had known that the
New Zealand Division was back in the line.

On 7th April, two days before our attack went in, 289th Regiment
had sent out an order which started: 'The enemy had carried out
extensive regroupings of his forces. Opposite our divisional sector
recently part of 78th (English) Div. was replaced by 2nd New Zealand
Division with 5th Brigade forward. A major enemy offensive must be
considered possible any day now.'

Meanwhile General-leutnant Reinhardt had been calling on his
troops to hold the Senio. 'You are well aware that on the stop-banks
and dams of the Northern Italian plains you are defending Germany
and you protect the backs of your hard-pressed comrades in the East
and West of the Reich,' one order stated. His men were called on to
use 'ability, cunning, malice and hatred' to defend the banks, and were
offered fourteen days' special leave and 100 cigarettes for the best suggestion for building dug-outs and gun-pits.

Later still the officer who had commanded this sector was to tell his
story. He was General-leutnant Graf von Schwerin, who was an old
enemy of ours. He had been with Rommel in the desert, until Rommel
sacked him. Then he had commanded a division in France, till
Rundstedt sacked him. In Normandy British troops had captured notes
of telephone conversations in which opinions about von Schwerin's
bungling had been expressed in no mild terms by his superiors. These
we had, in December 1944, written into pamphlets which were fired
over to greet the Graf when he arrived to take command of 90th Panzer
Grenadier Division at Faenza. He was stung to reply by firing back

others full of abuse for Freyberg. The Count had, however, continued to get promotion and the Senio offensive found him commanding 76th Panzer Corps opposite us. He later surrendered on the banks of the Po, driving in in a beautiful staff car, followed by a truck containing his bulky personal luggage.

Schwerin said that the decision to stand and fight on the Senio was taken by Hitler himself. Both the commander in Italy, General Vietinghoff, and the Army Commander, General Herr, had wanted to do just what we feared they might – withdraw to the Santerno twenty-four hours before they thought our attack would come in. Operation 'Leonidas', the heavy shelling on the night of 6th April, had originally been arranged to cover his withdrawal. Hitler, however, in his bunker in Berlin, intervened once more, instinctively and disastrously. He sent out a signal cancelling the withdrawal. But what about the artillery programme? Was that to be cancelled too? No, there was nothing in the signal to say that it was. So, rigidly and incomprehensibly, the Leonidas programme was fired, using up the bulk of the army's munition reserves.

The next morning I went forward with the General to the Senio. The narrow, dusty road which led towards the stop-bank ran for its last quarter of a mile though country which was only now losing that chill, suspended, deadened atmosphere of ground which is being fought for. The shell-pitted fields; grass torn and trampled, or else lush and evil, covering unseen minefields; the shattered farm-houses still marked with the Red Crosses of the regimental air posts; the signs marking company headquarters; troops wearing their steel helmets, and carrying their arms; two wounded men walking back by the road edge; and over all the marks of the shelling – smashed and splintered trees, like plants broken off halfway up their stems, shallow craters, with their dead, dried sterile earth, their burnt black edges, and littered jagged shrapnel covering the fields like the scabs of some ugly disease, all were there.

We made our way through the transport, New Zealand and Polish, which packed the road, through the gap in the stop-bank, and across the Bailey bridge marked 'Raglan' on the plan. On the far side the road ran aslant to the top of the stop-bank. Tracks, trodden clear by many feet, wound straight up from the water's side. We walked up one of them, treading carefully, our eyes probing the ground for anything which might be mines. Behind us, dirty, brown and meagre, the Senio swirled away between its black earthen banks. It looked contemptible enough between its cratered dykes, and with all the litter of war strewn around – German rifles, ammunition belts, old grenades, rags, paper the inevitable paper which covers every battlefield, with here and there the crumpled grey shape of a dead German.

The flaming had left great burnt strips at intervals along the bank. On the east bank a bulldozer was still at work clearing the approaches. The driver wore a khaki felt hat bent up at the sides like an Australian, and a green jersey. They were always given to individuality, these bull-dozer drivers. He gave the General's figure and red-banded cap no more than a glance.

Around us were the smashed remains of the stunted wire entangle-ments. Under this dark earth were the mines. It seemed unbelievable that the infantry had got across these banks with hardly a single mine casualty. The barrage had torn the fields about in part, but the main thing had been the daylight. There had been still light enough to allow the infantry to see the tracks already made by the Germans, and to run up them to the unmined top. The flame-throwing and the bombard-ment had kept down the heads of the enemy till our men were on top of them. Had we had to make this attack in the full darkness this would not have been possible. They would have had to move up the bank anywhere, through minefields as well as along tracks. But now the mine bogey of the Senio was laid. There were other bogeys aplenty ahead, but this one at least was conquered.

The western face of the far bank sloped down to the countryside below. In it the trees and houses and orchards and roads, torn by fire, lay dense and rich. We looked ahead over a sea of green tree-tops, with here and there the white and red island of a farm-house. To our left, distant in the haze, were the foothills above Route 9. Beyond them, invisible now, were the Apennines, where the Fifth Army, mostly Americans, with some South Africans and British troops, waited to attack towards Bologna. I placed my map on the bank top and orientated it. Bologna itself lay about half left, eighteen miles distant, swallowed up utterly in the greenness and the haze. To our right, equally unseen, was the township of Cotignola, which 9th Brigade had captured that morning and were now handing over to the follow-up force, and beyond it again was the town of Lugo, which the Indians were due to take. Straight ahead our forward infantry and tanks were now along the line of the Lugo canal, waiting for word to advance to the Santerno, and staring warily in the meantime either side of them. For we were now well ahead of the other Allied forces. We were not a spear-head, for that implies a point which slopes back gradually towards a base. We were thrust out instead, if not like the proverbial sore thumb, certainly like an aggressive forefinger, reaching out for the enemy's throat along the line of the Santerno.

The General came over and looked at the map. Across its uncoloured surface, the draughtsmen had inked in for me six wide, winding red bands. The first was the line of the Senio. Ahead now, like bulkheads barring the heart of a damaged ship, showed the others: the Santerno, beyond it the Sillaro, beyond it again the Gaiana, and finally, covering the plain immediately above Bologna, the Idice, where the Germans had constructed a line marked on their maps as 'Genghis Khan'.

Even at Bologna the lines did not cease. Curving round Bologna in a great circle, barring the way north, was the River Reno. Only when the Reno was passed could one face the new river system, which flowed west to east, rather than north to south, and which would bar our way when we turned towards the Alps – the Po, a broad blue line printed on the map, the Adige, and a dozen more. The job was only just begun.

'How heavy are his minefields on the Santerno?' said the General suddenly.

'As heavy as these – if not heavier. That was to have been his main line.'

'And the Sillaro?'

'There are fields there, too – but thinner.'

The General was silent for a moment. 'It cannot last for ever, this mined area of his. Soon we shall outrun his minefields, then we will outrun his demolitions, and then we will be able to go like hell.'

He turned down the bank. The round, enigmatic, alien, sometimes brutish faces of the Polish infantry in their trucks stared at him, as their strange lost army jolted forward on one more stage of their road into the unknown. By the bridge a boy with the black patch of the New Zealand engineers on his arm, and the single pip of a second-lieutenant on his shoulder, saluted. He was the officer who had commanded the platoon of bridge builders. His face was unshaven and tired.

'You wanted me, sir?'

'Yes.' The General studied him carefully. 'Tell your men they did a first-class job last night. Good work. Did you have many casualties?'

'Half a dozen. Mostly from shelling and mortaring at the start. The Huns did the approach road over thoroughly and one truck got ditched. We had to push it off with a bulldozer, and then another got hit and lit up the whole countryside.'

The officer turned his eyes from the General to the black meccano-like girders of the Bailey bridge. The wooden planks covering them rattled under the wheels of the Polish trucks. He was pleased, it was clear, by the General's words, but they were not his real reward. The bridge, erect and steady, had already provided that.

The conference that morning had been called in the gloomy dining-room of the farm-house which formed 5th Brigade headquarters. Both brigadiers could report complete success. Bonifant, his eyes red with lack of sleep, said: 'My people had a bit of trouble at the start, but they got OK eventually. Both battalions have now married up with their supporting arms.'

Brigadier Parkinson reported likewise: 'My party went according to plan without a hitch. All battalions have supporting arms up.'

Gentry for his part had Cotignola village in his hands, and was ready to hand over to 78th Division and rejoin the advance as soon as possible. The guns were up, ready to cover a crossing of the Santerno. The General wanted the enemy situation. 'About 1,200 men at the most opposite our whole front. There should be a hole in front of 6th Brigade,' was the core of it.

It took only a few minutes then for the General to give his orders. The advance was to continue at 12.30 when the morning bombing stopped. We would try to gatecrash the Santerno line before the enemy had it manned.

The Santerno river, a more formidable natural barrier than the Senio, with steeper, deeper sides, with the same powerful stop-banks, and with even more elaborate fortifications, had been prepared by the enemy as his chief winter barrier across the Po plain. The air photographs showed the Santerno line protected by concrete dragons' teeth, by wooden blocks to hamper tanks, by wire entanglements, and by plenty of digging.

In the sector towards which we were moving these banks were not single, but double. The river had been artificially straightened in front of Massa Lombarda and a new channel, protected by the same type of high banks, had been built on the eastward side. Beyond it, on the enemy's side, the old course of the river was still there, dry it is true, but with its winding grass-covered banks forming further bastions which the enemy could man and against which our tanks could be checked. To this Santerno line, some sentimental German staff officer had given the name of the Laura Line. Indeed all the defence lines from Cassino northwards, except the Gothic Line, had had girls' names.

The minefields were ample, both from reports of civilians, from prisoners, and from air photographs. It would take a heavy blow to dislodge the German forces if they ever manned these lines. But had they troops enough to do so? And if they had troops, had they time?

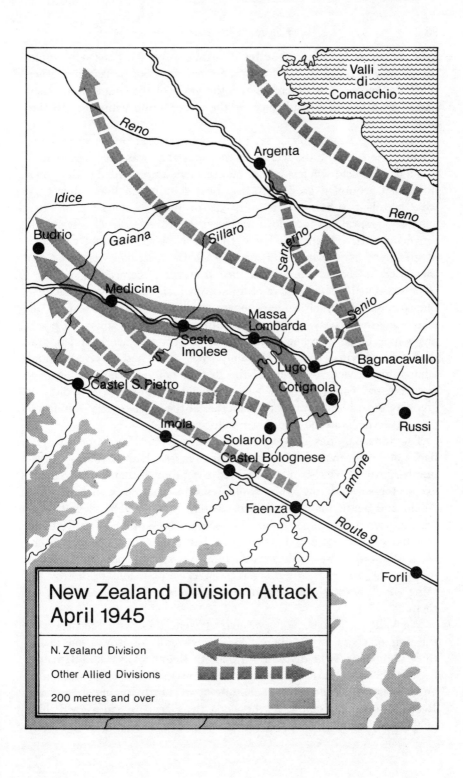

Valli di Comacchio

Reno

Argenta

Idice

Budrio

Gaiana

Sillaro

Santerno

Reno

Medicina

Massa Lombarda

Senio

Sesto Imolese

Bagnacavallo

Castel S. Pietro

Lugo

Cotignola

Imola

Russi

Solarolo

Castel Bolognese

Lamone

Faenza

Route 9

Forli

New Zealand Division Attack April 1945

N. Zealand Division

Other Allied Divisions

200 metres and over

Would they try to make time by attacking us on the flank now, using the roads which ran, parallel with the rivers, into our flanks from either side? For we were advancing across the grain of the country, and they had often attacked our advances in the autumn and winter in just this way.

Part of the answer to this lay in our own prisoner of war cage. Back there in the sunshine the scene this morning-after was like a regimental reunion. The field where we had the prisoners was crowded with figures in stained crumpled grey uniforms, some standing in lines while they were searched, others sitting in groups or lying in the sleep of utter exhaustion, sprawled face downwards on the grass. As truck after truck drove up with yet another batch the earlier arrivals would call cries of greeting: '*Ach Hans! Du auch! Und ist der Linke auch da?*' So they cried, as they enquired after their friends and comrades.

It was not that atmosphere of an army which still believes in victory, that atmosphere which we had known amongst prisoners of war up the whole length of Italy. This was the atmosphere of troops when peace has come. These men knew that the whole war was nearly ended, and that their personal war was certainly over. They had survived it, and what is more were prisoners of the British, not the Russians. So they were pleased enough. All of which was understandable, but did not give any great indication that the morale of the survivors who still faced us now on the Santerno would be much better.

The interrogations showed two things chiefly. The flame-throwers had not killed many, or wounded many, but had terrified a great number. Above all they had provided the junior leaders with soldierly excuse for surrendering. Who could resist in the face of such attacks? Again and again the NCOs asked us that question. The second thing was that we had torn a considerable hole in the ranks of 98th Division, but that we had not liquidated it. And that, after all, was what we were after. We wanted to smash it completely. We were not primarily anxious to cross the Senio, or any other river. We were anxious to destroy the thing which made these rivers difficult to cross – the German Army on them.

We had in all some 600 prisoners. I went back with the details of the unit of every one of them. We had virtually destroyed one of the three regiments of the division – the 289th Regiment; we had damaged badly half of 290th Regiment. But there was still left one battalion of 290th Regiment, and the two battalions of 117th Regiment, and the Reconnaissance Battalion. At the worst the Germans had a good third of the division left. I checked with Corps. Was 90th Panzer Grenadier

Division on the move from the mountains yet? Could it come into the line against us on the Santerno? No. No sign as yet. And on our flanks? The parachutists opposite the Poles were still holding on the Senio to our left. To our right the enemy opposite the Indians were going back slowly, but were definitely going back. Was there another division which could be brought up to the Santerno? No. All were identified elsewhere in Italy. So that when the General telephoned I could tell him that there was nothing in the enemy situation to make gate-crashing the Santerno line impossible.

All that day our four forward battalions, having got a few hours sleep in the morning, probed forwards towards the Laura Line on the Santerno. But the going was slow. On the left 6th Brigade were bombed by Flying Fortresses and Liberators as they were forming up to advance. The Brigade suffered 70 casualties. On the right 5th Brigade ran into determined opposition from Tigers. They had captured an enemy map which showed that all the German Tiger tanks in Italy – twenty in total – were opposite our front when the Senio attack was launched. This forced 5th Brigade to fight back hard with their Shermans through-out the afternoon. The infantry had moved forward under cover of a barrage, but it was difficult for the Shermans to keep up with them. The country was a maze of natural anti-tank obstacles – vines strung on wires, close-packed orchards, abrupt steep ditches. The enemy's resistance was patchy, but stubborn. Bitter fighting developed at many points amid the fresh spring foliage.

The pattern of it emerged from the front line reports. 'D Company of the Maoris was engaged by four German machine guns. Without hesitation Private Nia Nia led his section in a charge which silenced four posts, killed eleven Germans, cleared some houses and took four prisoners at the cost of one man wounded.' It was in these attacks that the Maoris used for the last time in the war their favourite weapon, the bayonet.

It was dusk before both brigades had reached the roadline just short of the Santerno. Here they were to rest until nightfall, and then to seize the near stop-bank, just as we had done on the Senio, to be ready for a further set-piece assault.

The battle of the Sherman v the Tiger, which was being fought out this sunny afternoon in the orchards of North Italy, as in a hundred other places in Europe, had already extended into the realm of political controversy. The reports of the debates in the House of Commons, in which Mr Stokes used to challenge Churchill about the inferiority of our own tanks, made fascinating reading for our Armoured Brigade when

they appeared in the army *World Press Review*. It was my job to collect
and assemble the facts about our battles with the German Tiger units,
and I am certain that our tank regiments had not the slightest doubt
about their views in the argument. The Tiger was definitely superior,
as a tank in close country, against anything the American and British
Armies put in the field. Its armour was impervious to all but a special
type of shell, used in the Sherman with the seventeen-pounder gun – a
type of shell and gun which never became available in Italy in
quantity. The Tiger's own 88 mm gun could shear through the armour
on the Sherman without difficulty. In a straight-out fight there could
be no question as to the result. I know which side the 4th New Zealand
Armoured Brigade would have put its money on in the duel to which Mr
Stokes challenged Churchill – Stokes to use a Tiger and Churchill a
Sherman.

Why then did the British Government not copy the Tiger? The
answer is that the Tiger was a heavy defensive tank, and we needed
tanks for swift offensive fighting. We could not afford a sixty-ton
vehicle like the Tiger, as we could not afford to build big bridges which
would be necessary to shift it across the roads and rivers in our path.
For the retreating Germans the situation was easier. They could use the
normal civilian roads and bridges, which were usually capable of taking
up to seventy tons weight. The ordinary light Bailey, however, carries
thirty tons only, and the Sherman weighed just under this – some twenty
eight tons. The second factor was that the Sherman had a far more
dependable engine. The Tiger's engines gave trouble over any distance.
The carcasses littering the roads north of Rome after the May 1944
offensive were some proof of this – as well as of RAF bombing. It is
doubtful if the Tiger could have stood up to the punishing road work
which our tanks were to face in the next few weeks.

Our own tanks went forward however, with their tails in the air.
For they knew that it was not to be solely a fight of New Zealand tank
against German tank, of Sherman against Tiger. We had other weapons
too. In front of Florence and in the autumn mud north of Rimini our
tanks and artillery had worked out a prescription for dealing with
Tigers. This involved hammering them, not only with fire from our
own tanks, but with fire from medium artillery, and with bombing and
strafing from the air. The infantry on the ground would report 'Tanks
firing from the farm-house at the road junction 280375. Suspected
Tiger.' The air op – the little, hovering Auster aircraft – would move
over and take a look. The infantry brigade would call down one of the
'Cab ranks', the lines of fighter-bombers who circled constantly on call

above our advance, on to the house. The bombing and rockets would drive the Tiger, which was probably hidden in a barn with its gun poking out of a window or through a hole in the wall, on to the road-way. The artillery observer, in his Auster, would wireless back to the full regiment of medium guns. In a few minutes the 4.5 shells would go roaring over, pounding the road of the tank's retreat. If a seventeen-pound shell might not do much harm, this 4.5 certainly could. Then the Shermans would move up for the kill, trying to catch the harried tank on its more vulnerable flank or rear as it swung round looking for further cover. If it once got into cover the aircraft would attack again. It was a complicated method, but it worked.

CHAPTER SIX

The Battle of the River Lines

We did gatecrash the Santerno. Our infantry and our tanks, pushing forward among the trees and vineyards and orchards, across the narrow canals and ditches and thin green fields and round the farm-houses and the villages, got to the road parallel to the river, by last light. By 1900 hours they were able to report that they were firm on the last road before the river.

The Santerno looked as ugly an obstacle in reality as it had in the air photographs. It was like the photographs we had seen of the Siegfried Line. As our patrols only too soon proved, there were wide minefields. Carefully camouflaged gun positions and dug-outs showed in the near bank, and beyond that in the far bank. The only remaining bridge was down, too. It had been hit that afternoon accidentally, when our artillery were registering on it.

Against this line the infantry advanced just before dawn the next morning – 11th April. Once more they went in four battalions abreast – the 24th and 25th, who had assaulted the Senio, on the left, the Maoris and a fresh battalion, the 23rd, on the right. They got the near stop-bank with hardly a fight, and on the left secured the far stop-bank firmly. The river, though in a more steeply sided channel than the Senio, was waded by the infantry. There was only scattered enemy resistance on the banks themselves. Not until the morning got under way, and we pushed out to take the bends in the parallel dead river-bed as well, did the counter-attack begin. With shelling and mortaring, the remains of 98th Division tried to get us off the banks and to stop the bridges being built. For bridges were urgently necessary to get our own tanks over. They, it was found, could not ford the stream.

But the bridge builders were sprayed by fire from Spandaus, and made little progress. Our infantry on the far stop-bank, and in the forward loops, were counter-attacked by Tigers. One Tiger pulled up right alongside a house in which the Maoris were sheltering. Two Maoris tied anti-tank mines to its tracks, and waited hopefully, but when it moved off they failed to explode. Only when darkness came were the bridges finally built, and the tanks able to pass over.

Even so it was to take another day of fighting before we got the Germans back from the river and behind Massa Lombarda, which stood square and solid on the map, like a medieval fortress barring the roads forward.

The Germans held strongly, despite the pasting they got, particularly from the air. April 11th was a field day for the fighter-bombers. We had them hitting everything we could get information about – gun positions, signal centres, headquarters, ammunition dumps. The Desert Air Force never went better than in these final days in the Italian plain. Their armoured control cars, their tentacles and 'Rover Jacks' and 'Rover Peters' and 'Rover Davids', long, rakish scout cars which looked like armoured Rolls-Royces, were grouped around the truck from which Colmore Williams ran the air support in our headquarters. His truck in turn was parked a few steps only from our I truck. Overhead, above the battlefield, circled the planes on cab rank, waiting to be called down on targets, and endlessly, in their neat noisy sixes, came up out of the eastern skies further sorties bound for specific targets.

During the afternoon of 11th April, seven German infantrymen were captured on one of the forward banks of the river. They were hurried straight back for interrogation. We found they had been in the line only an hour or so, and that that morning they had passed a house where General Rheinhardt of 98th Division had set up his headquarters. His trucks had just been moving in at the very moment they came through. Where was it? About here? On the map they worked it out for us. It was undoubtedly the Villa Seraglio, in square 2347. It took exactly three minutes to walk across the crushed hay-field to Colmore's truck, and give him the reference. It took him one minute more to pick up the microphone, call up the cab rank overhead 'Hullo Red Two, hullo Red Two'. Red Two answered, the sharp Australian voice of the pilot coming over the air unmistakably. Colmore gave him the reference, the house, the directions. It needed little imagination to picture the pilot, 4,000 feet overhead, one hand on his controls, his eyes glancing down to the map bound with rubber band round his thigh. 'O.K. I've got it.'

As I walked back to my truck I could see the first planes peeling off for their dive. The first bomb was a near miss. The second hit the casa dead on. For three hours, so later prisoners informed us, the headquarters of 98th Division ceased to function.

We worked at our side of this battle from a new area, between the Senio and the Santerno, for we had moved across soon after dawn, on the first of many moves. The stop-bank was in this sector smashed, as at Raglan filthy, and littered with rubbish, old weapons, and here and there the still unburied dead. When our trucks moved slowly over it, and down the narrow roads on the far sides, we moved back as it were from spring into winter. Here the shelling had brought again the leafless trees, bare fields and blackened earth. Every house was hit and gaping – the beginnings of that trail of destruction and ruin which this battle was to drape in a broad band across this lovely plain. In the farmyards were the entrance to German dug-outs, and every field had its slit trenches and shelters.

Through all this the marks of the barrage showed as if some line of giants had gone forward, crashing down trees in their path, gouging the ground. The fields were a rash of arid, dead-looking craters from the twenty-five-pounder shells; the trees were splintered and bare. It was easy enough to imagine why men surrendered, when they had waited in dug-outs with this storm of hot, swift metal moving steadily towards them like a brush fire.

We pulled into the grounds of the Casa Tambanelli where some wealthy Italian landowner had had his pleasant summer home. Now it was hit by bombs, and the garden battered – though not badly – by the barrage. Judged by some standards, the owner of the Casa Tambanelli had got off lightly. It was not like one big house just west of Forli, where the building and gardens had been literally stripped bare. That was the classic case in this area of war-time destruction. The house, damaged by bombing, had been demolished to provide bricks for road-making in the winter – there is no metal in the Po plains. The beams had been carted away for firewood and for dug-outs. The trees which had once embowered it had gone too for firing. The grounds had been churned by tanks and trucks and bulldozers into a morass of mud and clay, with only the line of stones to show where the ornamental garden or a rockery had stood. Only one thing remained – the foot and shin of a marble statue, with a piece of iron jutting out of the top where the rest of the body should have been grafted on. It was like a monument to destruction itself. No, by comparison Casa Tambanelli had got off lightly. We parked our truck in the shade of some big trees, noted with some satisfaction that there was a deep German slit trench right alongside and got on with the business of finding targets for the bombing.

The 26th Battalion, of which my brother was adjutant, was in the battle now. They had been drawn in at short notice. At midday on 12th April the battalion had been moving up to fill a gap which had developed between the 5th and 6th Brigades. While they were actually on the move forward, their infantry strung out in single file along the roads, their anti-tank guns being hauled forward across the tightly-jammed bridges over the Santerno, the General decided to launch a full-scale attack towards Massa Lombarda with both 5th and 6th Brigades. Brigadier Parkinson went forward to Spalding Bridge over the Santerno and there sought out Colonel Fairbrother, the Invercargill accountant who, in his late thirties or early forties, commanded 26th Battalion. Could he get his battalion on to the start line for the attack in three hours time? By all military precedents this was very short notice. Yes, Fairbrother thought he could. He contacted over his radio his company commanders, called them back to the bridge and there issued his orders. The companies at once deployed and moved towards the start line with their tanks, fighting pockets of opposition on the way, arrived on time, and took part in the attack.

'Monty' Fairbrother got a DSO out of this campaign, and he deserved it. He had a hard tongue, but he was a good leader. Above all he had a capacity for making swift decisions. He had already shown this particularly on one occasion in the desert. A British battalion in the early days at Alamein had taken part in a disastrous counter-attack, and had had to lie out all day in front of our minefields. After dark they were directed back towards a gap through the mines. Our sappers had been warned to stand by to close the gap as soon as the English were through, to check an expected early morning push by Rommel. Fairbrother, then a staff officer, went to the gap and with a radio gave directions to the English troops whose Bren carriers clanked and banged in the night ahead. They came directly towards the gap in the pitch blackness and then suddenly swung away south.

'What is the matter?' queried Fairbrother over the air. 'Why are you moving south? I say again. Why south?'

'We have run up against wire around a minefield. We are trying to get round it.'

Fairbrother calculated quickly. The gap had to be closed, and these troops brought in before midnight, for an artillery programme was to start then. It was a quarter to midnight now. At once he said: 'That minefield is a dummy. Come straight ahead through it.' The clanking turned and moved back.

The watchers at the gap waited. 'Is it a dummy?' queried the sappers.

'I'm damned if I know, but if it isn't it's better that they get caught in it than caught in our shelling,' was Fairbrother's reply. The noise of the tracks came nearer, nearer, until suddenly through the darkness the first Bren carrier appeared. The minefield had been a dummy one all right. By midnight the battalion was through and the gap closed.

The attack into which Colonel Fairbrother led 26th Battalion this afternoon of 12th April cleared the way to Massa Lombarda. By dusk at least four Tigers had been reported as K.O'd and the air op. was signalling tanks and trucks and horse-drawn transport moving out of the town to the west. Against the lovely sunset glow the cab rank fighter-bombers were on to them like the wrath of God.

*   *   *

Under the sluggish misted sky of early morning the infantry of the dismounted Divisional Cavalry Battalion were moving up. They marched along the roadside, ten to fifteen yards apart, moving swiftly. Each man carried his pack, with the white enamel mug tied under the strap and a shovel on top. The gear caught your eye more than the man himself. Some carried, some wore their steel helmets. Their rifles or Tommy-guns were slung over their shoulders. Their black boots were grey with dust below the anklets which bound in their battledress trousers, yet they left only rarely a footprint in the soft dust which was constantly powdered and coated anew by the passing lorries and jeeps.

Here a man carried a stretcher; there the red cross of a first-aid haversack showed up against the khaki; yet another man held the barrel of a heavy machine-gun over his shoulder like a log. Behind him strode a corporal with mortar ammunition, carrying the holder with its three containers in his hand like a suitcase, grotesquely, for all the world as if he were a week-ender hurrying to the train on Saturday afternoon.

Their faces had the set, silent, apart, almost hypnotised appearance of men about to go into battle. Already these men moved in another world, in the world of absorption in the fight and in personal survival which started just over the river, ahead there in the mist where the flat crunching bursts of incoming mortar shells sounded clearly. It was a world from which we in the jeeps and the passing trucks were separated by no great distance on the ground, but by an immensity in life. Across this distance they regarded us without rancour, without even interest. One man called some remark to a friend striding ahead of him, who answered with hardly a turn of his head. For the most part they marched silently, quietly, fatalistically, steadily, accepting but not pretending to like this lot which events had thrust upon them. Above all one felt their individual loneliness, their almost terrible apartness. They were not individuals in the ordinary civilian sense, but soldiers caught up in something as wide and unchecked as an ocean wave. Yet amidst this each remained, at this moment, alone in himself. No one else now could carry the burden of responsibility which rested on his shoulders like these weapons, this impedimenta, the dual responsibility for doing his task and if possible preserving his own life.

Their road branched from ours where the oblong black metal sign-plate marked with a white fernleaf and 'Main 63' directed us towards 6th Brigade headquarters, towards the morning conference. By some trick of memory that conference of 12th April is stamped in my mind more clearly than any other of this time. There was little reason why it should have been. The setting was as usual. Once again we were in a bare dining-room in a small farm-house. Over the maps, spread on the heavy wooden table, the General and the brigadiers leant, silent. Above the mantelpiece were snaps of round smooth Italian men and plump women, alongside gaudy religious cards. Clashing with these was a china mask of a girl's face, the kind of thing which would have gone better on the wall of a demi-mondaine's flat, a sophisticated girl with plucked eyebrows, bright cheeks and shining, tightly-drawn china hair. Her slant eyes looked down into the semi-gloom – for there were trucks backed up against the windows outside – where the red tabs showed up on the collars of the commanders and the staff officers. Their faces, as they gave their reports, were tired, lined, yet concentrated, unexcited and above all confident. You could feel then how thoroughly these men knew their jobs, and knew each other, and how confident they were of themselves and of each other. The strain, the responsibility, the complete absorption in the task in hand brought out the best in these faces, just as love can bring sudden beauty to the face of a woman who might otherwise pass unnoticed. In other places, at other times, these men had their full share of human faults and foibles, but here for this moment they were intent and, in some unmistakable way, fulfilled and complete.

This morning the decisions were taken even more swiftly than usual. The infantry were all over the river, the bridges were completed, 9th Brigade was getting ready to pass through and take over from 5th Brigade. There was a minimum of discussion. 'Have you got any mediums which can deal with tanks beyond Massa Lombarda, CRA?' queried the General.

'Yes, I have some mediums here – and here.' Queree pointed with his pencil to the map. His tone was as unemotional as a shopkeeper who says: 'Yes, you can have three pounds of sprouts and one of onions.'

'How many field regiments are across?'

'Two. The others are moving now.'

Hanson, unshaven, sleepless and yet still powerful, told of the bridges. Bonifant spoke eagerly of the Maoris' attack. The General listened to them quietly. For the first time I noticed that his hair was very grey above the ears. He suddenly looked all of his fifty-five years. Yet he counselled speed. As always his role was that of urgency: 'Push on, push on as hard as you can, Ike. He's not far from bursting.'

Outside the farm-yard was crowded with trucks, staff cars, cooking-stoves, dixies, a tank or two, motor-cycles, jeeps, command vehicles. Kiwis in grey jerseys ate porridge and drank tea out of their oblong, grey mess tins, greeted each other, stared with curiosity but no awe at the officers who came and went from the conference. Amidst all this an old peasant shuffled to and fro to one of the barns, and a girl came out with a bundle of washing. Dark-eyed, white-faced skinny children watched the dixies and the red jam on the white bread in the men's hands. In the road beyond the gate-way the traffic whirled past, the dust rising constantly like a smoke screen; and at the corner files of the Divisional Cavalry showed, where they marched still towards the battle.

* * *

We knew Massa Lombarda well from the map and from air photographs. It lay like a black griddle across the green line of the secondary road connecting Ravenna with the mid Po plains. As befitted a town amid these flat, squared, regular fields, it was a place of straight streets, set at right angles, of two and three storied plaster buildings, and of no distinction. The Baedeker on the shelf in our truck did not mention it – and rightly. It did not have, like the similarly dull Bagnacavallo, even the convent in which had died Byron's natural daughter by Claire Clairemont, Allegra. It did not even have the fine church tower of Solarolo, that other dull village in which the Germans had set up an artillery observation post throughout the winter.

We had found, among piles of captured documents, a postcard picture of the Solarolo church, with gleeful notes by one of the observers that here they had stayed in relative immunity throughout the winter; 'The Britishers did not shell the church,' he wrote. In the same bundle was a Nazi propaganda card saying the British had destroyed that other classic observation post, Cassino Monastery, out of pure wantonness. No, Massa Lombarda had none of these distinctions. It had only a German headquarters on the outskirts, well and truly bombed; several supply depots; and a name which lent itself to mild wisecracks. 'How do, Massa Lombarda – Solarlo you've been troubled,' the Maiu Westers would drawl in imitation South minstrel accents.

It is with some reluctance, therefore, that I must now record that on the edge of Massa Lombarda we were to spend a dirty afternoon under the guns of the almost destroyed 98th Division. We had moved up to a new position in an orchard right on the side of the town early in the morning. The drivers and orderlies, sensible men, noted with decent concern that it was no day to go travelling. It was Friday, 13th April. The Santerno line looked even more formidable as we wound up through its anti-tank barriers and across the small ravine formed by the high banks. The fields beyond were again gouged by yesterday's barrage.

Massa Lombarda itself had all the signs of a town which had just passed out of the front line. There was the stench of death, of dead troops lying unburied in the ditches and dead mules in the road-ways and dead civilians under the ruins of bombed houses. Smoke and dust still rose from the houses which had been hit all along the main street of the town the day before, when we had bombed the retreating enemy. Smashed carts, papers and equipment lay around. Telephone lines were broken and trailing; and the streets were chill and empty, as if an icy wind blew. Only a few civilians were stirring, mostly partisans who, red-scarved and Sten-gunned, were moving around greeting each other with delight. They had, I learnt later, utilised the night hours to carry out as thorough an épuration in this little town as in any area of Italy. Even wounded Fascists in the hospitals had been dragged out and shot. This was one of the areas where German and Fascist repression had in their time been very harsh and, as elsewhere in Italy, the partisan reaction was equally fierce and ruthless. All around the town was the sound of gunfire. Some of it was from our own guns, but only too much of it had that flat ugly crunch of incoming shells.

The orchard in which we were setting up headquarters was a beautiful spot – long green grass, wide green paths between the rows of trees, the trees themselves heavy with blossom. Our truck was pulled in romantically under a big cherry-tree. Bruno Secundo, who had shared our billet in Matelica, directed us in. We were not there long before a troop of twenty-five-pounders arrived in the field next door and began to dig themselves in. They dug, I noticed, good deep pits and slit trenches. Clearly they expected counter-battery fire. This did not look very reassuring. For the hard fact is that a headquarters cannot dig itself in to face bombardment: it cannot, with efficiency, work in holes in the ground. It needs big maps, tables for planning, space for con-ferences. It needs many vehicles grouped together in a relatively small space, so that the different arms can make easy contact. With its wooden-walled office trucks, it is peculiarly vulnerable. With one eye, therefore, on these guns – (for field guns, it must be remembered, not only give out shells, but attract those of the enemy) – I set my driver to work digging slit trenches, and started work myself at my desk in the truck, feeling as if I were not five feet, but fifty feet in the air, and in full view of the enemy.

The clerks I noticed, were not long in following suit. I heard one of the runners say : 'When I see the I blokes who are supposed to know about the enemy, start digging, then I start digging, too.' There was no particular reason why this orchard should be shelled, but there was very good reason why the roads behind it, and to one side, should be done over. With the main street of the town blocked by our bombing, as the Germans knew, the chances were that we would have to use these side roads.

It must have been just before noon when the first salvo was fired. I heard the unmistakable, rounded report of a gun pointing towards us. The sound wave from a directly hostile gun, once heard, is not easily forgotton. The shells burst just at the foot of the orchard, where the air tentacle vehicles were. I took my telephone and my papers into the half-finished slit trench and continued working from there. Half a dozen wounded men, one with his face terribly cut by shrapnel, came running up the grassy track from the orchard end. I stared up with hatred at the cherry above my head. It represented neither beauty nor fruitfulness, but only danger. For a shell hitting it would burst in the air and rain its shrapnel down on me in my hole, instead of bursting into the ground and spreading over the surface flatly, missing those below ground.

Then developed a maddening morning. The forward battalions were to move up to the Sillaro that afternoon, and assault across it that night. My own brother's battalion would be in the assault. So would Vic Milne's and my friend Ken Joblin's. I was trying to work out the enemy strength on the line, so that the guns could be spread rightly, and the attack put in in adequate strength. It was, to say the least, difficult to concentrate on such calculations.

Sammy Martin was working in a trench of his own. 'Must be three 105s of 198th Artillery Regiment,' he commented cheerfully across the orchard. 'Just across the Sillaro by the sound of them. Look out, here they come again.'

From the north-west came the sound as of taps on a heavy drum. One, two, three. I would have portrayed it as three round black daubs. The sound spun out of them like wire, closer, rising to a whistle, a whine, a screech, crescendoing into a smash and breaking into a host of tiny sounds as the fragments sped over the area. The ringing of the phone through it sounded maddeningly normal and civilised.

By lunch-time the fire died down. The optimists – particularly those whose work took them into the big shrapnel-proof armoured vehicle which housed the operations room – had it all reasoned out. 'He'll soon shoot off all his ammunition. Just getting rid of his dumps.'

About one o'clock the General sent for me. The Corps Commander was in his caravan. I was to come over and give them the enemy picture. I had just got about as far as the fact that we had identified two companies from 26th Panzer Division moving on to our front when the triple tattoo sounded again. It came from the clear sky in the very direction that the General's caravan was facing. Did he hear it, I wondered, my mind filling with the thought of the time he had stopped his car on the most heavily-shelled road at Cassino to listen to a nightingale?

The General sat up. 'Shelling?' he queried.

'Yes, sir.'

He seized the Corps Commander by the arm. 'Out you get into the ditch, Charles. I can't have you getting killed in my headquarters.'

They moved smartly into the shallow grassy irrigation ditch; I followed with equal alacrity. The General's ADC came across with steel helmets. The conference continued in the ditch.

The divisional conference that afternoon met in a farmhouse. Its brick walls looked solid enough against anything but a very heavy shell. It's surprising how reassuring nine inches of brick wall between you and the enemy can be. Maybe you are safer in a slittie in the open, but there's something about a house. So that when they did us over thoroughly about three-thirty it assumed the proportions of a lot of noise rather than a lot of danger.

Yet when I got back to the truck the drivers were busy pulling the gear down. 'Orders to move, sir. Move at your own time to a new location. There's been a lot of chaps hit.'

Martin was packing the jeep. 'Bruno Secundo has had it,' he said. 'They hit the area all round the mess during afternoon tea. He lay down in one of the ditches, but the shell hit the tree above and burst on top of him. He was killed immediately. Des was lying right behind, and never got touched. I can see now how the padre got his M.C. He was sprinting around the place like mad with shell dressings. They got two senior signals officers, too, and some others.'

'Where were you?'

'I was looking at the Tiger with a bloke who came up from the Air Force to check on it. The RAF claim it, and the Shermans claim it. So when the heavy shelling came we tried to get inside.'

'Did you?'

'Not a chance. The inside was packed with seven jokers as it was. I lay in the ditch and felt naked.'

We packed the truck and the jeep in double time. But the guns left us alone till we trundled out, down the road where we could get back to the job of examining the enemy situation with a more generalised and less personal interest, where we could get our minds away from these deaths, which were all the uglier because the end of the war seemed so near. One reason indeed why Bruno Secundo had been given this safer headquarters post was that he had already had more than his share of frontline fighting.

At the new area a group of partisans with red scarves were waiting. They had been stopped by our own troops down by the river bank as suspicious characters. Enthusiastically (they were not yet disillusioned) they explained that they wanted to help. They had been told that there were several Germans hiding in this area. One they said was patently an officer. Gold braid had been seen on his shoulders. Could they not carry on with the search?

It took only five minutes to get their papers checked and to set them loose. At the same time we put part of the Headquarter's Defence Platoon out on the same quest. 'Any prisoners you can get will be valuable,' I told the bearded partisan leader.

He grinned. '*Si, si. Prigionieri,*' he said.

Half an hour later there were shots down by the river bank. An hour later the partisans were back. They had found the Germans, three of them. One was certainly an officer. Where was he? Ah, he had tried to escape. A very foolish fellow. '*Molto stupido, molto stupido.*' But here were his documents. And they handed over a blood-stained bundle.

I opened the top pay-book. *Hauptmann.* So he was an officer all right. An anti-tank gunner. Two passport photographs fell out of the book. The face on them might well have come from a stock propaganda shot of the stern SS man. Here were those deep-set eyes, that hard thin mouth, that cheek crossed with duelling scars, that sleek yellow hair, that square German head of the ideal Nazi type. Every detail in the book bore out the picture. The man had been in the SS from the early days of Hitlerism; his list of decorations filled a whole page at the back. 'Medal for the Einmarsch into Austria: Medal for the Einmarsch into Czechoslovakia: Medal for the Polish campaign: Iron Cross Second Class in France. Served with the infantry in Russia: Transferred to the anti-tank gunners at the end of 1943: Iron Cross First Class in the Crimea for destroying two *feindlicher Panzer Kampfwagen*. The medal of the Iron Cross, its ribbon stained crimson brown above its red, black and white, lay amongst the papers.

The *Hauptmann's* book was full of photographs of Storm Troops and of soldiers, of sisters in white blouses and dark skirts, of a heavy-built father with close-cropped hair, of other young officers with the same relentless faces. This was the type Hitler had loosed on Europe, brave, desperate, efficient. Now he had come to his end in an Italian field, shot down by an Italian farmer's boy with a Sten gun, shot in the back I learned later, as he crouched in hiding.

CHAPTER SEVEN

Breakthrough

In the intervals of these activities we had still the ever-changing enemy picture to delineate. Had the enemy had a hard enough knock yet to go right back? No. By midday it had been clear that he was still going to fight for it not only on the next river, the Sillaro, but on the canal which ran on our side of it. Indeed he showed so much fight that we thought there must be fresh troops on the scene.

We had therefore to take two bites at the Sillaro cherry. That night the western sky and the black olive groves and orchards were lit by yet another bombardment as 'Operation Foxie' (was ever a campaign fought, whatever the reason, with such miserable code names?) went in against the canal. Gentry's 9th Brigade had now come in as the left-hand brigade, allowing 5th Brigade to drop out for a rest. The canal was crossed, and the infantry pushed on and seized both banks of the Sillaro river, where once again there were the familiar earthen flood-walls, though lower this time than before. There was no great battle to get them, as the enemy had adopted a new method. He was dug in, not on the flammable banks themselves, but some hundred yards farther back, where the barrage would be harder to direct on to his exact positions. The next day he proceeded to counter-attack us with some vigour, and to shell and mortar our troops in their slit trenches.

The enemy troops were a fresh formation. They were the 278th Infantry Division, a stock infantry formation of no distinction, known to us chiefly because of their loud-voiced, aggressive commander, General Hoppe. Of Hoppe we had a file of anecdotes, related by prisoners, telling of the way he ranted and raved at new drafts of reinforcements when they were paraded at his headquarters, promising them all the rigours of the Third Reich if they did not hold the line, and all its delights if they did. His force had been brought out of the mountains south-west of Bologna to plug the hole made by our advance. We regarded their arrival with some satisfaction. It demonstrated that 98th Division, which we had set out to destroy, had been largely wiped out. The prisoners from 278th Division gave a vivid enough picture of the thin files of the 98th Division stumbling past in the dark on the night of the change-over, muttering encouraging slogans like *'Rette sich wer retten kann'*, which we translated for the *Summary* as 'Every man for himself'. The arrival of this formation was also a sign that the wider campaign was progressing, for it meant we had drawn down one formation from the hills into the plain, and had made the mountain offensive correspondingly easier.

This was all the more important because the big Fifth Army offensive had by now got under way. They were hitting straight north towards Bologna, and making ground. 10th Mountain Division, the new American troops in whom we all placed great faith, were taking height after height, even if at high cost. For the first time our heavy punching in the plains looked as if it might bring not merely a gain of ground, not merely carry us to yet one more river barrier, but actually open the way for victory.

Another move which spoke of more open warfare was a change of command. We were informed that night that we were to pass from command of 5th Corps to that of 13th Corps. The name of 13th Corps evoked recollections of the swift campaigns of the desert. Their commander, General Harding, had led the 7th Armoured Division through much of the worst of the Libyan and Egyptian fighting, and had been BGS of 13th Corps in its greatest desert days. We had been with them in many actions there. We looked with satisfaction as their red-caps posted along the roads their red and black 'Leapin' Gazelle' sign, and as their trucks bumped past with desert camouflage and Egyptian number-plates. We even looked with a kindly eye on the suede desert boots and the polka-dot scarves which their staff officers affected, in cheerful indifference to the ridicule which the 'Two Types 'cartoons had thrown on such garb. Their very presence seemed to indicate that the horizons were opening out.

We farewelled 5th Corps, however, with regret. They had been our companions through the hard, cold winter of 1944-45, that winter which was in so many ways the worst of the war, because it seemed the most unnecessary. We had been given such ample grounds for believing that the show would finish in the autumn of 1944 and we had decided from all the reports that it could have been finished if Eisenhower had strengthened Montgomery's hand in the autumn, instead of handing out reserve divisions to every American commander who came and asked Ike for 'a little help and I'll be in Berlin by Christmas.' So that the winter fighting had had the bitterness of disappointment and of postponement as well as of cold and mud. This dull harsh fighting period had been spent by us under 5th Corps, and our bonds with them were the solid bonds of adversity. So I said good-bye to John Crawley, and taunted him that we would reach the Alps first. His own answer was cheerful enough, for 5th Corps were making progress to the north. It looked as if they would rapidly break open the Argenta Gap and get to the Po first.

There were other encouraging signs, too. The next morning at our conference a new figure had made his appearance – a British colonel who commanded a regiment of the 12th Lancers, cavalry in armoured cars. They had now come under our command. Had we not known something of British cavalry regiments from desert days, we might have put down Colonel Savile as 'just another Pommie', for he looked shy and worried, and he blushed when the General first addressed him. Yet like so many of his kind in the desert, he turned out to be the extremely efficient commander of a very efficient regiment, which was, in the pursuit which now lay ahead, to write one of the more spectacular pages in its history.

His Staghound armoured cars were already crowding on to the roads behind us, feeling their way out along innumerable back paths and tracks to watch our flanks. We needed them. We were now well out in front of both the Poles on our left and of the Indians on our right, and at any time the enemy might try to hit us from the north or the south. To guard against this the 12th Lancers' patrols were sent out to both flanks, the round, pink-faced English troops in soft berets staring out of the turrets, and their round voices contrasting with the sharper tones of the Kiwi infantry who greeted them with friendly satire as 'Chooms'.

Events continued to move swiftly. While the brigades fought a day of local battles on the Sillaro on 14th April, the enemy was going back slowly but markedly all along the front from the Tyrrenhian coast to the Adriatic. Towards Genoa the Fifth Army were pushing into the mountains and, glory be, had drawn in one of the regiments of the enemy's crack reserve division, 90th Panzer Grenadier. South of Bologna the battle for the last range of the Apennines was going ahead. On Route 9 the parachutists were giving ground slowly in front of the Poles, edging back along roads which we noted must bring them on to our front. Most spectacular was the fighting on the Eighth Army's right flank. A battle was under way there for a narrow strip of roadway, the high-banked Route 16, the main road from Ravenna to Argenta, and on to Ferrara. This road ran along the shoreline of a huge salty estuary lagoon, Lake Commachio. The enemy had breached the dikes to flood the low-lying marshy lands to the south of the Lake, leaving Route 16 as a narrow causeway running through the waters. This causeway they fortified, turning it into a formidable military obstacle. By any standards this constituted a narrow axis of advance for the three divisions which, under the plans for Operation Buckland, were to force a way through to Ferrara and up to the River Po. On the planning maps this route was listed as the Argenta Gap, but it was more truthfully the Argenta defile, a thin sliver of roadway through a wide, muddy waterscape.

It was here that the Allied strength in amphibious vehicles showed its value. These had been designed primarily for the D-Day landings, but they had their value here too. The Fantails, Dukws and Kangaroos enabled the 56th London Division and the 6th Armoured Division to mount a series of waterborne flanking attacks on the roadway, cutting behind the German positions and forcing them back from one strongpoint to another. Parallel attacks were made to the south by 78th Division. All along the line we were leaning against the door very hard. A few more blows with the battering ram, and we would be through.

A few more blows. They sound simple enough. They were not so simple in terms of men lying face downwards, clutching the Italian dust on the slopes of the stop-banks, crumpling in the chaos of bombed and shelled farm-yards. Steadily the war diaries of the fighting units were sketching, in unemotional detail, the reality of those sunny April days on the Romagna plain. Our Divisional Cavalry report read :

> Throughout the day both B and D Squadrons had to accept mortar and shell fire which steadily whittled down their numbers. Snipers too were claiming their quota. D Squadron alone lost four killed, three to snipers.

Other reports rounded out the story :

> In the face of machine-gun fire and grenade fire Corporal Rawson led his section across the river and silenced three enemy posts.

> An assault gun was set on fire by Sergeant Mitcheson, who dashed towards it with a Piat and at very short range scored three direct hits. Its crew then fired on him, but he killed three of them with his Tommy gun.

> At dawn Corporal Anderson left the house which the two platoons occupied and armed with a Tommy gun walked towards the Germans in their trenches a quarter of a mile away. Others from C Company went to support him. As Anderson grabbed at an enemy rifle about 30 Germans rose, dropped their weapons ,and moved forward. Then Anderson fell, his left arm (later amputated) severely shattered by a concealed German Tommy gunner.

Second Lieutenant Vazey left his tank to observe the enemy from the stop bank and returned to direct his Troop's shooting until his tank was knocked out and he was wounded.

Lance Corporal Hutchinson of 10 Platoon made a solo dash over the crest of the bank, killed a German, wounded another and took a prisoner.

We found ourselves theoretically occupying 350 yards of stop-bank with nine or ten men on one flank and three on the other. All the platoon commanders were wounded, two sergeants dead, and the third wounded.[1]

Reports of this kind, coming back day after day, translated themselves into the grim arithmetic of the casualty lists, the price of our success.

Again and again now in the General's caravan I heard the word 'casualties'. Again and again at conferences the word 'reinforcements' was mentioned. Already our losses were getting near the figure at which the General was determined that he must ask for us to be taken from the line. It was with concern that he laid down the plans for yet another set-piece attack, to break the opposition in front of the Sillaro, and carry us through towards Medicina.

In this pause, as in the other on the Santerno, Colmore Williams and the RAF were giving the Germans what was perhaps the worst time from the air they ever had in Italy, except at Cassino. All day we phoned Colmore the targets which we secured from the prisoners, from documents, from the air op. All day the brigades sent in their targets too. All day the sky was filled with planes circling, planes diving, planes coming up out of the east and south, moving across the blue like footballers in formation, We reduced Sesto Imolese village, just across the Sillaro, to literally nothing but dust and rubble. We harried every point where the enemy might be. We carpeted his assembly areas and supply dumps with pattern bombing by mediums. We hit headquarters after headquarters. How the Germans felt under this we needed no telling. We had been on the receiving end of air attack in Greece and Crete and at Tobruk and Alamein. But one diary which we captured told the story in terms vivid enough to be worth quoting. It was written by a member of a German Nebelwerfer Regiment. This soldier wrote :

Continuous attacks by fighter-bombers and shelling directed by air op. In wave upon wave bombers come over. Four fighter-bombers attack us and score direct hits in signal centre, burying and killing eleven men, wounding nine. We spent the rest of the night and day searching the ruins for bodies. Sjt. K. still believes he can throw his weight about.

Discipline has deteriorated badly. Again we move our positions another six kilos to the north. Night and day fighter-bombers and shelling. No more mail comes up. Are our parents alive? When will the battle finish? New signals centre set up in Sesto Imolese. Again we change our positions, again the fighter-bombers come, and shelling. All the Nebelwerfers have been wiped out. Two new Nebels come up. No more proper organisation exists. The paratroops keep clearing out. I had a row with Sjt. Kahle. He has had a great opinion of himself and thinks only of his own life. A man can go to hell for all he cares. It is senseless to keep on fighting. We are supposed to stop tanks and it is always the same people who make a bolt for it. The Italians are happy that the Tommies are coming. Another change of position. Two wounded. Utter chaos. The break up of the German Army has begun.

In these circumstances it was surprising that we encountered hard fighting along the roads west of the Sillaro before the break-out from the stop-banks were complete. In the confusion the German tanks and our own infantry got mixed up, the infantry thinking, as they heard the clank of tracks on the roads behind them, that the bridges had been put through in record time, and that our own Shermans were arriving. A jubilant company commander sent back his thanks for the armoured support. A harassed battalion commander wirelessed back to him to look again. The company officer looked, and found Tigers instead of Shermans. So the infantry had to turn and use their Piats. They knocked out three of the Tigers, and one self-propelled gun.

It was, however, a lucrative attack. We took 557 prisoners and wrote off the greater part of the already depleted 278th Division. We found, too, bigger fish than 278th Division in our net. From the areas opposite our left flank we had sixty prisoners in the flattened steel helmets and the unmistakable overalls of the parachutists. They were from 111th Parachute Reconnaissance Battalion, and they had fought like fury before they were captured.

Their story showed clearly that the pressure of battle had now squeezed on to our front the parachutists who had previously faced the Poles. So our enemies of Cassino and Florence were in front of us again. Our hopes of a break-through at the Sillaro, our hopes that this attack might be our

last set piece assault were gone. We knew these parachutists would stand
and fight, and so it proved. After a relatively swift move forward for two
days we found ourselves, on 17th April, facing a solid line of parachutists
on the Gaiana river west of Medicina. Their steady, efficient ground fire,
their heavier artillery, their maddening Nebelwerfers all showed that
battle was again necessary. We were to mount it with one New Zealand
Brigade and one Gurkha Brigade, the 43rd Lorried Infantry Brigade.
It had been brought under our command to ease the strain on our
own men.

The battle of the Gaiana river was to attract little attention in those late
April days of 1945. Amidst the thunder of blows which were falling on the
Third Reich, the hammering which the parachutists of 1st Para Corps
got on the Italian front went almost unheard. Yet we can claim, I believe,
that few nails were driven into the coffin of Nazism more thoroughly
than this. On the Gaiana we were able to bring down such a blow on to
the best German infantry on the Italian front that from then on, with
steadily increasing speed, the way to the Po and the Alps opened up.

I have called the scene of the action, as do the maps, the Gaiana river.
On the ground it is no more than a ditch, a straight irrigation ditch like
a canal, crossing the Ravenna-Bologna road just beyond Medicina. At
any other time you would never have noticed it; there are dozens of such
ditches to be encountered in an afternoon's drive on this road. The Gaiana
had straight, parallel flood-banks fifteen to twenty feet high, and a black,
muddy stream which could be waded by men but not crossed by tanks.
On the banks of this barrier, as good a natural anti-tank obstacle as one
could find, the parachutists dug themselves in. They prepared to prove, as
they had done so often, that they could hold where the ordinary German
infantry had yielded.

We came up against the Gaiana line of 17th April. This time the 9th
Brigade was on our right, and on our left were the Gurkhas. We needed
them. Our casualties had mounted further. I had heard that morning
that Vic Milne had been hit. He was wounded in the wrist on the Sillaro.
Ken Joblin too had been wounded in the face. They were only two of
many. We were glad too that it was the Gurkhas who came to us. We had
fought the battles of Faenza alongside them in the winter. They were
pouring into the area already, their small round yellow faces peering like
the faces of children from the back of their many trucks, their shoulders
marked with the badge of crossed kukhri knives, their equipment neat and
soldierly.

As if to mark the importance of the occasion, we held the divisional conference on the morning of 18th April in a bigger room than usual. It was on the front floor of a stone farmhouse as spacious as a small castle. From the windows you could see across the fields to where the shells burst already behind the line of the river. The General interrogated me closely on the enemy layout. Were we sure the parachutists were there in strength? Yes, we had identifications from six full battalions, in the line or in reserve – two battalions of 12th Para Regiment, two of 10th Para Regiment, one of 4th Para and one of 11th Para Regiment. Tanks? Yes. The few remaining Tigers had been moved off our front, but his half-dozen Panthers were still opposite us.

Would the enemy be sure to stand and fight on the Gaiana? There was every sign that he would. He had now committed all his reserves, and was fighting hard on every front in Italy. 90th Panzer Grenadier Division was fully committed, partly towards the west coast, partly south of Bologna. 29th P.G. Division, which started to leave for the Western front, had been recalled to try and plug the Argenta Gap. A break-through anywhere would threaten all his fronts.

'Very well, then,' said the General. 'We will break him here.'

The brigadiers' reports bore out the fact that the Gaiana was strongly held. There was a good deal of sniping, a lot of Nebelwerfer fire, and on the Gurkha front there had been local counter-attacks. It was the Senio all over again. We had the near bank generally under our control, while the enemy had the far bank. The banks, moreover, were low enough to ensure that the flame-throwers, if used, would reach the far bank without fail.

'The situation,' commented Brigadier Gentry, in his somewhat academic manner, 'is most suitable for flaming.' Brigadier Barker, the tall, countrified Englishman who commanded the Gurkhas, concurred: 'I agree with the technique of withdrawing and then stropping him up,' was his view.

The full-scale attack was set for 2100 hours that night. That would give ample time for the bridges, said Hanson, but he must insist on having some infantry left with the sappers to give them protection. On the Sillaro his men had had to stop bridging in order to go and fight German pockets left behind. And the Gurkhas wanted a slightly slower rate of advance than usual.

'My fellows have very short legs, you know,' said Barker.

The General disagreed. 'They have short legs but they move them mighty fast. They'll keep up all right.'

The General and the CRA hurried back to their headquarters to bor-row or bully more guns out of every formation they could – Corps, Army, neighbouring divisions. The Wasps and Crocodiles were being hurried forward along the crowded roads. Back in our headquarters area, in a field of uncut hay, we checked again the estimates of the enemy.

It was a superb day, sunny and brilliant. The trucks and caravans of divisional headquarters – as those of practically every unit in the division – were parked in the open, in the strips of pasture which lay, like football fields, between the rows of vines or poplars. Had one been in a mood for beauty, this was beautiful indeed – the leaves moving in the slight wind, the purple and golden flowers amongst the trampled grass, the larks singing very high up in the hazed sky. But it did not move one as beauty should. There was nothing one could enjoy in this or in any such scene which served as a background to war. Its very loveliness did not console, but intensified the sense of bitterness and strain and weariness, the distorted sense of time, so that some hours were as long as days, and some went in meaningless swiftness. Here, as in the desert, as under the cypresses in the Florentine Hills, as even in the quiet of Matelica, beauty brought always a taste of gall. It looked beautiful, but it did not feel beautiful.

It was almost melodramatically appropriate that this battle, which, given good fortune, should be our last major action in Italy and perhaps in the war, was to be waged against the parachutists. They had been our opponents in many areas from Greece to Italy. They had dropped on to us on the Corinth Canal in 1941, and in Crete. In Cassino 1st Para Division had been our opponents in what was perhaps the ugliest battle of the Western war. In front of Florence we had met 4th Para Division. 12th Para (Sturm) Regiment, which now occupied the left flank of the Gaiana, had provided the glider-borne troops who had led the assault on Crete. On just such a sunny day as this we had stared up through the olive-trees at their slow, wide-winged, silent craft swooping down on to us. The 12th Storm Regiment was something more too than just one unit in a big corps. From it had been drawn the cadres to rebuild the parachutists after Crete, to transform them into the elite of the German Army under Nazism, brutal, strong, with an almost masochistic willingness to die.

The long sunny afternoon wore on. On every side guns were moving in to take part in the bombardment. Harried artillery staff officers were having a terrible job to find room to disperse them all. The air thickened with haze and vibrated with the bombers, never absent from the daylight sky. At last dusk came, and with it the cool sweet spring night.

Ten minutes before the barrage was due to start the phone rang. The General wanted me. I found him pacing the grass alongside his caravan.

'Give me your estimate of the enemy strength again.'

'A maximum of a thousand, sir.'

He did a quick sum in his head. 'We've got three regiments of five fives, and eight field regiments, plus the 105th Regiment. That's 192 field pieces alone. They will fire about 100,000 rounds. That gives us 100 rounds for each individual paratrooper from the field guns without counting the mediums. I wouldn't like to sit under that – it's a worse barrage than any other there's been this war.'

His phone rang. 'Yes, Barker – yes – did you test the market at dusk? The Hun was still there? Good. We're giving you the greatest bombardment we've ever put down.'

The General came back outside. It was very still in the dark. Voices called from the men's mess truck where the cooks were bedding down.

The General took up his interrupted line of thought. 'This will be the most important battle we have fought in Italy.' He chuckled : 'They're worried sick at Corps and Army that we're going to shoot off all their ammunition tonight. So we are. But we are the only ones in position and ready to do so, so why shouldn't we ?'

He had some right to feel proud on that score. We were well in the lead now. We had been able to build bridges swiftly and to get up the ammunition and move in the guns, and get the fire plans drawn up in time to mount this series of massive attacks. It was in this labour of war, as much as in the fighting of war, that the physical strength and education and above all the sense of responsibility of the ordinary Dominion private and gunner showed up. Ever since the first Senio battle these efforts had enabled us to deploy and use in its fullest scale the immense mass of material that is a modern army's equipment. Can you blame us then if our sappers felt fine when, day after day, the neighbouring troops borrowed our bridges to pass over their tanks and guns, because their own bridges weren't yet up? Or if every day our infantry nodded their satisfaction as they saw on the map the red bulge of their line nose out a little farther in front? So that this evening, when we had insisted on more than our rights in ammunition, we had got it.

Yet up here in the darkness I could see the General was frankly nervous. He had to justify this tremendous expenditure of shells. He had to show results, German casualties in dead, wounded and prisoners by the morrow. Above all he was gravely worried about our own casualties. Even with the Gurkhas to help this must be our last attack, or at the best our last but one. Yet he knew the division was desperately anxious to be in the open warfare which must come soon, and which had been promised to the Eighth Army all the way up Italy. He knew too, that we were better fitted, from our desert days, for open warfare than anyone else in Italy.

2130 hours. The barrage opened with a roar on right and left, with a splitting crash from the battery of 3.7s behind us. The flashes lit and flared like a hundred thunderstorms. The trees around us changed from lumps of soft, slumberous darkness, to shapes of green and yellow. The whole western sky was alive with bursting shells.

It looked appalling, far far worse than the Senio. It moved the General to a rare moral judgment about the enemy. 'I hate these paratroopers,' he said suddenly, 'they represent all that is worst in the whole Nazi system.'

At ten o'clock the flame-throwers went in. Their spurts of flame, red under the lightning flashes, showed again, again, again. All along the line of the river they glared, red and ugly. The black smoke mounted up into the stars. The assault was on.

Despite all this, the parachutists did not give up easily. Though the prisoners who came back were dazed and horrified, they totalled less than 200. Their casualties on the ground appeared, in the dark, not very numerous. It looked at first as if the battle had paid none too high a dividend. We carried the Gaiana line, and advanced deep beyond it, but ground was not what we wanted. We wanted to destroy the German Armies in Italy this side of the Po, so that they could not get back into the Alps. At first it looked as if this time we had failed.

It was only when I went forward to the river line itself early the next day that I realised that this was not so. We had indeed hit the enemy as we wished. The first count of enemy casualties had been too low. Along these banks in the stream, in their trenches, in houses and holes behind, lay the massed dead. Few battlefields in this war can have presented the picture of carnage which the banks of the Gaiana showed that day, this spectacle of Germans killed by the barrage, or caught crouching in their holes by the flame-throwers, or slaughtered in a hundred other ways. You did not see dead in great masses in this war in the west. Men were killed in their thousands and tens of thousands, it was true, but they fell over wide, wide areas, so that the individual saw few of them and was spared the full impact of horror. Not so on the Gaiana. If anyone wants to run an anti-war exhibition in the future I commend to his attention the photographs which record the carnage in the Gaiana area. There they lay in all their ghastliness, the youth of Germany, the pride of Hitlerism. It is not for me to describe them in detail. Let it be enough to say that they lay like the very embodiment of sudden brutal death.

And we who had planned the killing of these men? What feelings had we, in the sunshine? My first reaction was, I believe, a very usual one.

It was a sense of awe and fear at this spectacle of death which might have struck down any one of us. It had hit them, but had fate willed it might have been us instead. Nor did these boys appear as individuals, even in their individual deaths. Their bodies were still just part of that generalised thing 'the enemy' at which you must hit, or he will hit you. They were items to be washed out of our path, not people who had known hopes, fears, ambitions, who had lived and longed to live further.

In all honesty, however, I found I could feel in myself little pity, but only disgust at the waste of it all. These boys, whose lank and matted hair now trailed in the filthy waters of this meagre canal, represented the waste of a whole generation in the life of a country and of Europe. Parents had laboured and worried and saved to bring them to manhood, and then Hitler and his system had taken them and led them to this end, to this evil death in the service of evil. They were utter waste, wasted and dangerous in life, wasted completely in death, the final price of Hitler and the forces who had brought him into being. Any man who ever said a good word for Nazism should have been taken that morning to the Gaiana, to stand there and see amid the sunshine and stench what this faith could do even to those who professed it.

Even with these casualties, however, the enemy still appeared to have parachutists enough to make one further stand – the Idice. The Idice was another Santerno, with generous stop-banks and prepared defences of wire and diggings, and some mines. It had been constructed as the final inner defence for Bologna, to it had been given the impressive name of the 'Genghis Khan' position. On to it the survivors of the Gaiana were now pulling back. There we had to face them again. Very well. The General was quite clear about what should be done. If they wanted another blow like last night's, we would give it to them. He urged Queree to get up all his guns again, and more ammunition.

'I hope the enemy do man the Idice,' the General said. 'Then we can destroy all the more of his forces south of the Po.'

So the next day 9th Brigade and the Gurkhas were pulled out to rest, and 5th and 6th Brigades came forward for yet one more riverline battle. For it we were promised all the corps artillery.

But it was weary work. Were the Germans never going to crack? They must be hearing the news on the wireless, the reports that the Russians were on the edge of Berlin and the Americans and the British racing across Western Germany. Even in Italy the Fifth Army were now close to Bologna, with the worst peaks captured. 5th Corps on our right had won their long battle of the Route 16 causeway, had broken through the Argenta Gap, and were heading towards Ferrara, the big provincial centre which guarded the main Venice road bridge across the Po. Yet here we were on our eleventh day of consecutive hard fighting, and instead of having a break-through we were still getting minor counter-attacks on our flanks, exposed further by our new advance.

There were, it is true, some signs of the impending end. Among the 300 parachutist prisoners taken on the Gaiana, there was one genuine officer deserter, the first we had ever had from the parachutists. He was, moreover, an old-time Nazi – a tall, heavily-built man whose figure, quite apart from the silver braid on his shoulders, singled him out in the cage. I gave him a cigarette and we talked in the sun. He had been with the Condor Legion in Spain in 1936 and 1937. He said he had never been through a barrage like that of last night. It was worse than Velletri, where all the artillery of the Fifth Army had been concentrated for the break-out from the Anzio bridgehead. The casualties from the shelling had not been heavy as his were experienced troops, well dug in. But the effect of the flame-throwers had been final, and in the close fighting afterwards his troops had had many losses. And the enemy's strategy? It was, he said, to fight us to a standstill. If the battle could be kept moving we could break them; if not they would settle and hold. Why then had he deserted? He shrugged his shoulders. The war was lost anyway, whatever happened here. Why wait and perhaps be sent to Germany, to fall a prisoner to the Russians, where here you might get to America? America, ah! He rolled his eyes in mock delight. He had been there as a seaman on a liner in 1926. What a country! What *Mädchen*! Yes, he hoped he would get to America.

I thought of this deserter's attitude the next morning, when I had to make a quick judgment about the enemy's condition. I had been wakened by Colmore Williams. The Royal Air Force wanted to know whether they should bombard Budrio, the small town which lay across the road from the Gaiana to the Idice. If we hit the entrance and exit of it we could hamper the enemy's retreat, perhaps block the withdrawal of much of his material. They had twenty-four medium aircraft laid on for the job, and they wanted an immediate reply.

Was it worth it? We might do the Germans a little harm; we would certainly do Budrio a great deal. These bombs could block the roadway only by destroying the houses on the town edge. It was not, it is true, our job to take those factors into consideration. Our job was to hit the Germans with every possible weapon, regardless of whom or what got in our path. At that moment as we stood there at the tailboard of Colmore's truck, our trouser cuffs soaked with the heavy dew, the cooks busy with breakfast in their truck beyond, and the shadows almost solid black in the trees, I realised more than at any other time the power of these weapons which science had put into our hands. Colmore was in his late twenties; I was in my early thirties. Ahead of us, in their homes, in their cellars, cowered the Italians of this small town which had played no part in history, ancient or modern. The decision of whether or not their homes were to be destroyed, as part of the destruction of the enemy, rested with us. Back on the airfields the mediums were bombed up, ready to start. We had to flash them their target within five minutes.

We had seldom had this worry before, for all the way along our route till now there had been enough German resistance to make every blow, wherever delivered, essential. We had pressed our prong of 'the fiery rake' deeply into the soil of this strip of Italy along which we had advanced, unhesitatingly. But was it now justified? I found it hard to believe that it was. I could not honestly say that we could damage the enemy to any extent by going for those roads. His guns were almost certainly back behind the Idice, his troops would not be stopped by holes in the road.

'What do you say to this alternative target – plaster the main lines of the river just north of the town?' said Colmore. I agreed with some relief.

'Yes. Let Budrio stay put.'

Colmore wrote out his signal, giving the river bank target. We drank down chipped enamel mugs of tea which his batman had brought, and went back to shave.

The rest of that morning we prepared for one more set assault. By midday however strange things had started to happen. 5th Brigade had not only reached the Idice bank, but had two companies of Maoris across with hardly a fight. An hour later, at the afternoon conference, Brigadier Parkinson had even more surprising news. He had one battalion on the far stop-bank, while to the left 26th Battalion had found a ford and at this moment were crossing with their tanks.

'Which ford, Ike?' queried the General. With his walking-stick Ike pointed it out on the map. The point of the stick rested across the black line drawn to mark the boundary between our sector and that of the Poles.

'It's in the Poles' territory, Ike. We've no right to be there. They might start shooting you up at any time.'

'Can't we get the boundary changed? If we have to shift north then we will have no ford or crossing, and we will lose the fruits of the battle on the Gaiana. My people are full of running and if we have to give up that bridgehead then we will have to fall back on B bank and call it a day.'

There was no mistaking the bitterness in Parkinson's voice. He certainly did not want to pull back. For the first time since these battles had begun there was real tension in the conference room. After all, we were over the river, with tanks, without a fight. Were we going to have to withdraw just because some staff officer at Army had drawn a line with his pencil on a map at this point? Surely the boundary could be changed more easily than another bridgehead be won?

The General shook his head : 'I've taken the boundary question up on Army level, and it's too late to get it changed.' Parkinson was about to say something, but he checked himself, and filled his pipe instead. I thought of 26th Battalion up there now, pushing out confidently with their tanks, the first of the Allied troops to be really across the Idice, across the last dirty water barrier. They were going to take it hard, being ordered back.

Yet there was another side to the case. Boundaries have to be drawn in advance, for without them no Army could do any planning. A host of other things have to be fitted into them – supply routes, fire plans, operation orders. There was too the fact that if we pulled back we might give up a little ground, but it would be a worthwhile price if in return we caught the enemy on yet another river bank and trounced him hard again. With one more real blow he would surely be finished completely. Casualties, not ground, were what we sought to wrest from the enemy.

The General adjourned the meeting while Parkinson phoned to his headquarters for the latest reports.

Ike came back, looking in a thoroughly black mood. A full squadron of tanks was across. 'Well,' said the General, facing the room like a minister facing an angry Parliament. 'What do you think now, Ike?'

We waited for the storm to break. But Ike swallowed his wrath. He paused for a moment and then said quietly : 'After all, the Hindenburg Line was broken by one man who hopped over the barbed wire when the Germans weren't looking. I think this line's broken in the same way. Let us use the ford, and push our stuff over, and turn north, and clear a bridgehead in front of our own stretch of the river.'

The last war simile hit home. The General grinned, and slowly gave way. He did not like abandoning the chance to smash the enemy again, but he decided upon a compromise. The 6th Brigade on the left would move across the ford, while 5th Brigade would still put in an attack under a barrage. Then he hurried back to his headquarters to sell this plan to Army, get the use of the Poles' ford, and stop the Polish artillery shooting us up.

Situations of this type in ordinary life, as politicians well know, often solve themselves it left to lie fallow for a while. In warfare they seldom do. They have to be dealt with rapidly, for the pace of events is always rapid. The General got on to the Poles immediately by phone, and to corps and army. They agreed to leave us the ford, and to go through our bridgehead the next day. It was an excellent compromise. The next morning the fruits began to tumble from this tree which we had been shaking so long and so hard. By eleven o'clock the Poles were through us, and in Bologna, where they met the Americans of Fifth Army, down at last from the mountains. All along the front we were well over the Idice and heading north as well as west. The battle of the Po plains was finished. The chase was on.

Saturday, 21st April, was grey and cloudy, as if to mark by a change in the weather the end of one period of the campaign. But perfect sunshine came again the next morning when divisional headquarters moved over the Idice on the first stage of the chase northwards. Through the willows on our left the white walls of reprieved Budrio gave back the sunshine. To the west of the river the wind stirred the leaves of the ranked poplars which are the glory of the Lombardy plain. Steadily the country opened out. There were still ditches and lines of vines, but the fields were bigger, offering views now, not just glimpses. The farmhouses were massive, rich and well kept. To the south the mountains rose up behind Bologna, clear and blue, giving us a horizon at last. Peasants in their Sunday clothes walked to church along these unshattered roadways, for now the battle was moving too fast for real damage to be done. Church bells rang out across the lush countryside as we drove that morning to plan, not battle, but pursuit.

Martin went off in the jeep to contact the South African Armoured Division, which had broken out of the mountains with Fifth Army, and was moving up on our left. The 12th Lancers were racing ahead at speed, in their true role of cavalry advance guard.

We got out our detailed maps of the Po and the Adige, and Fred Kersh hammered at Corps for photo cover right up to the Alps. On the captured German maps the Adige bore its Teutonic name of the 'Etsch', that southern boundary of the Reich which in *'Deutschland über Alles'* good Germans are urged to guard *'Von der Etsch bis an den Belt'*.

It formed part now of the last German line in north Italy, the Venetian Line. This had been fortified as thoroughly as if it were the boundary of the modern Reich. The Venetian Line covered the forty miles between the sea and the Alps, running from Chioggia, at the southern end of the Venetian Lagoon, along a canal and then along the north bank of the Adige. From the river it swung northwards to the edge of the Euganean Hills, and from there to the foothills of the Alps and to Lake Garda. It was believed to be the strongest defensive line the Germans had built in Italy. Properly manned, resolutely held, it could block our path for days, perhaps even for a week or more. Until it was broken or pierced, we had no hope of advancing eastwards onto Venice and Trieste. The aerial photographs showed that the sector onto which we were directed, around Este and Monselice, was studded with gun emplacements and field fortifications.

At our headquarters VIPs began to gather. Field Marshal Alexander came in the afternoon to visit the General, and Mr Harold Macmillan, then the Minister Resident in Italy, arrived towards evening. I felt that afternoon as if we had come out of a long tunnel, or a dark green forest, into the sunlight, as if we had lived and fought this last fortnight not, as in fact, in brilliant sunshine, but with a great darkness over everything. The end of it all seemed suddenly in sight. That night we slept amidst wild irises in a hayfield north of Bologna, under a notice warning German convoys that this was a zone 'Infested with Bandits' (Bologna had long been a partisan area of significance). Even the German aircraft who spent half the night circling around dropping butterfly bombs along the main road did not spoil our sleep.

Above Bologna the Reno river curves in a great horseshoe. We were inside the curve; the parachutists and the remnants of the other divisions who had fought us on the plain were moving back inside it too, to cross it to the north, en route for the Po. They could not hope to stand and fight on the Reno, for at both ends Allied forces were already across the river, and moving up the far bank to converge (we hoped) at the top. From the east 6th British Armoured Division were driving north-west; from the west 6th South African Armoured Division were also on their way northwards. But the parachutists were agile enough to hold both these thrusts, and to get back across the Reno and retreat towards the Po. We followed them hard.

Bridge-building, not fighting, now determined the rate of our advance. The Reno was a much bigger river than any we had crossed to date. It was midnight on Monday before the bridges there were through. By mid-morning the next day 24th April, we were on the south bank of the Po. We reached the Po almost directly north of Bologna opposite the small town of Bondeno. There was no bridge at this point – nor indeed had the Allied air forces left a single Po bridge standing. The Germans had used ferries to cross in this area, and their great notices '*Zum Po*' still sign-posted the route. It would have needed no such marking, however, even had we had no maps. For the approaches to the river were littered with the abandoned material of an army, some blown up and destroyed, some just left, mile upon mile of it. We spent much of that day checking up on it. Under the constant air attack it was clear that a hundred local Dunkirks, each worse in its way than the 1940 evacuation, because here the attackers had held complete control of the air, had taken place. Trucks, horse-drawn wagons, cars, caravans, guns lay abandoned or burnt on the roadside, tipped into ditches, run into fields. Hundreds of supply and artillery horses roamed the fields, the magnificent draught horses of Hungary and Germany. Amongst the trucks we captured the documents of the 4th Parachute Division, including their own books on the Crete campaign and their victory there over the '*Neuseelander*' in '*Einsatz gegen Kreta*'.

How strong would the enemy resistance on the Po be? To the west the American 10th Mountain Division was reported to be already across the river on a bridge built with seized enemy material. They were doing superbly. Could we in our sector risk an immediate daylight assault? The forward troops thought they could They would line the stop-bank with tanks, shell the opposition bank for all they were worth, and push out in their rubber and canvas assault boats. An officer, just to prove it was possible, got over and back without attracting fire. The Po was, of course, a completely different proposition from any of our previous river crossings. At its narrowest at this point it was 300 yards wide, and it flowed swiftly. It could certainly not be waded, and a bridge could not be built in less than twenty-four hours, so that any tank support would have to be ferried over by our one motor ferry. The operation was more like a seaborne landing than a river crossing, needing ducks, amphibious tanks, and assault boats. We had, or were getting, the gear for this. Tank transporter after transporter were blocking the roads as they hauled forward ducks, motor-driven assault boats and the pontoons. Amphibious tanks with canvas floats deflated against their sides, like children's waders, were on the roads too. Eagerly the forward battalions planned to attack that afternoon.

But the General would have none of it. 'No. We wait till darkness, and the proper artillery support. We might get away with it but we might run into heavy casualties.'

Brigadier Bonifant was disappointed. He held to his argument. 'Both battalions are sure they can make it.' The General shook his head. He remained adamant even when the two 5th Brigade forward battalion commanders were sent for, and ordered to report direct to the conference. If ever anyone could have convinced the General that the attack should go in immediately, it was these two men. They came in with the white dust of the roads heavy on their faces and uniforms, and that hardened, taut look of the good soldier. They were genuine veterans of this war. Both had been with the division from the earliest days. One, Sandy Thomas, of the 23rd Battalion, was in his twenties still, the other Alan McPhail of 21st Battalion, was in his thirties. Thomas, tall as the General, fair-haired, boyish, was probably the New Zealand soldier of this war who most closely resembled the Freyberg of the last war. Under the dust on his battledress tunic were the ribbons of DSO and MC and Bar. His first MC had been won escaping from a prison camp in Greece. Badly wounded (he had only just argued the Germans out of amputating his leg) he had escaped from Salonika, spent a winter in the Greek mountains, made several attempts to sail the Aegean and had been driven back by wind each time when just off the Turkish coast. Finally he had come down through Turkey to rejoin us in Syria, just before Alamein. There he had taken off his coat, and rolled up his trousers to show the General the scars which covered his body. The General responded by taking his own coat off and showing him what the trench fighting of the last war had done to him. In Syria Thomas had gone back to his old battalion. The bar to his Military Cross had come as a company commander in the desert. Now, since the Sangro, he had commanded the 23rd Battalion, till this afternoon found them on the banks of the Po.

McPhail, alongside him, was a different type, quiet, much slower, but very steady and clear-headed. He was one of those men whom you would never think of in peace-time as belligerent, as he took the tram day after day to his office, or on Saturday afternoons to play a reliable but unspectacular game of football. Yet in the war he had emerged quickly as a leader. He too had a double MC won at Thermopylae and at Alamein.

Each made his case with fervour. They were sure they could cross. It was no real risk. But the General held firm. No daylight attack would go in if there was a risk it might mean higher casualties. It was too late in the war for such things. So the two colonels went back to their jeeps outside to cancel, over the air, their orders for the attack. Disappointment was writ large on their faces. The full attack was then duly planned for that night.

Whatever might have happened in the afternoon, the crossing went perfectly at night, except that the floating tanks sank ignominiously. The enemy opposition was slight, coming only from tired coast-watching troops hurried down two days previously from north of Venice. The main army was in full retreat to the rear, racing for the next water barrier of the Adige.

So we spent an agreeable enough 25th April – the Anzac day on which, thirty years ago the original ANZAC Corps had gone ashore at Gallipoli – bridging the Po. In the sunshine it was like a regatta. Motor-driven storm-boats and ducks filled with Kiwi infantry and gunners plied to and fro between the banks. The wide river was blue under the clear sky, and the banks bare but for a fringe of young poplars on the far side. Engineers, their brown torsos bare to the sun, hauled pontoons and boats into position. Men off duty swam from the edge of the motor raft, which slowly carried across Sherman after Sherman. The bulldozers snorted and thundered as they tried to make some order out of the chaos of huge bomb craters. Hanson strode amongst them, completely in his element, controlling this job as he had controlled so many bridging jobs in remote New Zealand valleys. Slowly, pontoon by pontoon, the bridge spread across the river.

The Po, at which we had stared so long on our map, our goal since we first reached Italy in 1943, was crossed.

CHAPTER EIGHT

Partisans

'Major Shirley would like to see you, sir. He's picked up some message of importance on the radio.'

The signaller pointed across the open field to the signals lines, where John Shirley was bending over a small receiving set. So John's curiosity had unearthed something else. He was always discovering strange things, for he was a great deal more than just the wit who had made his wisecrack into the American air force microphone. He was a first-class radio expert, the second-in-command of our divisional signals, and in field telephony he had made one technical contribution of considerable importance to the war. He had hit upon the fact that the Germans, in the static conditions of the winter front, had revived one of the intelligence techniques of World War I. I had consulted Shirley because I was struck early in 1945 by the sudden improvement in the enemy's knowledge of what we were up to. Documents which we captured in raids on the Senio stop-banks and interrogation of prisoners showed that they had detailed knowledge of which Allied troops were opposite them, and dangerously exact foreknowledge of our movements. At that time our telephone lines from rear headquarters to the fighting units went through the streets of Faenza, slung in a thick swathe along the upper floors of buildings, and looped across street corners. I suggested to Shirley that enemy agents might be tapping there.

He had another explanation. 'No need for them to do that,' he said. 'They just have to lay a line in parallel with our field telephone lines along the front and they can pick up, by induction, what we are saying. It was standard practice by both sides in the trenches in the last war'. This theory set off a furious debate within Eighth Army Signals. Their experts were divided into those who thought we had indeed hit upon something important, and those who thought we were talking nonsense. General Freyberg backed our view, and when we returned to the line in April we took with us generators to produce interference with any interceptors the Germans might be using.

And they were indeed eavesdropping as John Shirley had predicted. When we overran the stop-bank we captured their intercept posts, and their records which showed that our counter measures had reduced the value of these listening posts severely. Later in Padua we were to get even more striking proof of the store the Germans had placed by these World War I techniques. Records of their Signals Headquarters showed not only that these methods had been used along the Senio Line, but that they had played a dangerously valuable role at Cassino. Our telephones to our forward units in the ruins of Cassino had been laid along the railway embankment. But the rails continued into the German-held sector, and served as efficient conductors of our telephone messages. Page after page of telephoned discussions, and telephoned orders between the troops in Cassino town and the commanders to the rear were on record in the enemy files. The value of this information to the Germans in that close-knit struggle must have been very great.

But on this morning in Northern Italy it was John Shirley who was doing the intercepting. 'Listen to this lot,' he said to me, handing over his earphones.

Through the static an Italian voice was talking rapidly: 'Radio Genoa, Radio Genoa,' it said. Then a voice speaking broken English took up the call. 'This is Genoa. Patriot Radio Genoa. The patriots this morning captured all of Genoa. The German garrison has surrendered. We have many prisoners. Send help quickly. Allies, send help quickly.'

I telephoned the intercept to Corps. Yes, Army had got the same message. The partisans had captured Genoa, and there was fighting in Milan and Turin. The industrial north was in revolt, and the Germans were surrendering everywhere. The partisan movement was carrying out the task it had prepared for – the seizure of power in time to prevent the Germans carrying out their immense programme of wrecking factories, warehouses, railway stations, roads, docks, bridges, all the massive machinery of modern society.

We were ourselves now for the first time in proper partisan country. As we had thundered northwards that morning, over wide roads unscarred by bomb craters or demolitions, with their telephone lines intact by the roadside, their houses undamaged, their fields green and untrampled, we were met by organised partisan forces, not the fragmentary units we had encountered on the Romagna plain. The New Zealand Division had, until this stage, had little to do with the Italian partisan movement. The bulk of our force had therefore little reason for believing that they would be anything but just another crowd of Italians like those we had encountered in the desert – boastful, showy, sometimes brave but at other times unwilling to make even a token fight.

With the simplistic approach of wartime the New Zealand soldier was ready to attribute this to a basic national flaw, and swept aside any alternative explanation that the Italians had never had their heart in this war, had had no incentive to fight alongside Germans they disliked against the British with whom they had traditional links of friendship. Even the fact that Italian mountain troops had fought well alongside us in the winter of 1944-45 was taken as the exception which proved the rule.

This impression had been only slightly modified by our experiences in the advance from Cassino to Senio. Except briefly in Florence we had had practically no contact with organised partisan units, as we had been fighting a type of warfare in which they could be of little use. We were an assault division, put in deliberately to crack with our massive artillery and our trained infantry the most strongly held parts of the enemy line. In such fighting the partisans could do nothing. No partisan movement is intended as an assault force. Its prime value is as a sabotage body behind the enemy lines. When the battle finally reaches its home area, a partisan unit is of use only when the battle is so rapid, or the ground so difficult, as in mountains or woods, that it can wage effective guerrilla action alongside the main battle.

Yet by the autumn of 1944 the partisan movement in Italy had developed to proportions which rivalled those of the French Maquis. It had sprung into existence all over Italy, but particularly in the north, after the armistice of September 1943, when the open German occupation of the country began. The partisan units were based originally on two main forces – scattered Italian army units which had taken to the hills when the armistice came, and militia bands organised by the Committees of Liberation. For many months the two forces regarded each other with suspicion, and maintained independent policies. The ex-army units tended to be conservative and monarchic, and came gradually under the influence of Italian staff officers, such as Major 'Mauri' (his real name was Martini), organiser of the Blues in Piedmont, and General Fiore of the Green Flames in Lombardy. Both were officers steeped in the tradition of the Italian Officer Corps. The Committees of Liberation on the other hand were composed of representatives of the six chief underground parties – Socialist, Communist, Christian Democrat, Action, Republican and Liberal.

All these parties had begun by forming their own units with distinctive names, such as the 'Justice and Liberty' of the Action Party, the 'Matteoti' of the Socialists, the 'Il Popolo' units of the Christian Democrats. The most numerous were the 'Garibaldi' brigades, formed originally on the cadres of the Communist Party and of anti-Fascists who had fought in Spain. The name of the Italian national hero was adopted so as to attract recruits of all parties in the resistance, but the leadership was usually in left-wing hands. In some areas, as for instance the Romagna, the Garibaldi Brigades represented almost the entire Resistance movement. It was their red scarves which we came to regard as the usual partisan badge. In the Udine region in the north-east, however, the Osoppo brigades were important. They were drawn from all the non-Marxist parties, wore green scarves or green shirts, and took their name from a mountain near Udine famed for a peasant rising against the Austrians in other days.

The first fully organised partisan bands, apart from scattered groups in Naples and the south, were encountered in the winter fighting of January and February 1944. A group operated then in front of the Eighth Army in the Pizzo Ferrato area and around Casoli, on the Adriatic coast. The main partisan forces were not encountered, however, until the spring offensive of May 1944. First contact was then made at Aragni, south of Rome. As the Fifth and Eighth Armies moved northward into the mountainous country north of Siena and Perugia and closed in on Florence and the Gothic line in the Apennines, more and more partisans were contacted, and more and more evidence became available of their work. These partisans were carrying out the prime function of a guerrilla movement, the harrying of the enemy's lines of communication. Throughout the long summer of 1944, when victory throughout Europe seemed so close, the Italian Resistance movement did valuable work against the rear of Kesselring's armies. This was their main contribution in 1944, just as the final rising was to be their major effort in 1945. During this summer no German car or lorry could move through the Apennine passes without guards and without being in convoy, and captured German documents constantly showed what trouble and casualties the partisans caused to the enemy.

In the battle for Florence in early August that year they demonstrated their value in liaison with an advancing army. The Germans blew all the bridges across the Arno except the Ponte Vecchio, which they blocked by demolishing the historic houses built on its approaches at both ends. The partisans cut the fuses leading to the houses on the south end of the bridge, but the Germans repaired these, and when the demolitions took place a number of partisans were buried in the ruins.[1] The partisans then managed to lay a telephone line across the rest of the bridge, and through the ruins, which they used to give information to us about German activities within the city. Over this line they pleaded with us to launch an immediate attack to their aid when some of their forces launched attacks within the city against the Germans. But the rising was premature. We were still held up by strong German rearguards in the southern suburbs, and they suffered severe casualties before we reached the heart of the city. This incident was to find expression in emotive, if inaccurate form, as part of Roberto Rossellini's post war film classic, *Paisa*.

Once, however, our forces had linked up with them the partisans were able to speed our pursuit of the Germans by showing us where minefields were laid, and where obstacles had been prepared. Indeed watching where the Germans placed minefields was one of the most useful tasks the partisans discharged, and they were taught, in propaganda broadcasts from Rome, how to pronounce the word 'mine' so as to be of immediate help to advancing troops.

British and American policy moved cautiously in its contact with these new Allies. There were many in high places who regarded them with the same suspicion and distrust as did our division. No one it seems had contemplated that, if the Italians were in Churchill's words 'to work their passage', the crews would come aboard in red shirts, flaunting revolutionary banners. The military mind preferred the grey-green uniform of the reformed Italian Army, even if it had been the uniform of Mussolini. Throughout 1944 the Allied policy was to co-operate with the partisans until their area was liberated, then disarm them, and disband their units. Those individual partisans who wanted to see further service were recommended to enlist as individuals in the new Italian Army which was being formed under Allied guidance in the south. Large numbers of partisans did so enlist, urged on by all parties, in spite of the strongly Monarchist tendencies of the many New Army officers. No partisan units were kept in being or incorporated as such in the new army.

Though the Allied officers who actually dealt personally with the partisans were enthusiastic about the movement and energetic in supporting it, there was a weight of distaste and reluctance hindering policy at many stages. Fifth Army had greeted many of the partisan bands in the Apennines by putting them into internment camps. The Poles, inflamed by the undoubtedly anti-Soviet feelings of those rank and file who had been in Russian prison camps between 1939 and 1941, were liable to arrest anyone wearing a red scarf. The Brazilians, it is true, found them most useful allies, and often used them as a forward screen. But many other formations looked on them as did our troops, as excitable bands of adolescents who might be more of a nuisance than help.

This policy, however, gradually changed under the impact of events.

The official attitude grew warmer. Field Marshal Alexander had early laid down a policy of full co-operation, which was in the later months of 1944 interpreted more generously. Partisan units in the north were being sent considerable quantities of arms and supplies by parachute. Allied liaison officers contacted them. The military and Committee of Liberation bands acknowledged the common authority of a new unified military command, called the CVL (Corps of Volunteers of Liberty), which operated under the political direction of the Central Committee of Liberation in Milan. The man chosen as military commander, by agreement between the Allies and the Italian Government, was General Raffaele Cadorna, son of the Italian C-in-C in the last war. He was dropped in by parachute in August 1944. It took two months of hard negotiating, in back street apartments in Milan and in forests in the Apennines, before local partisans would accept his authority. They did so only when two northern leaders were appointed as his deputy commanders – Signor Parri of the Action Party and Luigi Longo, a Spanish war veteran of the Communists.

In the winter of 1944-5 the strength and value of the movement received sudden publicity from the actions of the Bulow Group around Ravenna. 'Bulow' was the *nom de guerre* of an Italian officer named Boldrini, who formed a powerful partisan unit, 28th Garibaldi Brigade, in the pinewoods north of Ravenna, that same Pineta di Classe in which Byron and the Carbonari in their day had hidden their dumps of muskets and powder. They gave the Canadians considerable help in the capture of the area, and Bulow (the name in local dialect means 'Bull') was awarded the Gold Medal (the Italian VC) at a formal parade attended by the Eighth Army commander.

Throughout this winter the partisan liaison officers on AAI and at Eighth Army had been struggling for full recognition and retention of the partisan forces as fighting units when we advanced into the north. The chief partisan liaison officer at Eighth Army was Major A. Colquhoun, and he and his assistant, Captain Rendall, a Cambridge history scholar, waged a constant administrative battle to that end. They placarded their office in Cesena with publicity about partisans – photographs, press cuttings, statistics. A booklet, *Facts About Partisans*, was issued to troops. Its cover showed a young partisan, rifle in hand, shoulders draped with bandoliers, side by side with his young wife and two children. In particular Colquhoun and Rendall battled against the view that there was a danger in Italy of a repetition of the ELAS rising in Greece, and that in consequence the Communist and other left-wing elements in the partisan movement should be restrained.

This fear was most clearly expressed by Churchill in a speech early in 1945 about 'the wild and fanatical politicians of the north.' But in the situation in Italy, as in France, it was recognised by the parties of the Left that a revolution was simply not on the cards. Stalin certainly held this view, and held the official Communists back from any such adventure.

The Communists were at this time playing a dominant role in the Garibaldi brigades, a role for which their organisation and discipline equipped them. They and the Action Party had run the only major strike against the Axis in the war – the General Strike in the spring of 1944 in Northern Italy. They had had experience of underground work from the days of Mussolini. Some of their exiled leaders had been able to slip back across the border from Switzerland; others had returned from Russia. Their party line was to organise resistance to the Germans, and this they carried out straightforwardly. They were prepared to serve under any leadership in the Garibaldi brigades which the Committee of Liberation thought best, but often they were able to assert effectively their own claim to such leadership. Yet the Allies continued to regard them with concern, particularly after the winter fighting in Greece. The policy which Britain and America should adopt towards the partisan movement in the 'red' areas such as Milan and Turin, once these were liberated, was debated endlessly. It was a complicated question, as it was linked up with a struggle for power between the Government in Rome and the Committees of Liberation in the north.

Just before the spring offensive of 1945, however, under pressure from the Eighth Army, the official policy came out more strongly in full support of the partisans after liberation as well as before. Bulow's troops were allowed to retain their organisation and given British arms and transport to fight alongside the Allies. Plans were laid for organising, for future service alongside the Allies, seven partisan brigades, with full equipment and transport, out of the forces known to be ready in the north.

In our winter fighting around Faenza, and in our preparations for the Senio offensive, we had known little of this. The Romagna plain around Route 9 had been an important partisan area in the late summer of 1944, but the Germans had moved through it ruthlessly with the gallows and the firing squad. In the town square of Forli, Corbara, the young champion footballer who had been the most spectacular and romantic partisan figure of that year, and his mistress, Inez Versari, who had fought alongside him to the end, were hanged by the Fascist authorities. Posters carrying their names as martyrs covered every wall in the town when we moved through it to and from the front. But the repression took much sting out of the movement, which the character of this flat country, with its easily guarded rivers, hampered greatly. All that remained were members of two groups, the SAP and the GAP – Squadre d'Azione Partigiane and Gruppi d'Azione Partigiani. They carried out spying missions and minor sabotage jobs in the area. But they worked on their own, with sporadic contact by messenger to Corps and Army, so we, at divisional level, saw little of them.

We had, however, two Italian liaison officers with us from November 1944 onwards to maintain contact with these groups. These men did something to break down the divisional soldier's reserve towards partisans. Neither of these officers was a regular Italian soldier. One was a mining engineer whose wife and children still lived in enemy occupied territory near Milan, the other a diplomat. They were both brave and energetic, and they fitted in well with the forward troops. Yet in general the suspicions remained. An Eyetie was still an Eyetie, whether he wore a red scarf or not.

There was, however, one important group of New Zealand troops who were strongly pro-partisan. They were the escaped prisoners of war. An increasing number came through our lines now every day, and each of them was fervent in his praise of the partisans and the ordinary peasants, just as he was bitter in his detestation of the Mussolini Republican Fascists. All these escaped prisoners, often aged beyond recognition by a year or two in hiding, had the same stories of peasants shot, of houses burnt, of partisans who had hidden them or organised their escape.

One such man came forward to us on the evening we were bridging the Reno. He was a New Zealand sergeant who had been hidden in North Italy since the summer of 1943. He had been brought off from the coast north of Venice by motor torpedo boat. Now he wanted to go back, to contact the partisans and other prisoners, and be with them when we advanced, so that he could fight this final battle at their side. For over an hour he showed us on our maps the partisan position in his corner of the country. Would he be allowed to go back? At Base they had said it was difficult. A returned prisoner of war should be sent home at once. Only the General could rule against that procedure. So he came forward now to seek permission. He had with him a young, sunburnt American officer, with eager eyes, who was due to go back the next day into the area by Venice.

'Wait till you get there,' he said 'We've a whole army waiting for you. Those guys are good.'

If I recollect rightly, the sergeant got the permission he desired, but he never was able to use it. The battle moved too quickly for him. But I remembered what his American friend had said. The guys were to prove good indeed.

CHAPTER NINE

The Race Under Way

The doorway at the back of the truck darkened with three figures, Heyden, with the latest balance sheet of enemy identifications from the PW cage, a runner with a bundle of defence overprints showing the Venetian Line, and my driver with the *Union Jack* and the *Eighth Army News*. The driver got his word in first.

'There's some real horror stuff this morning, sir. Pictures of these concentration camps in Germany piled high with corpses, like logs outside a sawmill. I knew they were bastards, the Tedeschi, but never as bad as that.'

We turned aside from prisoners and defences to look at the illustrations of Belsen. I needed nothing to remind me of what Nazism could sink to. My years as a foreign correspondent in Spain, in Austria after the Anschluss, and Prague in 1938-39, and Germany itself again and again in the thirties had made its nature very plain to me. But even to my already convinced mind these photographs were shocking. To the troops who saw them now, as they jolted forward in the back of their three-tonners towards the Adige river, they were one more stimulus to an aggressiveness which already ran flood tide.

I gave one of the most ghastly pages to Heyden. 'Stick this up in your truck when you're interrogating, and ask them what they say about it, Mickey.'

'I will – but I know in advance what they will say – *Greuelpropaganda.* But we've got some newcomers which I thought you ought to see for yourself.'

'What are they – parachutists?'

'No. Four Russian girls and a German who speaks perfect English and says he's an anti-Nazi. There are a couple of hundred parachutists as well. The girls were said to have worked in a hospital, but it isn't hard to guess what job they did.'

'Right – but let's just look at these defence overprints first.'

Across the map which covered the area from the Lido to the Euganean Hills a fine tracery showed the gun positions and trenches of

the Venetian Line like blue veins on a hand. Once again now we faced
fortified river lines – the Brenta, and beyond it the Piave; beyond that
again the Tagliamento. The maps showing, from air photographs and
agents reports, the latest defence positions had been flown up to us only
that morning. We were now between the Po and the Adige, far ahead
of Army headquarters. The one bridge across the Po was in such
demand that the only way they could get the photographs forward was
by Whizzer. The Auster which carried them had circled over us
five minutes before and bombed our signal strip neatly with the
bundle.

They looked formidable, these defence lines, but what troops had
the enemy to man them with? Everywhere he was in full retreat.
Everywhere Allied forces were thrusting out – Americans up Route 9
towards Milan, Americans and South Africans across the Po towards
Mantua and Verona. The British 6th Armoured Division were moving
across the Po and coming up on our right, and farther right still 5th
Corps were forcing a crossing of the Po north of Ferrara.

'Come on – let's see your Russians,' I said. 'We'll give the artillery
the maps, for what they are worth.'

The prisoners were in a field at the back of a small farmyard. They
lay in the sleep of the exhausted, or sat and talked, or stood in groups.
The Kiwi guards with Tommy-guns under their arms leant on the gate
or stood in the evening sun under the trees. The four girls sat apart in
a small adjoining field. Three of them had heavy, round Slav faces, with
deep-set eyes red-rimmed with weeping. They could have been any age
between eighteen and thirty. Their faces had the heavy pallor of the
ill fed. The fourth stood against a tree, just staring with a dull, almost
animal hatred at the German prisoners waiting nearby amid the
trampled lucerne. Her dark hair was a tangled mass through which she
ran her hands as she looked out now at her former captors. Hate alone
was marked on her roughened face, hate such as I have never seen on
any other face. All the fury of an enslaved and despoiled continent
glowered in the eyes of that one Russian peasant girl.

The sound of their crying rose above the other sounds of the cage –
the murmur of German voices, the guards talking to one another, the
cookers hissing in the yard behind. One of the guards walked over with
a cake of chocolate. The two girls who were seated took it with
frightened smiles, the others waved it away, frightened still.

I was watching them when the English-speaking prisoner saluted at
my side. He addressed me in English, and I answered. It is a mistake
to speak to a prisoner in English. It gives him a sense of his superiority

over you, and tends to make him resistant. But I was tired, and anyway I didn't want to interrogate him. I just wanted to see what sort of an anti-Nazi he thought he was.

He was a bespectacled man in his late thirties, a lecturer in English from Hanover. 'I have always loved England,' he said – and I believed him. 'I have made this war with a very heavy heart. Very many Germans have made this war with a heavy heart.'

I showed him the photographs of Belsen. 'Enough Germans had light enough hearts to accomplish this.' He stared at the pictures. He shook his head. It was clear that he thought them to be fakes.

'Why, if you were against the war, did you do nothing against Hitler? Why did you do nothing to stop it?'

He threw his hands open in despair. 'What could we do? My friends and I, we were not Nazis. We hated the Nazis. But we were powerless. We had to do what we were told. But you must realise that all Germans are not bad.'

I realised that well enough, but I was not going to let him know it. 'How can we judge whether all Germans are good or bad, when you all fight us? Take your own case – what has been your job here in Italy?'

'Not a fighting job,' he said. 'I have never killed anyone in this war. I was in charge of a ferry across the Po. And believe me' – a note of urgency back into his voice – 'believe me it was not an easy job. We were bombed, bombed all day and all night.'

'Maybe. Yet even though you disapproved of Hitler you went on ferrying German troops across the Po to fight his battles. You ferried down men who killed our men, my friends. Why should it matter to us whether you did it with a heavy heart or a light one. You did it, as a nation. And as a nation you are all bound to suffer.'

As I spoke, I knew that I was asking the impossible. The kind of revolt which the Generals of July 1944 had been unable to carry out at the top was not open to a corporal in a corner of Italy. The Nazi techniques of repression saw to that. But the stacked corpses and the skeletal, flimsy limbs of the victims of Belsen which showed in the pictures in the newspapers in my hand raised just such impossible questions.

I waited for the German to reply, for him to make the counter charge which came to my own mind. He could have said, 'If we are all guilty, as Germans, what about those people in your own and other countries who, from Versailles onwards, encouraged the events which enabled Hitler to climb to power, and who truckled to him once he was in power?'

I waited for him to call attention to these beams in our own eyes. But he did not.

I pointed to the four girls. 'Do you feel no shame about that sort of thing? Does it not seem evil to you to take girls like that and drag them from their homes in this way, to be used as slaves?'

'It is ugly. But it is one of those things which come with war.'

'And these others. Do they feel no shame?' I pointed to the parachutists behind him. But before the question was out of my mouth, I had answered it myself.

In the mass they looked the embodiment of the outcome of years of Nazi schooling and Nazi training, physically fine and yet with a hard, relentless, arrogant bearing, even in defeat, which was both degenerate and repugnant. Many had long black hair, of almost effeminate length, hard mouths and hard eyes which met mine now with hostility and anger. They were typical of hundreds we had interrogated, youths untroubled by conscience, untroubled even by any contemplation of what they were doing, content to have handed their minds over to Hitler for a duration which could last throughout their lives.

Their eyes followed my arm as I pointed across to the girls, and several of them smiled with smiles which were half sneers. The anti-Nazi was studying now the photographs of Belsen, his face intent, but unconvinced. I saw then, not just these Germans in the sunlight in their crumpled uniforms, but all that they had wrecked in this country and elsewhere – the blackened, swollen, fly-encrusted corpses of peasants shot as hostages outside Arezzo; the tiny bits of flesh and clothing, scattered in the pine-woods, where they had blown up three partisans with dynamite, tied alive to the trees; the scarred wall of the village church outside Siena where on Sunday they had shot all the men, dragged from Mass. These crimes had been made possible by the military shield which these elite formations had provided, so that they seemed no longer soldiers but mere killers, with a sense of death and of the love of death around them.

When I turned to go the officer who spoke English said, 'May I ask you one question? What will happen to us?'

In my anger I answered him with a lie: 'You will be handed over to the Russians to rebuild some of what you have destroyed.'

Real fear spread across his face. 'You are very cruel,' he said, 'you would not be so cruel.'

And as I walked away I could hear the whisper run through the other prisoners, '. . . *den Russen übergeben.*' At least they were scared of that.

I walked back to the truck. Ahead the evening sunshine picked out, against a rain cloud moving towards us from the unseen Alps, the curve of the Euganean Hills. There Shelley had lived, on their slopes he had written many of his poems. There he had joined Byron and driven down to ride with him along the deserted sand-hills of the Lido. But there was no poetry in the Euganean Hills this evening. There was only the knowledge that they were full of Germans.

* * *

The main body of the division had crossed the Po on 26th April. We held the conference that morning in a dramatic enough setting, on the north bank of the river. The maps were propped up against the windscreen of the jeep and the General and the brigadiers and commanders stood round under the young poplars. In the background the traffic wound its way slowly across the undulating pontoon bridge, and up along the sandy roads which the Germans had cut through the small wood. We were now approaching the Venetian Line. On our front it lay eight miles to the north of the Adige, the German engineers having curved it away from the course of the river to take advantage of the high ground of the Euganean Hills.

We got across the Adige with little opposition – so little that the infantry in their assault boats were covered by fire only from the guns of our tanks, without artillery protection. But it was now raining heavily, and we settled down to yet another exhausting bridging job. The approaches were cut to pieces by bombing, and the huge craters made work on the approach roads very difficult. The last bombing had caught the German rearguard, who lay now in the craters along the banks in even ghastlier array than on the Gaiana. One man hung, head down, from the girders of the smashed bridge, his dead body lashed by the rain which had now come down on us for the first time since the offensive had begun. The bridging train, an elegant name for sixty three-ton trucks loaded with pontoons, and driven by Polish drivers, had got lost. On the far side of the river the parachutist rearguards were fighting with an ugly tenacity against our forward troops. The bridge was not open for trucks until three o'clock that afternoon, and the heavier bridge for tanks had only just been started. Our tanks had to be ferried over on the motor ferry, at a rate of three an hour.

Though General Freyberg had received no orders yet about any thrust for Trieste – and indeed Field Marshal Alexander was still without any directive from London or Washington to do so – we prepared for the break out when it would come. We had got trucks enough now to carry all the troops all the time, instead of using them, as in the slower fighting farther back, in relays to bring up, first the forward troops, then the reserves. Brigadier Crump, who had controlled our ASC since the early desert days had issued desert rations of water, petrol and oil, and food – three days supply of food at least. Every driver, with desert experience clear either from his own recollections or from those Old Digs who felt they were coming into their own again, borrowed or stole extra jerry-cans full of petrol and water, and stocked up with all the spare rations he could get. The artillery regiments were placed under the different brigade commands, so that each brigade could fight an independent action if necessary. The fresh brigades had come through, too, the 9th Brigade and the Gurkhas.

The division was champing to go. And no one champed with more vigour than the General. The infantry commander who had thought in terms of massive barrages had dropped away now; in its place there appeared the cavalry commander who was going to push on at the utmost speed. The General throughout this campaign – as throughout all actions so far as we could remember – had always been the most optimistic, the most aggressive, the most anxious to seize the initiative and smash hard. 'He's gone – he's bust – he's shooting off his dumps.' These sayings of his had become bywords among his officers, as he would urge the leading brigadiers to press on, on.

They were in part, I believe, an instinctive expression of the natural belligerency of the man, of his great physical and mental aggressiveness and energy, and in part a carefully calculated policy. Freyberg knew that his task as a commander was to maintain the constant dynamic which any force must have. So he called continually for every possible effort, pointed out every optimistic feature in the situation. His brigadiers and his staff knew this, and worked their views in with it, distinguishing between those statements which the General made as adjurations and those which were definite orders.

'Press on at full speed, press on,' he would say. 'Give them no rest.'

At times his staff and commanders would try to put the brakes on to this eagerness by pointing out reasons why it would not be possible. If the reasons were factual he would listen; if they were opinions he would listen too, but would be unconvinced.

By the morning of Saturday April 28th the General had to make a major decision. Should we race towards the Venetian Line and try to cut through it, gatecrash it, not with infantry but with tank and moving columns, or should we shape up and put in a set attack? The enemy still had troops to man the line. They were moving back on to

Padua, where 26th Armoured Division might still be in some shape. The parachutists were moving into the Euganean Hills. Other troops were on the Brenta and the Venetian Line was being manned.

If we could find a hole in the Line, and push enough stuff through, we could outflank it. Towards this end we moved. The 9th Brigade were directed towards Este, where the defence began from the foot of the hills. Here the secondary roads on which we were travelling joined the broad highway from Mantua to Padua. Here a bridge, if not blown, gave access over the canal which formed the core of the defence line.

It would be a risky move. To our right 5th Corps were not yet across the Adige. We would have to go alone, because the thin bridges over the Po could not bring up petrol enough for more than one division. It meant yet another of those sweeps into enemy territory which we had made in the desert. For over an hour that morning the General discussed it with the corps commander, while the forward infantry and tanks probed towards Este.

At one o'clock I turned on the wireless for the BBC news. The Russian and American forces had linked up in Germany. The partisans in Milan were rumoured to have captured Mussolini. General Dittmar, the German military spokesman, had surrendered and described the situation as hopeless. Then the telephone rang. Ian Whigham, the G2 I of 13th Corps was on the line. 'The Yanks say they are through the Venetian Line and north of Vicenza.' I started across to the General with this news, when the phone went again. It was the artillery IO.

'The air op. reports that the Este bridge is intact and that the armoured cars of the 12th Lancers are almost on it.'

This time I sprinted across to the General's caravan. He was already in his jeep, with his ADC climbing in the back holding the General's revolver belt and steel helmet. He had the news direct from the CRA. 'I'm off to Este,' he said. 'Whips out!'

He drove off down the narrow track towards the gateway. The next time I saw him, twelve hours later, we were in the outskirts of Padua, well behind the remnants of the German Army on this front.

Though we could not know it at the time, this swift decision to plunge forward with our flanks unprotected was the decision which was to change the fate of the city of Trieste.

CHAPTER TEN

Operation Merlin

We were halted in the half moonlight, and above the bark of the frogs and the engines running I heard a nightingale in the woods. They were woods which ran up the sheer slopes of the hills, the silent and menacing Euganean Hills which seemed to lean over us as we waited on this long straight road, built up on an embankment beside a canal. Voices of men hauling a bogged half track out of the mud on the flat below sounded very clear. Suddenly from the hills there rose a green very light, then a brown one, answered by a red farther away, then another, then another.

'There are the parachutists, anyway,' said Martin. We were studying the map by the light of a torch in the front seat of the I truck. Ahead of us, behind us, jammed nose to tail, stretched the trucks and jeeps and caravans of divisional headquarters. Beyond, to the front, began the guns and Bren carriers and trucks of 9th Brigade. Behind began the fifteen cwt. trucks of the Ghurkas.

'Let's see – that last town we came through was Monselice – Este must be six miles back – we must be at least a mile up this straight stretch of Route 16.'

Yellow and direct on the map, Route 16 ran north-eastwards towards Padua. We were twelve miles beyond the Adige, twelve miles deep into enemy territory at least four miles beyond the Venetian line. Virtually unmanned, it had been breached after no more than a skirmish. Away to the south the searchlights, making a blister of white on a cloud, showed where the front had been, where to a large extent it still was. Gun flashes lit up the sky. They seemed far, far behind us.

It was just ten p.m. Ever since seven o'clock that evening we had been moving through the flat, thick country north of the Adige. It had been chilly, with rain just clearing away. In village after village the crowds had increased, lining the streets to shout 'Adios – Viva', and 'Ciao', which meant a mixture, so far as we could see, of 'Hurrah – Good luck – and Good-bye'.

Girls threw us flowers hastily gathered from the fields, and white elder blossom torn from the roadside trees. In one village I asked when the Germans had left.

'*Ieri sera* – last night,' and they had left '*molti morti, molti morti.*'

What dead Germans? No, '*molti morti Italiani.*' The parachutists had wanted bicycles, and had shot down half the men of the village in seizing them. The *fratello* of this woman, the *zio* of this boy, had been shot in their own homes.

These were no romantic villages, but were mostly lines of squalid semi-detached labourers' cottages, with white sheets now hanging in surrender and greeting from the windows. We were in the area of the big estates, the paid labourers, the absentee landlords. No wonder it had nourished the partisan movement well. The ditches were still full of German ammunition dumps; the bridge at Este was still bumpy where the demolition charges had been dug from the roadway. Then we were right in under the hills, with their rocky slopes black and sheer with a ruined castle at one point and the two small towns of Este and Monselice with snipers' shots ringing in the streets, until we made our first halt on the long straight Padua road.

From woods which lay below us, grey in the moonlight, came now the occasional chock, chock of a sniper's rifle. Again the very lights rose from the hills to the left, answered by others more distant, then by one which seemed to come from a bare quarter of a mile away.

I walked forward to the ACV – the armoured control vehicle. At long last, after so much slow-moving fighting, the ACV was fulfilling its proper function of motorised command post from which a battle could be controlled on the move. It looked like a London bus with blank walls of solid steel, and was indeed just that. On to a bus chassis had been built one steel-walled compartment about the size of a small ship's cabin. At one end were the radio sets and the signallers in contact with the brigades, the artillery, the 12th Lancers out in front, and Corps. Crowded around a desk in the centre were the GI, and the others, his junior offices, his G2 and his G3s. One G3 marked up the movement of the battle on big maps on the wall; another put down in the log all the information received, the orders given out. From this cabin, even if it were swaying along at thirty or forty miles an hour, the battle could be controlled. With difficulty I squeezed myself into its crowded, brightly-lit, warm space.

I looked at the map. A tiny red mark with 'Div. Cav.' on it showed like the half crescent of a red moon just on the edge of Padua. 'Going like a steam engine,' said Gilbert. 'Place was half captured by partisans when we got there. What do you make of these lights to the left?'

'Remnants of 1st Para Corps, I should say. It's a good job we've got this canal between us and the hills. They could do us some damage if they cared to put a few mortars on to this road.'

'Yes. The sooner we get to Padua the better. This is about the unhealthiest stretch here, right under the hills. But they may be in too much confusion to think of attacking. And the very fact that they can see those searchlights away to the south must make them a bit puzzled. For all they know we might be their own stuff.'

When I climbed out into the darkness the nightingale was singing again. It had started to rain, soft rain, good growing weather. Then calls came down the column, and the engines revved up, and we moved forward another mile. At the next halt a jeep came down the road from the direction of Padua. The driver was calling: 'Where's the I truck?' In the back he had three German officers. They had blundered into the column a mile farther up, retreating towards Padua.

One was a colonel who was commanding a battle group of survivors. He was a quiet spoken Bavarian. He agreed the war was lost, climbed into the ACV with me, and showed us on our own map the line he had been ordered to take up with his troops. It was clear the Germans still hoped to man the Brenta beyond Padua. Between us and the coast the whole German line was in retreat. With luck we would cut them off. I took his own marked map, found a military policeman, and told him to drive me on the back of his motor-cycle along the column till I found 9th Brigade headquarters and the General.

All along that wide straight road up which we were racing stretched the vehicles of the forward division. Here in the darkness, along the edge of the road which shone under the rain, the fighting units of the forward brigade lay like some shining, oiled mechanism, a thing of machines rather than men. Here were the long-barrelled seventeen-pounder anti-tank guns, gun after gun, limber after limber; here the twenty-five-pounders, one after another behind the great 'quads' which hauled them; here were the Bren carriers, their Brens and Brownings thrust out, ready, their crews huddled up asleep or standing talking by the roadside; and here, mile upon mile, the trucks with the infantry, the cavernous canvas-shrouded three-tonners, where the glow of a match would show up brown faces, steel helmets, the glint of rifles and shovels. Here the ambulances, water trucks, supply vehicles, in endless lines. If the parachutists had had one glimpse of this it was little wonder they did not interfere.

The General was with Brigadier Gentry in the ACV from which 9th Brigade were, even then, controlling the advance of the forward infantry through the streets of Padua. We were across the very branch of the canal where the captured colonel was to have taken his stand.

'We've plenty of prisoners for you,' said Evans, the 9th Brigade Intelligence officer. 'The partisans had 3,000 when we arrived. They'd been fighting a battle here for twenty-four hours.'

We were in Padua ourselves before dawn, going swiftly forward through darkened streets where people ran shouting '*viva, viva,*' dark figures with outstretched hands, clapping, crying. We turned our trucks into a small bare square in front of a church. The defence platoon deployed into the surrounding buildings to deal with snipers whose shots still echoed up and down the quiet street. I spread my bed-roll on the truck floor and slept.

Only rarely in life does experience thrust itself on you in great chunks, to be munched hastily, greedily, unreflectingly. This Sunday into which we now woke, on the edge of Padua, was to provide us with just such fare. The day was grim and grey in its starting, but in its finish it was as bright as the sun which shone on the canals of Venice or on the wall of the Alps ahead, as strong and sure as the great Italian flags which everywhere flaunted their red, white and green against the blue sky.

I woke just before six. The shots still rang out, single shots that drew no answer, and that spoke more of partisans on patrol than of fighting. But I was glad to notice the tanks just ahead of us, guarding a bridge into the town. In the grey dawn they were reassuring. At once information began to pour in. It came chiefly from partisans. Much of it came from the Eighth Army liaison officer who had entered Padua the evening before with the foremost tanks of the 9th Brigade. He was a dark-eyed, voluble and friendly Montenegrin, one Captain I. M. Radulovitch. Radulovitch had been a journalist before the war, and until 1942 he had served with the Royal Yugoslav Army units in the Middle East. But he had been critical of King Peter's policy, and had got out of his own army and into the British. He was a first-class partisan liaison officer. He spoke good Italian, and his English was perfect too – far better than ours.

Radulovitch had caught up with us just south of the Adige. When we began probing towards Padua I sent him forward to work with the 9th Brigade. There, north of the Adige, he had got his first message from Padua telling of the partisan success. The city was in their hands, they said. But they wanted support quickly.

These messages Radulovitch took to Brigadier Gentry that Saturday morning, as the 9th Brigade probed towards Este. Gentry reacted with a mixture of scepticism and of that swift leadership which was his great strength.

'Are you sure these messages are reliable?' he asked.

Radulovitch was by no means sure, but he took a risk. 'Yes, I think they are.'

Gentry studied him closely. 'All right then,' he said finally. 'I accept your word for it – we'll push the tanks ahead fast – but you can go with the front tank and make contact with these partisans of yours – if they are there.'

For Radulovitch it was undoubtedly one of the most critical moments of his life. He was backing his judgment with his own skin. He must have had an anxious time as he clung to the turret of the foremost Sherman as it edged its way into Padua. It was dark by now, and the rain made visibility very poor. The outer streets were deserted. Only when they reached the small square where we were to put our head-quarters did they encounter anyone. The square was filled with shadowy figures carrying rifles. Radulovitch called to them in Italian from his place on the tank. Inside the tank itself the crew stood to their guns. This might well be still the German rearguard. But the reply from the men came back in Italian. They were a partisan company, holding this sector of the city, and had good news to tell of the rest of it. Radulovitch was entitled to his pride when he heard the radio operator inside the tank calling back to the brigadier in the 9th Brigade ACV: 'Partisan liaison officer reports contact made with Padua partisans. City in partisan hands. I say again, city in partisan hands.'

Now Radulovitch stood by our truck in the grey Sunday dawn and gave us the rest of his news. There was fighting in the Euganean Hills between parachutists and the villagers; three German tanks were at a point just over the Brenta; another group of enemy farther east; a German column retreating from the south. I marked them up on the map. Outside in the square women walked through to Mass, speaking excitedly to a priest with skin astonishingly yellow above his black cassock. They took little notice of the shots which still sounded, and were much more impressed by the sight of the troops shaving, their mirrors propped up on the side of their tanks, or of the white cloths on our mess breakfast-table.

One partisan arrived in great indignation. Someone had stolen his radio. A British soldier in khaki had looted it from his flat. I sympathised, but I knew the chances of recovery were nil. His arguments became unreasonable.

'We fight for you, and then you do this. It is not right.'

I got unreasonable too. 'You fight for us? Who the hell do you think we are fighting for, here in Italy?' I would like to think he got his radio back, but I'm sure he didn't. An infantryman in the middle of a battle is not always exact in his definition of what is, and what is not, legitimate enemy booty.

As soon as I could I checked up on the story of the partisan battle of Padua. It was worth the trouble, for it is an almost classic example of what a good partisan movement can do when it is well led and well co-ordinated with an offensive by regular troops. Padua was the controlling centre of the Italian partisan movement of the north-east, or, to give it is full Italian title, the centre of the Commando Militare Regionale Veneto of the Corpo Volontari della Liberta. It had been selected for this purpose for the very reason that we had selected it as our objective in the drive forward. With eight important roads radiating from it, it formed the chief communications centre of the province. The partisans throughout north-eastern Italy had, however, had a bad winter. They had been subjected to severe German and Fascist attacks, for the enemy tried to break the movement and keep his lines of communication open before the spring offensive. Yet in the spring the *partigiani* had regathered their forces, and when April came they were in good shape. From the time of our attacks in the Po valley onwards they started small local actions, chiefly with the object of securing arms and ammunition. On 25th April, once we were across the Po, the real rising began. From then on throughout the whole of the area from the Adriatic to the Alps a thoroughly well organised rising took place. Village after village, town after town turned on its Blackshirt and German garrisons, seizing strong points from which to resist the counter-attacks of enemy columns. Though we did not know it fully on this morning of Sunday, 29th April, the whole of northern Italy, from Padua to the Alps and the Isonzo, was in organised revolt. Without their aid in seizing and preventing the destruction of the bridges across the many rivers and canals, our further progress would have been slow indeed. Even our advance to Padua that night had been largely made possible in the time by the action of a railway worker at Monselice, who had removed the demolition charges and prevented the blowing up of the bridge.

In Padua itself the main rising had begun on the night of 26th/27th April, when we were advancing from the Po to the Adige. On the morning of 27th April the Fascist Italian authorities in the city asked for terms, and finally signed an unconditional surrender to the Committee of National Liberation. There still remained, however, the problem of the German forces in the city, and in the area around the city. Among these forces were the remnants of 26th Panzer Division which had been sent back to prepare for a stand on the Venetian Line. Against these troops, wherever they were to be found, the partisan command now launched their own forces. A Tiger tank was captured intact in the city itself. German columns were shot up, and assaulted at many points. Then, on the night of 27th April, there arrived in Padua the formidable figure of Lieutenant-General von Arnim, the commander of 26th Panzer Division, an old desert campaigner who had fought under Rommel. He sought, and arranged, the unconditional surrender of the remnants of his division to the partisan command. He was not long without companions of his own rank. A short while later three German staff cars drove into the city from the south. They were stopped, and their occupants captured. Among them was the commander of the Ferrara area, General von Alten. Within a few hours he and von Arnim were joined by the general who commanded the Padua region. When we arrived there all three were ready to be handed over to us. In all the partisans of the Padua zone alone took over 15,000 German prisoners, and killed 497 Germans in the scattered but intense fighting. Their own losses were 224 killed. It was no inconsiderable achievement.

Over 5,000 of these prisoners were held in Padua that Sunday morning. We could not take control of them, though the partisans sent us a delegation asking us to do so. All we could do was accept their chief prisoners, including the generals. The prisoners were now becoming an embarrassment. We had no spare troops for guard duties, and yet the partisans were anxious to hand over their prisoners to us. They sent a delegation to arrange the transfer. John Shirley was with me at the time, waiting to hear our interrogation of a German signaller who had all details of the enemy radio Intelligence system at Cassino.

'What about cutting down and bringing your signaller and these generals up here, John?' I asked him. 'The defence platoon will lend you a truck or even a tank if you like. Maybe you'd better take a tank. I gather the centre of the town is still pretty unhealthy.'

John certainly brought them back in state. About mid-morning there rolled into our square a Sherman, followed by a crowd of Italians. On the front rode John, Tommy-gun in hand, like a mahout on an elephant. Behind him, hanging on to the tank with one hand, and holding great white flags in the other, were four German officers. The scarlet hatband of General von Alten was vivid amid the grey. With them, clutching on to every corner of the tank, rode red-scarved partisans and Kiwis.

I put General von Alten in a room in a disused office building with the other officer prisoners, arrogant young men with cruel insulting faces. With them was one SS girl, in civilian clothes, her good looks nullified by the lack of any trace of sympathy or kindliness. When I came to arrange their departure for the Adige they gave me the Nazi salute. The General asked for permission to take with him a basket filled with cognac bottles; his ADC the meanwhile was sneering with the other officers at the 'Neger' outside the door, nodding his head towards the Maori guard. So I gave the basket to the guard instead, and went back to the task of trying to persuade someone in the ACV to stage a battle against a column of Germans whom frantic partisans reported as advancing into Padua from the south. This proved to be a column of retreating Germans who thought that Padua was still in their hands. The 25-pounders of 4 Field Regiment were deployed in their old desert role of anti-tank guns, and knocked out three German tanks before the enemy surrendered.

There had been some short sharp battles in the early hours of that morning to secure the two bridges over the Brenta River, one leading to the autostrada and the other to the winding Route 11 to Venice. Had we not got these bridges our advance would have been seriously delayed. The defenders of the autostrada bridge gave up readily enough, perhaps because they realised that the bridge was so badly damaged that we could not use it for vehicles. But the smaller bridge at Ponte di Brenta was intact, and held by a strong German force with armoured cars and two 105 millimetre guns.

In the darkness a troop of New Zealand tanks drove straight at the bridge, carrying infantrymen on their backs. They took the Germans by surprise, knocked out one of the guns and two armoured cars, and were able to wireless back within ten minutes that the bridge had been captured intact. The attack had been so sudden the enemy had no chance to explode the charges laid under the bridge. This meant that the way eastwards was open, and in the morning our armoured cars pushed on towards Venice, twenty miles ahead.

Soon after midday we packed our trucks, and stood ready to move towards Venice the moment we got the word. That word was 'Merlin', the code name for Venice. It was just after one o'clock when it came crackling in over the wireless from the 12th Lancers. Their forward troop was over the causeway into the city. The autostrada was open; the more southerly road had still Germans on it. The General directed 9th Brigade along this road, to clear it, and Divisional Headquarters were directed to follow.

We went speeding off through the streets of Padua. Now the flags were out, the streets crowded, every window full of people cheering, crying, waving banners, shouting. They threw flags to us which went up on the vehicles, thrown over the canvas canopies or around the guns, the bright colours of Italy. As we drove on the sunshine broke through the ragged April clouds. At the eastern exit from the town the morning's fighting was still marked on the ground, with smashed buildings on either side of the bridge, and two destroyed armoured cars and a 105 mm. gun, its barrel crazily in the air. The next crossroad was guarded by a patrol of Lancers, the villagers staring at the armoured cars drawn up facing south. Still the crowds cheered, and still we raced on.

The rain came again as we continued on the road to Venice. We wound along beside a river, beside high brick walls above which showed the trees and bushes of big gardens, and through villages which merged into one another, with only a few fields between. The rain grew harder, and we waited with it lashing the windscreens of the trucks as the tanks thumped away and the Spandaus and our own machine-guns rattled just ahead. A column of German prisoners, guarded by partisans, and looking very scared, stumbled past. One man was held up by two others, his face pale, his arm a shattered mess. The troops in the trucks greeted the partisans with cries of '*Ciao*'. There was no lack of respect now for the partisan movement.

Then the rain dropped away and the sun came out and we raced on. It was real canal country, with one big waterway parallel to the road, and others intersecting it every half-mile. They were bordered by big houses and big gardens, the old-time estates of Venetian merchants and nobles. On the great horse-chestnuts the candles were out, pink and white, and there were beeches and poplars, rich and soft as velvet and silk. Partisans rushed up and down in commandeered trucks, and crowds were gathering. We met their welcome at its first breath, for the foremost troops on this road were only twenty minutes ahead of us. On the faces of the people who streamed now from their houses, still unsure whether or not they had been liberated, were written relief and a great, almost uncomprehending joy and amazed happiness. In one place we halted outside a small park. Past its wrought-iron gates came a man with a face as white as an invalid just risen from bed. His wife and two small girls were with him.

'This is my first day out of hiding for a year. A year in a cellar. A year,' he kept repeating.

Another halt, this time amid fields. On the right was a great clump of trees, soft and steeped in sunshine behind their wall, like the trees of an Oxford garden. Behind them rose a thin, red-brick campanile, sheer and beautiful. The bell in it was being tolled fiercely, madly, ringing in freedom. Other towers rose from the villages ahead, the high towers of a flat country.

It was at this bend that the machine-guns had fought out, twenty minutes before, their brief battle. A group of German coastguard troops, heading north towards the mountains whose blue shapes on the horizon spelt home for them, had fired on our Bren carriers. It had all been over in ten minutes. By the roadside lay a smashed handcart, with looted bags strewn around, and the inevitable litter and paper. Propped up against a tree was a badly wounded German soldier, his face grey with pain, his lips moving. Fifty yards from the road, in a ditch which ran across the fields, lay his companions. They had been caught side on and mown down by the Brownings in the carriers. They lay as they had been hit, dying and wounded in a crumpled grey muddle in the grassy green ditch, fifteen or twenty of them. The partisans had already taken away their weapons. One man looked up imploringly, saying nothing. Another, a middle-aged man, formed with his lips the words '*Ich habe Schmerzen – Schmerzen.*' The face of another, lying on the top of two dead men, was grey already with death.

There was no doctor there, but a small priest came hurrying over the field, bending over the men to capture their last confessions. In the fields around troops and peasants searched the other bodies for loot. A group of photographers drove up in a jeep and filmed the ditch. The priest posed bending over the bodies, and then turned again so that they could photograph him with the sun just right. From the church tower the bells cried their joy. On the green fields the sun was bright on the wet grass and the hills which the men had hoped to reach, the blue foothills of the Alps, shone clear and blue like a promised land. Slowly, groaningly a wooden cart filled with straw wound across the field to collect the wounded, and a red cross orderly took charge of them.

Then we were off again, for the maddest drive of all. This time there were no pauses. We rolled on past the great oil refineries, past partisans who saluted or clenched their fists, up the concrete ramp of the auto-strada leading towards Venice. Then, like a vision across the green fields and the shining sea, was Venice itself, with the dome and campanile of St Mark, and the brown roofs clear against the immense sky, remote and serene beyond the factories and cranes and oil tanks.

We did not go along the causeway towards the city, but swung left for Mestre and the road to the east. At the corner an officer waited with a jeep. When he saw me he drove alongside and gave me a message from the partisan Intelligence unit in Venice. The city was in their hands, the harbour was undamaged, there were still some pockets of enemy there, but they were being dealt with. Our own troops – tanks and a company of infantry – were on the scene.

I read it as we turned into the streets of Mestre, the industrial suburb on the mainland opposite Venice itself. Here the flood of excitement was running even higher. Noise and people jammed the street. Here were partisans with red flags, red shirts, red neckties. Here were flags and banners; men, women and girls. Above all girls. Were there ever such girls as those of Mestre on this Sunday of liberation? Brown faced, aquiline, sunburnt, lithe girls with shining hair and with greeting and invitation in their eyes; northern Italians with blue eyes and sweeping eyebrows and high cheek-bones in round faces; girls in white cool frocks with flared skirts like Americans, smiling, waving, laughing. This spectacle of a liberating army affected the women a thousand times more than the men. This knowledge of an enemy gone, this relief from the years of occupation and of war, this end of the tension of the last few days and hours, this prospect of peace – all of these found expression in their greeting to these sunburnt men from the other side of the world who waved to them now from their vehicles, from the thundering, swift-moving tanks and trucks and carriers and motor-drawn guns which themselves spoke of power and conquest.

The Italian men greeted us warmly enough, with relief and with thanks, but in the eyes of the girls there was something akin to ecstasy. Some threw us kisses, some threw their arms wide as if they would embrace us all, in their exultation; others smiled quietly, and called to us 'Ciao, Ciao,' as we moved on eastwards through winding streets. We smiled till our face muscles were stiff, we held out our hands till they were almost tugged off. It was no mean reward, the greeting of these people of Mestre in the April sunshine.

So it went on, mile after mile, till we were in open country again and we became suddenly aware of the Alps rising blue and white and sheer above the northern plains. On our right was the sea. Flanking the road were the trenches and earthen redoubts of the elaborately prepared coastal defences. In one village children sat on a grassy canal bank and chanted 'Viva-i-nostri-liberatori.' In another partisans led back four terrified prisoners. And as the afternoon shadows lengthened into evening my eye caught, for the first time, a white kilo stone under the white-boled trees. On it in black were the words 'Trieste 125 Kilos'. We were on the final road. That night our forward troops were on the Piave, another great river like the Adige or the Po, where the German and Italian lines had rested in the last war after the retreat from Caporetto. It was undefended. The troops who should have manned a canal position between it and Venice had surrendered at the first shot of our tanks, and were now crowded into the yard of a farm-house. The banks of the Piave itself were held by partisans. Our patrols crossed the river by boat and joined them on the far bank; our engineers set to work to build a bridge. The division spread out into the fields on either side of the road and gathered energy and supplies for the last bound. For now our orders were definite. They were expressed in one word 'Trieste'.

CHAPTER ELEVEN

'Avoid Combat in the Balkan Area'

These days which had brought us at long last across the defended river lines and out into the Friuli Plain had also seen the question of Trieste come back swiftly into the centre of the discussions and planning of Caserta, Washington and London. The issue of Venezia Giulia, which had been shelved in March, was now very much to the fore. Suddenly it seemed possible not only that we might get quickly to Trieste, but that we might even, after all, get there before the Yugoslavs.

Field Marshal Alexander had waited deliberately until he was sure the Po was crossed and the enemy were in disarray before he sought a clear directive about action in Venezia Giulia. He was aware that in the earlier part of April the Chiefs of Staff had their hands full with the great battles along the Rhine, and across the North German plain. He was aware too that until the enemy front was broken in Italy the pattern for any advance on Trieste could not be foreseen. Much depended too on the pace of the Yugoslav advance into Venezia Giulia. If they got to Trieste first – as seemed possible – the making of ambitious plans for attacks from Italy would be a waste of time. But by Tuesday, 24th April two cardinal facts were clear. One was that the German Army in Italy was near the point of collapse; the second was that there still remained a chance, faint but seizeable, that the Eighth Army might get to Trieste before Tito. The advanced units of the Yugoslav Fourth Army were held up before the main German line at Rijeka – (to give Fiume its Yugoslav name), though the Yugoslavs were trying to outflank the German positions and move onto Trieste. Slovene partisan forces were in possession of large parts of Venezia Giulia; but the big Italian cities of Gorizia and Trieste were still firmly in German hands. It might be several days before they fell. A swift thrust towards Venezia Giulia from Italy might just forestall the Yugoslavs. It was certainly worth trying.

Plans were prepared by Alexander's staff at Caserta for an offensive directed on Trieste, and were despatched to London and Washington. They reached the desks of the Chiefs of Staff on Wednesday, 25th April – the day we bridged the Po, the day the German envoys began their final

negotiations in Switzerland for a surrender on the Italian front, the day
Mussolini left Milan on his last journey towards the Swiss border – and
to his death at the hands of the partisans.

Alexander's plans envisaged not only an advance around the northern
curve of the Adriatic from the Po crossings, but a seaborne move on
Trieste and the more southerly port of Pola. The British Foreign Office
was quick to see the advantage of such a swoop, and Sir Orme Sargent,
head of the Foreign Office, wrote to the Prime Minister the next day
warmly supporting Alexander.

> If we could get to Trieste before the Partisans gain possession, either
> by battle or by German evacuation, it would greatly facilitate the
> American and British plans. Our chances of getting the Yugoslavs
> to withdraw from Venezia Giulia and of getting the Soviets to agree
> to their doing so would be much greater if we and not the
> Yugoslavs were in possession of Trieste at the moment of the German
> collapse.[1]

Churchill's comment was laconic and decisive. 'I agree,' he minuted. He
then set about infusing the operation with his own energy and eagerness.
He urged the Chiefs of Staff to give Field Marshal Alexander immediate
approval to move on Trieste, and to allow him to hold back in the
Adriatic enough landing craft for this purpose. Landing craft, the key to
all seaborne operations, were always in acute demand, and the Americans
wanted those in the Mediterranean to be released at once for the war
against Japan.

The Prime Minister added a footnote to his instructions which gives us
a glimpse of how, even in wartime, the traditional British weekend had
survived. 'In view of all that may happen in the weekend,' he minuted on
Friday, 27th April, 'I hope that the Chiefs of Staff will keep in close
contact and above all not be off scramblers' – scramblers being the
top-secret telephones.[2]

But Winston Churchill's central aim was to get the Americans to see
the need for urgency in the race for Trieste which had now opened up. So
that Friday he sent off a telegram to President Truman.

It was only a fortnight since the new President had taken office, but
he and Churchill had already been drawn into contact by cable, and on
24th April had had a long discussion by telephone, chiefly about the
Russian intransigence over Poland. Churchill had sensed at once the
capacity of the new President to see to the heart of the matter. He
appealed to him as frankly as he would have done to his predecessor for
a swift decision on the issue of Trieste.

The plan for the Anglo-American occupation of Venezia Giulia has been hanging fire in Washington for a considerable time; with the result that Field Marshal Alexander is still without orders. It seems to me vital to get to Trieste if we can do so in the easy manner proposed and to run the risks inherent in these kinds of political-military operations.

Churchill added a sentence which to a lesser man than Truman might have seemed patronising: 'The late President', Churchill continued, 'always attached a great importanec to Trieste, which he thought should be an international port forming an outlet into the Adriatic from all the regions of the Danube basin.' He concluded 'the great thing is to be there before Tito's guerillas are in occupation. Therefore it does not seem to me there is a minute to wait. The actual status of Trieste can be determined at leisure. Possession is nine points of the law. I beg you for an early decision.'[3]

Truman gave one without delay. He instructed the Chiefs of Staff to give the green light to Field Marshal Alexander. Indeed Churchill got more than he wished for. Truman authorised not only the capture of Trieste and Gorizia but also the installation of Allied Military Government over all of Venezia Giulia, even over areas already in the hands of Tito's partisans. This had long been favoured by the American High Command though the British thought it unrealistic. The instructions acknowledged that Soviet co-operation would be needed if the Yugoslavs were to accept this Allied control over an area which Tito claimed, and most of which was already his. The British and US Governments, Alexander was told, were considering the best method of seeking such co-operation. These formal orders were issued by the Chiefs of Staff on Saturday, 28th April. Our advance into Padua and onto the Piave that day, and the next, were therefore part of a new directive – not merely to defeat the Germans but to forestall if possible the Yugoslavs' capture of Trieste. The race for Trieste was on.

Over the weekend Churchill's advisers saw two dangers in the orders given to Alexander. One was that these went too far. If we aimed to secure control over the whole of Venezia Giulia, we were aiming at something beyond our grasp, and in doing so might impede our efforts to secure the areas still within reach – Trieste and Gorizia. There was the risk too that the decision to seek Soviet support for our long-term policy of controlling all of Venezia Giulia might be misinterpreted as needing to clear with them our short-term aims of seizing Trieste, Gorizia and Monfalcone. This second risk deeply worried Churchill. He knew that

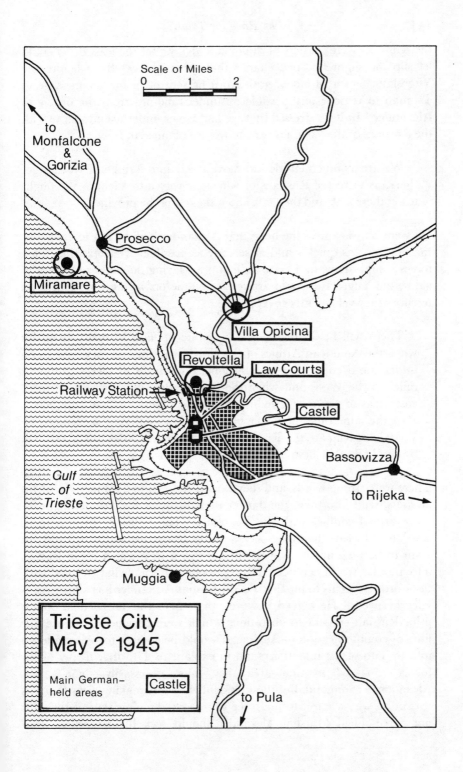

Scale of Miles
0   1   2

to
Monfalcone
&
Gorizia

Prosecco

Miramare

Villa Opicina

Revoltella

Law Courts

Railway Station

Castle

Gulf
of
Trieste

Bassovizza

to Rijeka →

Muggia

Trieste City
May 2 1945

Main German–
held areas   Castle

to Pula

the Russians were masters of diplomatic delay. Yet the least delay could let slip the slight but real chance that we might get there before the Yugoslavs. So on Monday, 30th April he sent off a further message to Truman to remove any possible misunderstandings from the orders to Alexander.[4] In it he stressed that we had never undertaken to clear with the Russians or the Yugoslavs any moves we planned in Italy.

> We are as much entitled to move freely into Trieste, if we can get there, as were the Russians to win their way into Vienna. We ought to get there first, and then talk about the rest of the province.

He went on to express the hope that Alexander 'will be left to carry out the plan . . . as quickly and as secretly as possible.' Whereas the Allied forces would arrive in Trieste as liberators, laying no claim to territorial gains, the Yugoslavs would arrive 'as conquerors laying their hands on territory they vehemently covet'.

> There will be a great shock to public opinion in many countries when the American Armies of the North withdraw as they have to do under the occupational zone scheme, on a front of several hundred miles to the West, and when the Soviet advance overflows all those vast areas of central Germany which the Americans had conquered. If at the same time the whole of the northern Adriatic is occupied by Yugoslavs, who are the Russian tools and beneficiaries, this shock will be emphasised in a most intense degree.

These were strong words, and they caused concern to Truman. He, or his advisers, read into them the danger that this dash for Trieste might involve armed conflict with the Yugoslavs. 'The Balkans,' the President was later to write, 'had long been a source of trouble and war. I did not want to become involved in the Balkans in a way which could lead us into another world conflict'.[5] His reply opened, somewhat sharply, with the words 'It seems to me that Field Marshal Alexander has all the guidance he needs.' He agreed however, that there was no need to obtain prior Russian consent to operations which were designed to secure our lines of communication to Austria. It would be enough for Alexander to inform Tito of his intentions, and to explain to Tito that if any of his forces remained in that area they must necessarily come under Alexander's command. But the President ended by making clear that this was in no way a remit to use force to remove the Yugoslavs if they did not agree. Field Marshal Alexander should seek further orders from the Chiefs of Staff 'before taking further action in the area in question if the Yugoslav forces there fail to co-operate. I think this is important, for I wish to avoid having American forces used to fight Yugoslavs or being used in combat in the Balkan area.'[6]

This policy stemmed not only from any suspicions the President held about Churchill's policy towards the Balkans. Truman was above all conscious that the war against Japan had yet to be won. He wanted to draw the Russians into it, 'thus saving' as he put it later in his memoirs 'countless American lives.'

But the orders to Field Marshal Alexander were clear enough. Even if the question of what should be done if Tito held his ground was unresolved, the Field Marshal had, by the evening of Monday, 30th April, a definite remit. He was free to launch the 2nd New Zealand Division towards Venezia Giulia, with instructions to secure Trieste, Gorizia and the lines of communication northward to Austria. What he could not judge was whether this move would be in time or not.

CHAPTER TWELVE

To the Isonzo

General Freyberg, with his headquarters installed close to the Piave, had been given only a very sketchy idea of these events. He had received firm orders to get to Trieste and open up the port as a base, but all he knew of the political complexities was that, as he noted in his diary, 'there was a somewhat awkward situation' because Marshal Tito wanted his Yugo-slav Army to get to Trieste.

We slept the night of Sunday, 29th April, after our advance from Padua, with the wall of the Alps clear under the stars to the north. The next day, while the engineers waited for the bridging pontoons to arrive, and the infantry probed towards the coast, where there were still pockets of Germans, I drove back into Venice. The partisan Intelligence group there had, I knew, telephone contact with many areas in the enemy rear. They could get us much information we wanted. It was a chance too, to see Venice itself at this strange turn of its history.

Venice absorbed the Eighth Army as it had absorbed so many other conquerors, with a quietness which indicated that all this fighting was a pretty vulgar business anyway. After the wild welcome of the mainland the day before, the canals of Venice were almost suspiciously quiet. But it was Venice, rather than the Venetians, which imposed this. It is one thing to cheer and shout at a column of trucks roaring through your street, where the movement and the noise of engines and the spectacle of powerful guns and tanks all help to rouse still further your excitement. It is another thing to sustain such feeling about troops in gondolas, or even in half a dozen motor-boats. No one can look like a liberator in a gondola. As we lolled back in ours that chilly morning on our way up the Grand Canal we looked more like tourists – and inevitably felt like them, too. Here and there people waved or cried to us from the upper window of a palazzo, or ran to look down on us, and smile as we passed under a bridge. But it was embarrassing rather than stimulating. We were thankful to get to St Mark's Square and hurry to Danieli's Hotel, where the partisan Intelligence group and the New Zealand occupying force had taken up their headquarters.

Thodey Force occupied Venice – a company of the 22nd Battalion and some tanks under Colonel Thodey of the 6th New Zealand Brigade. The tanks were parked by the railway station at the end of the causeway, the infantry spread around the gilded salons of the Royal Danieli Hotel, moving their gear into its bedrooms and mounting guard at the door. They were due to hand over soon to 56th London Division, which had followed us up the highway towards Venice the day before. In the meantime Thodey Force represented British power in the city, and incidentally staked a claim to Danieli's, as the best hotel in Venice, for a New Zealand rest centre in the months to come.

For in the midst of this drive forward the General had been determined that we would have Danieli's as a club. He knew Venice from pre-war days, and loved it. 'It was the one place which never fell below what I expected,' he said. And he was going to have the ordinary New Zealander see it as he had seen it, from the best hotel. He believed that good leave clubs were vital for morale. 'You can't treat a man like a butler and expect him to fight like a lion,' he would say. So we had staked out the claim which possession gave us.

These were, however, irrelevant details belonging to the future. The present found expression in a magnificent suite of the first floor. Here a group of Italians, organised originally by the American Office of Strategic Services, had set up their headquarters. Some of the OSS organisations which we had dealt with in Italy had been amateurish and clumsy. This one however was first class. These men were mostly well-dressed young lawyers and students who had been underground for months. Their leader, a peace-time racing motorist, had been dropped by parachute on the outskirts of Mestre a year before, wearing a city-style suit and carrying a rolled umbrella.

From these rooms, overlooking the Grand Canal and the lagoon stretching towards the Lido, we spent hour after hour collecting information by telephone from behind the German lines. For the Germans in their haste had failed to cut the telephone system. So we phoned to village after village up and down the rivers in our path – the Tagliamento, the Livenza, the Isonzo – finding out which bridges still stood and which were blown. We worked out which areas the partisans held and where the Germans were still strong. We even got through to the CLN at Trieste, but before we could do more than identify ourselves the phone went dead.

When I plotted this on my map it formed indeed an impressive picture. The tiny red marks showing partisan strong points covered the area from the Piave to the Alps as if the provinces were literally aflame. With the exception of one bridge on the canal just ahead of the Piave – a bridge where our engineers were already working – the partisans had seized and held the bridge system along Route 14 all the way from S Dona di Piave to the Isonzo. They had not done this without hard fighting. The rising at S Dona di Piave had started on 26th April, and 1,500 German prisoners had been gathered in in this area alone. The next day the Pellegrini Brigade farther east had captured the bridge over the next big river, the Livenza, and seized the towns of Ceggia and Portogruaro. They had had many counter-attacks in this area, and waited our arrival with some anxiety. In the Venice area the rising had begun on April 26th and fighting against SS troops and Blackshirts had gone on throughout Saturday, 28th April. Mestre had been liberated by the partisans on 28th April, after fighting which had cost them 110 casualties.

One bridge only on the road ahead appeared doubtful. The partisans were not sure that they could hold the auxiliary bridge over the Tagliamento, but they were posted around it, and would fight hard. We told them they had only twenty-four hours to worry about. We would be there after that time.

It was not surprising that the lines to Trieste had suddenly gone dead. When we reached there we were to find that since dawn that day the city had been in revolt against the Germans, in a complicated pattern of guerrilla risings aimed partly at liberating Trieste and partly at settling its future fate, of deciding whether it was to be within Yugoslavia or Italy. A witch's cauldron of conflicting politics and nationalisms had boiled over.

The leading authority of this period, Dr Bogdan Novak, whose book *Trieste 1941-54* is the definitive work on the subject, identifies five distinct groups, some operating openly, some working underground, who had been manoeuvering and waiting and planning for the moment when the German grip would be prised off the area.[1] All five were sharply divided upon whether their homeland should go to postwar Italy or Tito's Yugoslavia. These divisions overlapped and intermingled in a way which made for shifting alliances and enmities. Two of the main groups were above ground, operating with the permission of the occupying Germans. One of these was the Republican Fascists, the Party of Mussolini's desperate last stand in the North. The other were supporters of the Italian Prefect, Bruno Coceani, who administered the area under the Germans. He was a former Fascist who had refused to join the Republican Fascists, and his followers were mainly conservative Italian patriots.

At the same time Trieste had, like the other cities of German-occupied Italy, its underground Resistance Committee, the Comitato di Liberazione Nazionale – CLN – linked through Milan to the Italian Provisional Government in Rome. It was composed of representatives of only four parties – the Liberals, the Christian Democrats, the Action Party, and the Socialists. The fifth element in CLN committees elsewhere, the Italian Communist Party, was absent. They were linked with the pro-Yugoslavs in two pro-Communist underground bodies – the Slovenian Liberation Front, and the Italian Workers Unity Party. The Trieste Communists weer faithfully following the Party line, as set out by the Italian Communist leader, Toglialti, that it was better for Trieste to be part of a socialistic Yugoslavia than of a bourgeois Italy.

Each of these groups knew of the existence of the others. The double pressure on them all – to bring an end to the war, and to settle the future of their city either within Italy or Yugoslavia – brought them into a series of uneasy and suspicious contacts. The Prefect, and his colleague Mayor Pagnini were well aware of the activities of the CLN, but because the CLN wanted Trieste to be Italian they protected rather than persecuted them. Indeed when Mussolini's Republican Fascists arrested the Socialist representative of the CLN, the Mayor got him out of prison. For their part the CLN were drawn into talks with the Communist organisations to see if a united front might be formed to secure a take-over of power from the Germans. All had their private armies – the Prefect his *Guardia Civica*, the CLN some 3,000 men grouped in a 'Justice and Liberty Division' and a 'Domenico Rossetti Division' (Rossetti had been a nineteenth century Triestine poet and patriot). The Communists had some 2,500 Partisans in organised units ready to rise within the city. Trieste indeed presented almost certainly the most complicated political picture of any area liberated in the war.

These complexities extended beyond the confines of the city to the surrounding countryside. In the villages and forests and fields of Venezia Giulia no fewer than six organised armies, equipped with a formidable range of firepower, manoeuvered and stalked and watched and occasionally fought each other. The most formidable was of course the Yugoslav Fourth Army whose main forces had since 20th March been fighting their way up the Adriatic short to Trieste. Spread across the whole area, awaiting the Fourth Army's coming, were Slovene and Croatian Partisan forces, grouped in the 9th Partisan Corps. In some areas they held complete stretches of the countryside, with their own organs of government in the villages and the towns – the structure of local government which had given Eden such concern in his paper to the War Cabinet. This rested on a complete pattern of village district and provincial committees. It had its own schools, hospitals and relief services. In other areas the Partisans were still in hiding in the woods, or going about their business in the towns, their weapons hidden but oiled and ready to hand when the signal would be given. German troops were still strong enough to keep the organised Partisan forces away from the populated centres, the main roads, and the railways.

The leadership of these Slovenian and Croatian Partisans was pre-dominantly Communist. Ranged against these widespread and powerful pro-Tito Partisan forces were four anti-Tito military units. Two were of the area – the Slovene Littoral National Guard, and the Croat Home Guard. They each had their distinctive uniforms, were approved by the Germans, and operated only against the Partisans. Others came from the other side of Yugoslavia altogether. They were compact, well armed, well disciplined Serbian troops. One was composed of Serbian Chetniks. They were loyal to General Mihailovic, but had been split away from Mihailovic's other forces by the Russian advance on Belgrade. They had accordingly retreated across the country towards the West. The second was the Serbian Volunteer Corp, which Tito accused of having collaborated closely with the Germans in Serbia, never making even the limited resistance which Mihailovic's troops had shown. Each of these Serbian forces spread themselves over areas to the east of Trieste, living off the land, and fighting the Partisans. It was as remarkable a tangle of men and faiths and weapons as could be devised. Little wonder that in the White House, when his advisers briefed him on all this, Harry Truman was to declare that he was 'not going to get mixed up in a Balkan turmoil.'

Whilst these currents swirled and eddied in the surrounding country-side, within Trieste both the main underground forces – the pro-Italian CLN and the pro-Communist Slovene and Italian Partisans – saw clearly by Sunday, 29th April that either the Yugoslavs or the Western Allies would soon be in the city. Throughout Saturday, 28th April, as we thrust towards Padua, the CLN tried to get the German SS Commander, General Schaffer, to hand over power to them peacefully. The next day they tried also to arrive at a last minute deal with the Tito Partisan underground for Venezia Giulia to become a joint Slav/Italian territory, but this met with no success.

Then, late on Sunday the 29th, two rumours were brought to the four men who composed the directing committee of the CLN. The German SS, said one rumour, were quitting the city. Even more dramatic was a report that a naval flotilla was approaching the fort. This must surely be the Anglo-American landing force which had been so often forecast. On that belief the CLN leaders decided to make a swift bid for power.

They called out both their brigades of underground fighters, drew in a hidden reserve of sympathisers from the Mayor's Guardia Civica, and at four a.m. on 30th April launched their insurrection. They captured the Trieste radio station, seized the prison, and liberated 378 political prisoners. Their leaders took over the Prefecture, and constituted themselves as rulers of the city.

But both the rumours which had triggered off their action proved to be false. The German forces did not withdraw, and the flotilla proved to be composed of German and Croatian boats bringing in reinforcements. The German garrison, clearly following a well-prepared plan, moved into a series of strong-points – among them the Castle, the Law Courts, and the coastal fortifications. The CLN resistance fighters faced a hard battle, not an easy take-over.

Nor were the CLN long alone in the streets. The pro-Communist Partisans inside Trieste, ready to link up with the advancing Yugoslav Fourth Army, brought their underground forces into action the minute they realised that the CLN had risen. They moved into the centre of the city and joined with the CLN in besieging the German positions. Soon after daybreak they were joined by Partisans of the 9th Partisan Corps, who moved into the outer suburbs, close to the Slovenian-inhabited countryside, and sent columns into the heart of the city also. By the end of Monday, 30th April two guerrilla forces, one pro-Italian, one pro-Yugoslav, were therefore in arms and in action within Trieste. For the moment they were linked by opposition to their common enemy the Germans, but they were even more deeply separated on the question of the future of their city.

We had no detailed knowledge of these events that morning in the Danieli in Venice, only that in Trieste the rising had started. Even that seemed difficult to believe as one looked out at the Venetian streets.

In St Mark's Square the scene was astonishingly normal. Women sold food for the pigeons to the few Allied troops who had got into the city. In the entrance to the Campanile – the great bell tower – they were taking down the German price lists for the lift and putting them up in English. All the shops were still shut, but the crowds walked to and fro quietly. Enormous flags – the winged lion of Venice and the Italian tricolour – hung from the standards in front of St Mark's. There was a moment of excitement as a group of partisans came from a side street escorting a Fascist, surrounded by a curious, shouting crowd. The Fascist was a miserable specimen in all sooth, a meagre man in his late thirties with a blue cap on his head, looking like a railway porter. He carried a paper parcel under his arm and his face was white. He grimaced constantly, either from fear or indifference. They took him across the bridge which runs parallel to the Bridge of Sighs, and into the prison – that same prison in which Casanova in his day had been incarcerated.

The partisans could, I thought, have hauled in much bigger fish from the restaurant at Danieli's, which, but for the occasional khaki, looked at lunch-time as it must have done almost any day for twenty years. Suave, dark men in linen suits escorted their well-dressed women to tables where the glass and silverware gleamed in the light reflected from the lagoon. There were jewels and involved, expensive coiffures in abundance. Here, to Venice, the Republican Fascists had sent their wives and their mistresses for safety from the bombing. Here had gathered the wealthy of Northern Italy. Here, boldly enough, they waited to see what action we would take now that we, and not the Germans, were the masters.

It was a glittering scene, but it chilled the spirit, for it was irreconcilable with the realities outside, with the ambulances on the outskirts of Padua carrying back our wounded, with the crumped grey bodies of the Germans at the roadside the day before. I was glad to get away, and go lazily down the Grand Canal towards the causeway, past the palace where Byron had lived, past D'Annunzio's former home, through side canals where the gondoliers gave their sad warning call at the corners, back to the Piazza di Roma where tanks and trucks were jammed up in one great queue, surrounded by curious Venetians, and from there home to my truck on the approaches to the Piave.

We were woken that night by the sound of firing. In the darkness the shots became more and more frequent. Too frequent for partisans or snipers. They were followed by the flat sound of grenades. I crawled out of my small tent and looked eastwards. The sky beyond the field where our trucks and caravans were parked was lit by three fires, burning farther up the road in the direction of the Piave. It was just after four in the morning, but there was yet no real sign of dawn.

A dark figure came towards me, pausing at each bivvy and truck. 'Stand to. Everybody to stand to. GI's orders. Party of Germans have attacked the Field Park Company just up the road and taken some prisoners and trucks.'

I collected my Italian sub-machine-gun, a Biretta, and a beautiful weapon, from its clip inside the truck cab. The defence platoon sent a man over to say that they were deploying around the PW cage, which was in the farmyard right on the main road. We did not want any German attacks letting loose the 1,000 men there who knew very well that this was a headquarters. The firing and explosions continued up the road. At last the comforting sound of tanks rumbling up from behind us drowned them.

What was happening was clear enough. We were facing a local counter-attack. All the day before, while the bridge was being built, Martin had been working as hard as in any major battle dealing with reports of enemy pockets between the road where we were camped and the sea. Our thrust on Sunday had cut them off in their coast-watching positions, and now partisan after partisan came in with reports of bodies of enemy in many areas. The German turned 88 mm guns on to 9th Brigade, who had sent a battalion down to clear them out. But the area was wide, marshy and intersected by a host of canals, and it had not been completely mopped up by nightfall. It was from one of these pockets now that a substantial German force, organised and directed by officers determined to break back to Germany, had hit at an area where our engineers were encamped. They had chosen it because there a bridge crossed the roadside canal and gave them access to the roads northwards.

Their attack was skilful. They killed eight engineers, wounded 19, grabbed several vehicles, shoved into them as prisoners the other New Zealanders whom they had captured and drove away north. If they had cared to come up the road opposite which we were camped, instead of the next one to the east, they might have had the General as well, plus their comrades in the cage.

It was a small blow, and precisely what one had to expect in any thrust like this into the enemy's area. But it did not make the death of these men, on the second last day in which we were to be in action, seem any the less wasteful and sickening. The Germans accomplished nothing either, because they were gathered in by our tanks within six hours. Their morale had gone down considerably during the drive, as the Kiwis they had taken prisoner described how the campaign had gone, and assured them that escape to Germany would only bring them into the hands of the Russians. One German NCO was also foolish enough to hit a sapper to keep him quiet. When they were recaptured the sapper stripped off, demanded that the NCO strip off too, and then gave him a hiding by the roadside.

They were hauling a burnt-out scout car out of the canal when we drove forward at eight o'clock to the Piave for the day's conference. Behind the farm-house where the fight had been weary men were lining at the cook truck for breakfast after this night of fighting.

Yet the general news at this conference, the last we were to hold in this campaign, was good. We met, as on the Po and the Adige, on the north bank of the river, with the maps once again placed against the windscreen of the jeep. Behind us the trucks and carriers and guns of the Divisional Cavalry bounced and growled their way across the folding boat bridge. To the immediate north showed the brick buildings of S Dona di Piave. They looked new, and indeed they were, for the village had been badly damaged in the fighting of the last war. Across this river, though farther up, had been launched in 1914 the assault which cracked the Austrian and German forces and led the Italians to the victory of Vittorio Veneto – an assault which showed that the Italians, when they care, do fight well. There had been some British and French troops in the action, but the main assault had been Italian.

One of the Italian officers received a British Military Cross after the battle for his co-operation with his British neighbours. His name was Rudolfo Pacciardi, and he was to come into the limelight again in 1936, when he led the Italian Garibaldi Battalion of the International Brigade to victory against Mussolini's forces at Guadalajara, outside Madrid.

I thought of Pacciardi, now back as a Republican leader in Rome, and of Ernest Hemingway, bumping his way across these same roads as an ambulance driver, during the 1918 war, as we waited there in the morning sunshine for the General. The river where, in a *A Farewell to Arms*, Hemingway set his scene of the Italian police stopping officers during the retreat from Caporetto, was the Tagliamento, twenty miles ahead. It was from the Tagliamento now that the news was particularly good. The 12th Lancers, who had had their armoured cars ferried across the Piave the day before, reported that they had found a bridge across the Tagliamento intact and under partisan control. It was, I noted, the one we had telephoned about the day before. The worst obstacle on the road to Venezia Giulia had therefore been cleared. It might be possible to get right through to Trieste in this one day. That was at any rate now set clearly as our objective.

'We have to get there and open it up as a base from which the divisions moving into Austria can be supplied,' the General said. 'The Tito forces are fighting there, too. We should link up with them on the spot. To do it today, we have to be careful about petrol. For that reason all captured enemy vehicles must be left behind. We haven't petrol for them.'

As he spoke the General looked down on the traffic winding up from the bridge below. At regular enough intervals, amid the three-tonners and jeeps, were unmistakable Wehrmacht vehicles – Opels, Volkswagen, yellowish motorcycles, with German number-plates. The names of their new temporary owners were chalked proudly on the side. 'B Company

Cooks'. 'HQ Sigs – Hands Off'. 'Take those vehicles out of the column at once,' the General said to the APM. So the provost stood at the roadhead and diverted to one side the captured vehicles, till there were dozens of them lined up, while their indignant drivers and passengers, reduced once again to the back of their regulation three-tonners, ran, cursing and holding their gear, to climb on to the nearest passing vehicle.

Then we were off ourselves, through more villages of cheering crowds, along the tree-lined, superbly surfaced Route 14, through country which had not even been brushed by the finger-tips of war. Through Ceggia and Tezzi and Portoguardo, stopping sometimes, more often moving on, on.

At midday, when we were halted, a jeep caught up with us. In it, alongside an English partisan liaison officer, rode a young man with a lean keen face, and a sandy moustache. He was tall, and wore a uniform that looked like a cross between that of a scout leader and a Robin Hood costume – loose grey smock-like jacket, Sam Browne, a bluish scarf round his neck, a Bersaglieri felt hat with a feather on the side. He identified himself. He was chief of staff of the Osoppo (Right Wing) Partisan Group of the Udine area. They and the Garibaldi brigades were in about equal strength in the whole region, but the Osoppo were in this coastal belt.

The officer spoke good English. I learned later that he was Count Savorgnan di Brazza, of a celebrated family from north of Urbino. In the desert he had fought against us at Alamein, with the Ariete Division, a fact about which, for some reason, he was very shy. He need not have been. We had respect for Ariete – certainly more than for any other Italian desert division. He had just escaped from the Germans, who three weeks ago had arrested him and the other two leaders of the Osoppo. When he got away they came to search for his wife and children, but he had hidden them in time.

'That is not warfare, to take five-year-old children as hostages. It is the last act of mad beasts,' he said, a little naïvely, as if he had expected Germans to act otherwise.

I took him with me in my own jeep. As we moved forward he gave us details of the enemy layout. The Germans were still scattered along the coast road, and they held in some strength the old Venetian fortress of Palmanova, which still had the great walls of former days, so that it showed up on the map like a five-pointed star. And the auxiliary bridge at Tagliamento was indeed intact. In half an hour we were on it ourselves, a solid structure of logs and planks which had carried even our tanks. We moved over it and wound through villages and along secondary roads till we could link up with the main route again.

These villages, like almost all in this region, had been held now for several days by the partisans. Each had been turned into a small fortress with barricades of heavy logs and earth barring the streets. To them, as our armoured cars and tanks led the long divisional column into their area, we were not just an army which had expelled the Germans, but one which had come to the relief of their own fortresses. Their welcome tasted the best of all, because it was the welcome of men whose self respect ran as high as their joy.

I was glad, then, that their commander had found us and rode with us. For it was when they saw him in his partisan uniform that their cheering rose to its peak. It was raining now, driving rain that swept down from the Alps, but it made no difference to these peasants who jammed their narrow streets, who tore at the barricades with crowbars and axes to clear the route for us, who waved and shouted from every house. In each church tower the bells were pealing madly, and you could see small figures waving from alongside the swaying, jangling bells. When they saw the partisan leader with us their faces lit with an even fuller glow. They could greet us as fellow fighters, not merely as liberators, when they saw their own uniform in our midst. The partisan leader kept his face set and tense, but it needed little imagination to realise what he felt, as he returned into these villages whose fight he had directed through so many black days, with before and behind him, this massive, swift array of force, these tanks growling and thundering, these guns and trucks.

In San Giorgio, a little town twenty miles short of the Isonzo and the Venezia Giulia border, we caught up with the General. He was waiting for word about Isonzo bridge. If it was intact our way should be open right through to Trieste. Partisans and villagers crowded around him as he stood talking to the 12th Lancers commander. I introduced the partisan officer. As I did so a man in a red shirt came pressing through the crowd. The partisans at Palmanova were being attacked by the Germans. Could we not send help? The General, his mind fixed on his instructions to get to Trieste, shook his head. If we had turned aside for every pocket of Germans we would still be back around Padua. I noticed with relief that the partisan officer readily accepted the ruling, and urged patience on his followers. He was indeed eager that we should press on to Trieste without delay. We did in the end however manage to send off a troop of Lancers to see what help they could give at Palmanova. The crowd cheered furiously as the cars swung northwards.

The forward tanks were waiting in the square now, the wireless crackling and the operators chanting call signs: 'Hullo Victor Charlie Oboe, Victor Charlie Oboe calling.' General Harding, the corps commander, arrived, and stood talking with Freyberg. The clouds were still dark overhead, and the dust was laid by the rain. Then word came back that the Lancers had the Isonzo bridge. The General at once gave his orders for the advance to continue.

It was the last time the division would pass forward like this to battle. The General must have thought this too, for he remained there for several minutes, his red cap band towering above the villagers, and watched his force go by. First the tanks passed, starting up with a grinding roar, and then thundering on at what seemed breakneck speed. Their crews in their black berets stood in the turrets waving to the crowds, and their commanders, earphones clamped on their heads, gathered in the bunches of flowers which were thrown to them. Then the lines of Bren carriers, tossing as if in a rough sea until they got up speed, each with its Italian flag, the gift of some village on our way, and each with its smiling troops. Then the three-tonners, with troops on the top of the cab, and the backs jammed with troops sitting among their gear, the lean, smiling, alert, unbluffed New Zealand infantry, enjoying it all but deluded by none of it, bedecked with flowers but with their rifles and Tommy-guns ready for what they knew lay still ahead. They waved and shouted back to the excited Italians, but their faces showed that they knew the job was not yet over. These were triumphal marches to the Italians, but to the troops they were still the road to further battle.

The move forward on what was to be our last road stirred memories of other stages in the journey since 1939 – the clamour of guns, echoing, echoing, echoing on the road from Thermopylae to Thebes; the mountain road to Sphakia in Crete, with its miles upon miles of marching, weary, dysentry-ridden, hungry troops, the wounded stinking through their bandages; the desert in the dusk outside Tobruk, with vehicles spread to the horizon, so that the very ground seemed to move; the tarmac road over the Sinai desert, across which we had moved from Syria to Alamein, through a frightened Cairo; forward again through the broken line at Alamein; the trek around the unbroken line at Mareth; the cold, snow-bound and bombarded roads that led to Sangro and Cassino; the hot, dust-swept and bombarded roads that led to Florence and Rimini.

Many of these men, this afternoon in the Friuli plain, had known them all. They had seen it through from the start to this journey in the last days of the war. Never did they look better than on this final stage, as the provost nailed up the fernleaf signs on the roadside trees and the column gathered speed like a car slipping into top gear and thundered forward on the road towards Venezia Giulia. Chance had set this final march of ours on a road already well trodden by armies of the past. Here the

Roman troops under Augustus had tramped on their way to cross the Julian passes and push the borders of the Empire back to the Danube; Alaric the Goth and Attila the Hun had entered Italy in their turn by the same route; Charlemagne and the Venetians, the Habsburgs and Napoleon had moved their armies here. Now it fell to us, from remote islands on the other side of the world, to pass in our turn along this curving high road from Italy to the Balkans.

We had one further pause before we reached the Isonzo. The Lancers who had gone to Palmanova sent a dingo scout car chasing after us. In it, blindfolded by a coloured handkerchief, was an officer in German naval uniform. He commanded the garrison of marines in Palmanova. He was tough and contemptuous, and rapidly gave up any idea of surrender when he saw that we were heading east towards Monfalcone instead of north towards Palmanova. It was clear that he was parleying only to gain time.

'We have tanks heading for your town,' I said, lying in the hope he would surrender.

'We have anti-tank guns,' he replied.

'We will put our bombers on to you.'

'That is war,' he answered melodramatically – though I doubt if, in this safe corner of Italy, he had yet learnt just what sort of war that could be. But he was not to learn either. For we had no aircraft within call, and so we had to let him go back. That evening he duly tried to break out northwards with his forces, and lost half his men before he surrendered.

Into the rain-cooled afternoon we moved on. The gaunt hills beyond the Isonzo filled the horizon. The roadside looked bare, for there were no Italian flags now. Then, swiftly, we entered what the drivers rapidly enough called 'Titoland'. There were partisans everywhere, with red scarves and red-starred caps. Suddenly we were at the Isonzo, and twenty minutes later we entered the outskirts of Monfalcone. By the roadside they were posting up portraits of Tito, and writing '*Zivio Tito*' and '*Zivio Stalin*' on the walls, and marching in small columns with Yugoslav flags, and with Italian tricolours with the red star in the centre. Here again and again were the words '*Tukay je Jugoslavia*' – 'This is Yugoslavia'.

Suddenly, too, the atmosphere was completely changed. There was a difference, ill-defined but certain, between these people and these streets, and those whom we had met all the way from Piave. In the weariness, in the rain, the troops rapidly sensed the change. It may have been only that here and there a girl to whom they waved would turn aside instead of waving back, it may have been that the men shook their heads at our dog-Italian, but it was unmistakable. We felt like strangers in a strange land, as if at the Isonzo we had passed some unmarked but distinct frontier. As indeed we had. We had driven from Italy into what was to become a No Man's Land between Eastern and Western Europe, and like any No Man's Land it was extremely unpleasant.

CHAPTER THIRTEEN

The Other Side of the Hill

Only two and a half hours separated our arrival at the Isonzo from the overthrow of the German garrison in the area by Yugoslav partisans. The Lancers sent in their first report from the Isonzo bridge at 2.30 p.m. The official Yugoslav War History gives 1 p.m. as the time their troops captured Monfalcone and reached the Isonzo. Yugoslav time was an hour ahead of Italian time, so that by our watches they would have been there by noon.[1] The margin may indeed have been even less, because the capture of Monfalcone itself would probably have been taken as the event which was recorded, and the capture of the bridge was likely to have followed a little later By any standards it was a close run thing.

The first contact with partisan officers was recorded by the Lancers as taking place at 3 p.m. This meeting is not referred to in the Yugoslav History. That is not surprising, as they may well have lacked the signals equipment to send back a message which would find its way into the records They give 6.30 p.m. as the time when 'the head of the New Zealand column was on the Soca/Isonzo, where it encountered our units in the liberated city of Trzic (Monfalcone)'. This fits in well enough with the timing, at 5 p.m. our time, of General Freyberg's first meeting with the officer from the Ninth Partisan Corps. The History Reports that :

> Links were established with the Allied 2nd New Zealand Division. This Division had hurried that day from the River Piave in the hope that it would be able to enter the city (Trieste) before our forces.

That same Tuesday, 1st May, the Yugoslav partisans established a grip on Gorizia, and further up the Isonzo moved across the river into an area, long regarded as well within Italy, which had a substantial Slovene population. It was on that day, too, that the Yugoslav Fourth Army moved down from the hills around Trieste into the heart of the city where the CLN and the pro-Yugoslav resistance fighters had already got the Germans bottled up in a series of strongholds. These operations were the culmination of an offensive which had lasted five bitter weeks, and which had brought the Yugoslav Fourth Army one hundred and twenty miles up the Dalmatian coast, through mountainous country in the face of determined German opposition – the opposition of men who knew that they faced literally a fight to the death. It was an offensive in which the objective was clear – to get to Trieste, and round out the Yugoslav frontier at the Isonzo, before the Allies did, so that Yugoslavia would have, at any peace conference, that possession which was likely to prove all ten points of the law. It was also an offensive in which the Yugoslav commanders, driven on by this determination to be first into Trieste, accepted great risks.

As they moved up the coast, and along the valleys immediately inland, their right flank was continuously exposed to attack from the substantial forces which the Germans had in the interior of the country. Though these German formations were hampered by local Partisan activity, the Germans by then knew the countryside well, and were in a position, had they chosen, to strike hard and damagingly at the widely extended right flank of the Fourth Army. It was the acceptance of this risk – a highly hazardous military operation – and the constant, determined fighting of their troops, who suffered very heavy casualties in the process, that brought the Yugoslavs into Trieste and onto the Isonzo ahead of us by a narrow margin. In the event it was to prove too narrow a margin for them to secure exclusive control of the area. The door was still sufficiently ajar for us also to force our way in, in time to lay our own powerful claim to a share in the capture.

As the hard winter of 1944-45 drew to its end, and the Yugoslavs on their side of the Atlantic, as with the Allies in Italy, could prepare for one final offensive, the German front south of Trieste rested on a series of strongly fortified positions running inland from the small coastal town of Karlobag. Immediately inland it rested on the important road junction of Gospic. On the eastern side of the massive Pljesevica range the line ran along the course of the River Una, which curved from the high mountains north-eastwards towards the valley of the Sava. Through that valley ran the highroad between Zagreb, which was in German hands, and Belgrade, liberated in the autumn, and now the seat of Tito's Government. Offshore the Germans had garrisons and strongholds on the islands which lay, one above the other, in a line parallel to the coast – the islands of Pag, Rab, Krk, and Cres.

The basic strategy of the Yugoslav High Command was straightforward enough. The Fourth Army was to strike for Trieste by the shortest possible route, which was up the Dalmatian coast and through the port of Rijeka (Fiume), whilst fending off the enemy on either side. On its left, seaward flank this fending off involved no great problem. It was a matter of 'island hopping', of landing troops on each island in turn, overcoming the enemy garrisons, and providing a secure left flank.

The task inland, on the right flank, was much more dangerous, and more difficult. The road system which ran parallel to the coast some twenty to thirty miles inland had to be captured – and this route was strongly fortified and strongly held by the enemy. In addition attacks in considerable force had to be launched on German positions in the mountains and valleys of the interior, positions from which, if not subdued, the enemy could launch the counter-offensive onto the Fourth Army flank which the Yugoslav High Command so constantly feared.

The Yugoslav Army to which this spring offensive was entrusted was still young as armies go. Though many of its troops were seasoned fighters, with long years of intensive guerrilla fighting behind them, they and their officers had only limited experience of large scale, more formal warfare. Only in recent months, and in particular after linking up with the Red Army which had advanced into north eastern Yugoslavia the previous autumn, had the Partisan forces been grouped into complex, modern formations able to utilise a wide range of modern heavy weapons like field guns, tanks, and heavy mortars, and able to manoeuvre and fight according to complex plans and detailed timetables. The new Yugoslav Army had been organised very much on the lines of the Red Army, helped by Russian advisers. It had shown that it could learn rapidly, but it still had much experience to gain of operating as an army, and not as a series of smaller partisan units. Stalin had indeed taunted Tito, during the Yugoslav leader's visit to Moscow, with the inexperience of his troops, a taunt which Tito resented, and remembered.[1]

This new army had a mixed, if powerful armament Its enemies had provided a substantial part of its weaponry. Some had been captured from the Germans, some seized from the Italians when the Italian occupying forces in Yugoslavia laid down their arms after the Italian Armistice in 1943. Much had come from the huge quantities of Italian weapons seized when Sicily fell to the Allies. A resourceful Allied liaison officer had rushed to Sicily and persuaded the Allied command to let the Partisans have first rights to the material which had become suddenly available. The British and the Americans had rounded out these supplies, particularly with tanks. The American M3 General Stuart tanks, nicknamed Honeys, which had served well in the desert until the Germans introduced a more powerful anti-tank gun, found a new role with the Yugoslavs. They were well suited for use in close country, on narrow

AUSTRIA

Villach

Klagenfurt

Tarvisio

ITALY

YUGOSLAVIA

Udine

Gorizia

SLOVENIA

Monfalcone

Trieste

CROATIA

Rijeka

VENEZIA-GIULIA

Italo/Yugoslav
border 1939

Italo/Yugoslav
border since 1954

Boundary of Free
Territory of Trieste
(FTT) 1947–1954

Morgan Line

Zone A

Zone B

Pula

roads, particularly against an enemy who had himself few tanks – as was the case with the Germans in the Balkans.

All these sources provided also a good supply of that most essential of all weapons in this war, the field gun. The Fourth Army was strong in artillery, even if it was equipped with many varied types of guns requiring many varied types of ammunition. In the air, the Royal Air Force, operating chiefly from bases in Italy, supplied close support in battle, and bombed many bases. At sea, the Royal Navy gave support along the Dalmatian Coast.

The other element in the Yugoslav forces was provided by the Partisans. Though this name was often given to describe all troops under Tito's command, it belonged at this stage of the war more strictly to those forces operating in the areas from which the Germans had not yet been cleared. These Partisans were grouped in formal units, in brigades, divisions and Corps, though armed only with light weapons and mortars, and at times not fully mobilised. They occupied tracts of country into which the Germans penetrated seldom, if at all, where the villages were organised as self-governing units, and where the partisan troops, armed with Italian and German captured equipment, and some supplies brought in from the Allies, operated as a militia. They did some harassment of the enemy, ambushing some convoys and attacking some posts, but at this stage of the war their main task was to remain organised and ready to intervene in the battle from behind the enemy lines. Three such Corps stood ready behind the lines to aid the Fourth Army – the Ninth, Seventh and Eleventh Partisan Corps. It was the Ninth Corps we met at the Isonzo, as distinct from the Fourth Yugoslav Army which had made the main thrust up the coast towards Trieste.

One of the first tasks for General Drapsin, Commander of the Fourth Army, when he drew up his plans for the Spring offensive was to attack the enemy in the interior, in order to protect his flanks. This meant assaulting not merely Gospic, in the first major valley parallel to the coast, but tackling the much more formidable obstacle of Bihac, a substantial provincial centre deep in the mountains on the Una River. This task had become the more difficult because the Germans, well aware that an attack was coming, had pushed their fighting patrols up into the Pljesevica Range which flanked the Una Valley. This had not only given them a stronger position, but had cut across the lines of communication which the Yugoslavs maintained along this range with large areas further north which were already in the hands of the partisans.

The German forces facing the Fourth Army were of mixed quality. Some were high quality Jaeger formations – light infantry – skilled in mountain warfare, many drawn from Austria; some were mere routine garrison units; others were Croatian anti-Communists, the Ustachi Domobranchi or Home Guards. These were organised into full scale divisions, and were brave and skilful fighters. They felt themselves to be Yugoslavs fighting for their native land just as much as were the partisans, whom they regarded as already in pledge to the Russians. The Ustachi believed indeed that in aligning themselves with the Germans they were merely anticipating a pattern which they were sure must become wide-spread, under which they envisaged the Allies ceasing to fight the Germans and joining in a crusade against the Russians. Since the Yugo-slav Government regarded the Ustachi Domobranchi as traitors, neither side was likely to extend much mercy to the other.

The Germans had by now had nearly four years of experience of warfare against the partisans. They knew that they faced, in this final campaign, a terrible fight. Their only hope of survival lay in resisting as determinedly as possible until they were forced back, or ordered back to the Reich – though so long as Hitler held to his fanatical 'No retreat' policy, there was little likelihood of any such orders being issued. As a result the battles in this final stage of the war in Yugoslavia were particu-larly stubborn and particularly bloody. For the Yugoslavs this was the final drive to get the enemy out of their country, and to bring to an end these harsh hard four years in the mountains and the forests. They fought with great courage, in attack after attack on the numerous German fortified strong-points. The Germans showed comparable courage in defence, just as they were showing under the Allied air attack and the massive Allied bombardments on the other side of the Adriatic.

The Yugoslav plan was in three phases. The first was to break through the enemy forward troop positions. They knew that the Germans had no operational reserve, and would therefore find it difficult to fight a battle of movement. The second phase was to thrust forward up the coast and through the mountains, forcing a way to the main German fortified line above Rijeka, the Ingrid Line. The third phase was to break through that line, which commanded the main road from Dalmatia to Trieste, and advance on Trieste.

Their timetable was, in the light of later events, of interest. They did not envisage coming up against the main Ingrid Line until the end of April. They estimated – and rightly – that this line would prove very tough to crack; they therefore set the date for taking Trieste and reach-ing the Isonzo as 30th May. In the event they were able to get there some four weeks earlier – in nearly half the time.

Zero hour was set for 6 a.m. on Tuesday, 20th March. The attack began, as the official Yugoslav War History records, 'exactly at the ordered time'. The Fourth Army got away to a good start. They had infiltrated parties of troops through the German positions some days earlier, and had seized a point high up in the Pljesevica mountains where the main footpaths along and across the range crossed. This knot of paths was very important, for control of it prevented the Germans moving troops across this otherwise impassable barrier. The enemy garrisons in the Una Valley were by this stroke separated from those nearer the coast, leaving the Yugoslavs freedom to move along the range to attack the key inland centre of Bihac.

The fighting for Bihac was to last a week. It was typical of scores of such battles which were to take place in the ensuing weeks. The villages around had been turned by the Germans into strongpoints. So had the heights on the ranges on either side of the river. The bridge over the Una River had been blown. Each strongpoint had to be stormed, each hilltop seized in a series of constant attacks, which were frequently met by the Germans with counter-attacks. Finally one Yugoslav brigade managed to get across the river in rubber dinghies, and to clear much of the town. But the Germans retreated, as was their tactic, to a series of strongpoints – the secondary school, the railway station, the hospital. Here they held on determinedly.

It is not hard to envisage the scenes in this small Balkan town in those cold March days, with the snow still on the tops of the surrounding mountains, with the river swollen and brown with spring floods, with the meagre stone and brick buildings a mass of rubble, stinking with the fumes of burning timber, and explosives, and of the dead. We had known village after village and town after town like this on our battle up the mountain spine of Italy in the winter of 1943-44, culminating in Cassino. The cold, the squalor, the grey skies of a late spring, all seemed to give these ruined places a further sense of awfulness.

Now here at Bihac, as in so many other towns, the Germans found themselves in a type of mini-Stalingrad, cut off, fighting with no other hope than either to drive off the enemy or to force their way out, to find yet another defensive area, to face yet another siege.

The offensive of the Fourth Army was not a matter of broad, set-piece battles such as we were engaged in in Italy. It was a series of fights, for one strongpoint, one fortified village after another, with Yugoslav troops and their supporting Partisans thrusting, encircling, at times retreating under enemy counter-attack, and with German forces moving in small but powerful groups to hold this position, to thrust back against this other one. The Yugoslav maps of the campaign give an idea of this fighting. They are not covered with the broad coloured arrows – red for one's own forces, blue for the enemy – used to portray orthodox military advances and retreats. Instead they are a complex, writhing mass of red and blue arrows, crossing and interweaving not only with those marking the enemy, but with those of their own forces, as each side cut and thrust at the other. At times main German strongpoints are portrayed as dark blue circles, at which the red arrows jab and thrust like flames licking around a log. At other times the red and blue arrows intermingle as if two coloured panes of glass had been shattered and their fragments had fallen amidst each other.

On 27th March Bihac fell. The victory brought important results. The Germans had suffered heavy casualties; one Ustachi Domobran Division had been completely annihilated. For the time being at least the danger to the Fourth Army's right flank had been removed. Now the attack along the coast, and the island-hopping offshore could begin.

This attack went in on 4th April, at the time when we were settling in on the Senio, beginning to dominate the stop-bank, and preparing for our offensive which was to start five days later. Both on the coast road and on the parallel road inland the Yugoslavs made swift progress. Karlobag, where the German line met the coast, and Gospic, the provincial town in the valley parallel to the coast, fell quickly. Within four days the Yugoslavs were on the outskirts of Senj, half way to Rijeka. They had also cut the roads running up from the coast to the interior, splitting off the coastal forces from support from direction.

The assault on the island of Pag was less succesful. The Yugolavs had had little or no experience of carrying out landings from the sea, and there were delays in embarking and disembarking the assaulting infantry. But the air strike, mounted by the RAF, and the artillery bombardment went ahead on time. The landing parties reached the beaches well behind the bombardment, and the enemy had had time to regroup and prepare. Bad weather prevented the gunboats giving effective supporting fire. Indeed they fired on their own troops, and had to be ordered to stop their bombardment. It was not until next day that the main town on the island fell.

On the mainland the thrust up the coast continued. By 10th April Senj had been taken, together with the inland town of Jospidol. Part of the German forces had been splintered into small groups and took to the forests, where they were hunted down by the partisans.

The previous day the Allied offensive had been launched in Italy. The Yugoslav High Command knew therefore that it was now only a matter of time before the Germans in Italy must surely be defeated.

Though the Fourth Army was well ahead of schedule – the first ten days objectives had been achieved within two days – they decided that Drapsin must push on as fast as possible towards Rijeka and Trieste. This was to be done even though his right flank was now again dangerously exposed. Though the fall of Bihac had neutralised the danger of a German thrust down the Una valley, the Germans were in strength on other main roads running south from the important centre of Karlovac, itself linked by an excellent highway to the major German base at Zagreb.

Military prudence demanded that Drapsin should either clear this flank, or hold it in strength before he moved further up the coast. He decided however to split his forces, committing the main body to driving forward towards Rijeka, whilst sending two divisions out on the right flank to strike at the main German strongpoints, the towns of Slunj and Ogulin. These were on the roads running down from Karlovac, roads which stuck out on the map like two crinkle-bladed daggers pointing at the side of the Fourth Army.

After a series of forced marches through mountainous country the flanking divisions got to grips with the Germans at both towns. The mountain peaks covering the main road at Slunj changed hands twice before the Germans were forced back to Karlovac. For the moment the threat to the right flank was again contained. The main force meanwhile maintained its thrust towards Rijeka and Trieste along the coast and through the islands.

On the night of 11th April the island of Rab was taken. This time the landings went smoothly enough. The lessons of the failures on Pag had been swiftly learned. Indeed the attack went so swiftly that the two supporting Royal Naval gunboats were not called upon to fire. By the night of 16th April three more coastal towns had fallen – Novi, Selce and Crikvenica, and the Yugoslavs were approaching the outskirts of Susak, the town immediately across the river mouth from Rijeka itself.

They were now coming up against the strongest German defences, and the best organised German troops. The pre-war Italian-Yugoslav border had run northwards from Rijeka, along the River Recina and up into the mountains, which rose here to a height of 5000 feet. Mussolini had built a strongly fortified line to guard the frontier, and the Germans had strengthened and modernised it. As in Italy, they had given it a girl's name – the Ingrid Line.

It was manned by the German 97th Army Corps. This had two good infantry divisions – the 188th Mountain Division and the 237th Infantry Division, as well as German and Italian coastal artillery and coast-watching units. It was not under the command of the German Army

Group 'E', which was responsible for Yugoslavia, but came under General Vietinghof's Army Group 'C', against which we were battling in Italy. This was to enable the 97th Corps to protect the rear of the Germans in Italy, and to guard the coast of Venezia Guilia from the seaborne attack from the Allies which Churchill had so long advocated, and which the Germans had so long anticipated.

The 97th Corps had therefore had its eyes to the west towards the direction from which the Eighth Army might come. Now it had to swing round and face eastward, to meet this Yugoslav attack. The swift advance of the Yugoslavs had indeed shown up a flaw in the German military organisation for the area. Three separate commands now covered the breadth of northern Yugoslavia – 97th Corps, under Army Group 'C' in Venezia Giulia; to their east an occupation force under an SS officer, Rezener, who came under the German 18th Corps at Salzburg; and further east still, facing the 1st and 3rd Yugoslav Armies, Army Group 'E'.

There was still one strong enemy line covering the outer defences of the Ingrid Line. This was along the valley through which ran the main road and railway from Rijeka to Zagreb. On 17th April, the day on which on the other side of the Adriatic the New Zealand Division had reached the Gaiana River, General Drapsin launched a threefold attack on this line through the mountains, along the coast road, and onto the islands of Krk and Cres. Though the attack on the islands had to be postponed by twenty-four hours because of a sudden storm at sea, both islands were duly taken. Since only a narrow channel separated Cres from the mainland of the Venezia Giulia peninsula, it would now be possible for the Yugoslavs to land forces behind the Ingrid Line. Though this did not offer any very serious threat to that massive position, which was prepared for all-round defence, it did open up a further route towards Trieste.

By 20th April the main forces of the Fourth Army had fought their way, in three days of bitter fighting in the mountains, and against the guns of the coastal artillery, up to the Ingrid Line. They were into the outskirts of Susak, and had Rijeka under fire across the mouth of the River Recina. Further north they had some units across the old Yugoslav-Italian frontier, deep into the mountains where roads were few. But the main German defensive line covering the port of Rijeka and the main road system leading to Trieste was solidly intact.

April 20th was an important day on the Eighth Army front in Italy. By then the New Zealand Division and the other formations of 13th Corps were across the Idice, the last of the river barriers running down from the Apennines, and were wheeling round to face up to the River Po. 5th Corps had pierced the Argenta Gap, and were also near to the Po at Ferrara. The end in Italy could not be long delayed. One more heavy blow by the Eighth Army, and the way could be clear for them to move across the Friuli plain towards Trieste. Tito therefore decided that Drapsin must strike towards Trieste without delay, whatever the risks. One more Division was put under the Fourth Army's command, and the Army was told 'the general situation requires that you advance rapidly on Trieste'.

The problem which Drapsin faced was formidable. His direct path was barred by the Ingrid Line, which was very strong around Klana, where the main road crossed the frontier just north of Rijeka. The line here was manned by some of the best German troops in Yugoslavia, still relatively fresh, and with ample supplies. To break it would be a difficult, and perhaps prolonged task. To outflank it would be dangerous, for the Germans were in a position both to strike out from Klana from the south, and to strike down simultaneously from Ljubljana in the north onto any outflanking force.

General Drapsin decided that he must, however, accept this risk from the north – a very real one now that the fighting had come closer to the German base and communications centre at Ljubljana – and must attempt a wide detour through the mountains inland from the Ingrid Line. This was more hazardous than his previous advances. It was no longer a question merely of exposing the flank of his main army along the coast, solidly based as that was. He was now proposing to detach substantial forces who would be far from their supply routes, moving over difficult ground where the enemy held the roads. But it was his only chance of getting to Trieste quickly. To smash through the Ingrid Line and open up the main road from Rijeka to Trieste meant a delay of many days. The first assaults on that Line had proved that the enemy were in a very powerful position – at times their counter-attacks had the Yugoslavs reeling back. Indeed the Ingrid Line was never broken in all the hard fighting which was to follow. The Yugoslav commander therefore decided to send one division in a wide arc round to the north. He would also try to outflank the Ingrid Line to the south by landing troops across from the island of Cres onto the lower part of the Venezia Guilia peninsula. He called the waiting Partisan Corps into action as well. The 7th Corps were to give such protection as they could against any German move from Ljubljana, and the 9th Corps were to mass in the Trnovski Forest to the north of Trieste, ready to move onto the city and onto the Isonzo.

On the night of 24th/25th April, as we came up against the River Po, the main Yugoslav flanking movement got under way. There had already been heavy fighting, with the heaviest casualties of the campaign, on the Ingrid Line itself. Though the Yugoslavs had managed to secure one bridgehead across the Recina River which formed a natural anti-tank moat for the Ingrid Line, the Germans were able to contain this. The seasoned 188th Mountain Division was now fully in action, with devastating effect. Day after day the fighting continued for the main peaks and hillsides which commanded the river valley, and day after day the Fourth Army made no real headway.

Nor did the proposed thrust across the narrow channel from the island of Cres onto the mainland offer much hope of success. The weather had broken up, and though the convoy of landing boats set out in a heavy storm, only relatively light forces got ashore. It would be days before any substantial forces could be gathered there. All therefore depended upon the encircling move to the north, if Trieste and the Isonzo were to be reached before the highly motorised formations of the Eighth Army got a chance to break out into the flat North Italian plain.

Drapsin had already one division – the 20th – committed to this right hook. Now he added a new element. He decided to revert to the tactics of the old partisan days in the mountains. He told the commander of his 43rd Division, which had been engaged in the fighting on the northern edge of the Ingrid Line, to detach a brigade and infiltrate its units through the enemy lines towards Trieste. Moving by night, and through the forests and across the higher mountain slopes by day, it could, if fortune held, gather itself together behind the Ingrid Line and be able to advance onto Trieste by a shorter route.

The 20th Division was given the support of the Armoured Brigade, with its Stuart tanks. The 20th managed to get astride the road leading from Rijeka to Ljubljana, but only by hard fighting. The Germans had groups of fresh and experienced troops in the area, seasoned by months of fighting against the local Partisans. They had prepared many of the villages and hilltops as points of resistance. Even with the tank support, and their artillery, the 20th Division was unable to break through this well organised line, which constituted in fact the outer defences of Trieste.

By the night of Friday, 27th April the Yugoslav High Command had reason to be anxious. The Americans now had five divisions across the Po. The whole German front in Italy was cracking. Tito called on Drapsin for one supreme effort. The next day, Saturday the 28th, as we raced forward to Padua, the breakthrough which the Yugoslavs sought came at last. At the very north of the Fourth Army's flanking movement the German network of fortified positions gave way. The village of St Peter fell to a Yugoslav tank and infantry attack, and the township of Postojna was partially taken. The gap was not large, but it was enough. Just before midnight on that Saturday night, as we were entering Padua, a mobile group of tanks, infantry, artillery and engineers formed up in the darkness near St Peter, ready to move on to Trieste. At the same time the 43rd Division to the south had now managed to infiltrate all of its three brigades through the centre of the enemy position, across the mountains and through the forests, and was now gathering itself together for an attack on the city. Though the German 97th Corps, by its stubborn defence, not only held its main position intact, but still presented a threat to the southern flanks of these Yugoslav troops, Drapsin had now got two full divisions around the German line and onto the edge of Trieste. Elements of a third, the 9th, were making their way up from their crossing places from the Island of Cres.

At this point the Germans made a change in their command structure which was to give unexpected help to the Yugoslavs. The 97th Corps was taken away from the collapsing Army Group 'C' in Italy, and put under the command of Army Group 'E' in northern Yugoslavia. It was ordered by Army Group 'E' to hold its position at Rijeka at all costs. This made sense from the point of view of protecting the approaches to Ljubljana and southern Austria, but it meant that Trieste was left to fend for itself. There was to be no question of the strong and efficient divisions of 97th Corps being withdrawn to ring Trieste and hold it against the Yugoslavs, as might have been ordered had the Corps still been seen as part of the Italian battlefront.

The Commander of the 97th Corps pleaded to be allowed to break out northwards, where his experienced troops would have been a most valuable reinforcement to those covering Ljubljana and the southern approaches to Austria. But he was told to stay where he was, even if that meant being surrounded and besieged within his defensive lines. Army Group 'E' still hoped that they could gather together enough forces in the north to cut across the Yugoslav right flank. Had that been possible, they would not only have re-opened the link with Rijeka, but would have done heavy damage to the thinly stretched Fourth Army. In the actual conditions of the day it was, however, more of a pipe dream than a plan. In insisting on it, Army Group 'E' condemned the 97th Corps to destruction and imprisonment.

On Sunday, 29th April, the day on which we swept forward from Padua to the Piave, Drapsin issued his orders for the final attack on Trieste. He now had elements of three divisions on the city edge – with a fourth protecting their rear towards Ljubljana. The 20th Division with its mobile column of tanks and artillery was to move onto the city from the north east; the 43rd Division was to attack along the main road from Rijeka, on which it had formed up after its successful infiltration through the German lines; part of the 9th Division, which had made the landing on the peninsula behind the Ingrid Line, had made its way towards the southern edge of the city. In addition the 9th Partisan Corps, with its two divisions, the 30th and 31st, had moved out from the Trnovski Forest. It was given a double task. Part of its forces were to secure the northern suburbs and infiltrate into the city. Others were to capture Monfalcone, Gorizia, the upper Isonzo, and the Slovene – inhabited regions across the upper Isonzo.

This was the situation when, in the early hours of 30th April, the pro-Italian underground forces in Trieste, the CLN, ordered their cadres to rise and seize the city. Their rising introduced a new element into the problems facing both the German defenders and the Yugoslav attackers. For the Germans no co-ordinated plan of defence was now possible. Within the city they and their Italian Fascist allies could do no more than retreat to the series of strongholds they had prepared against this eventuality – the barracks, the port, the dockyards, the coastal defence installations, the Law Courts, the Castle, the high ground around the villa Revoltella, even the Sports Stadium. Outside the city they planned to hold as long as possible the ring of prepared positions at Villa Opicina an important road junction, at Basovizza, and those covering Muggia and the road to Pola.

These outer defences managed to resist throughout that Monday, 30th April. Basovizza changed hands three times in the course of the day. Opicina, which had been brought under attack by the 9th Partisan Corps on the night of 29th April, was another centre of hard fighting. The only significant Yugoslav forces which got into Trieste itself were those of the 9th Partisan Corps. They made their way in through the northern suburbs, and linked up with the Trieste pro-Slovene guerrillas, who had come out quickly onto the streets once they realised that the CLN had struck. By midnight the Partisans had the Trieste railway station and the approaches to the quayside under fire. But the main body of Yugoslav troops were at nightfall still held up o nthe outer fringes of the city.

Yet, as Tuesday, 1st May dawned, and the New Zealand Division gathered on the eastern bank of the Piave ready for the dash which would carry us into Monfalcone by the day's end, General Drapsin held Trieste within his grasp. He needed only to close his fist to crush the outer shell of the German defences on the hilltops and the knots of resistance within the city, and Trieste would be his.

He entrusted the final attack to the 20th Division, which had made the breakthrough at St Peter two days before, and to the 9th, which had moved up from the south. The 9th Partisan Corps were withdrawn, in order that they could concentrate on capturing the area up to the Isonzo. The commander of the 20th – unnamed in the Yugoslav War History (which indeed gives the names of no commanders at all, nor of any individuals who took part in this campaign) – decided to send two columns between the main strongholds at Opicina and Basovizza, which were meanwhile kept under attack. It was the old tactic of infiltration, but this time on a grand scale, led by Stuart tanks.

In the early hours of the Tuesday morning the columns were on their way. One headed for the University and the Military Hospital, with its main goal the stronghold of the Law Courts. The other cut across the city further south, sending part of its force to link up with the 9th Division troops who, using captured German lorries, were coming in on the Rijeka road. Another part was directed onto the barracks, the Castle of St Justin, and the waterfront.

The Yugoslav forces came down into a city already partially held by the CLN and the pro-Slovene underground fighters. Their official War History makes only glancing reference to this fact. It reports that when Yugoslav troops reached the Piazza Garibaldi that day 'they linked up with the Slovenian-Italian volunteer unit, which had participated in fighting around the castle. In co-operation with this volunteer militia, whose ranks were steadily increased by more and more Trieste citizens, the battalion continued their attacks towards the coast'. One later passage says that 'in the Trieste battle, in addition to the Slovenian-Italian volunteer militia, our forces were also aided by towns-people who possessed arms. The support of these people greatly helped the final clearance of the enemy from the city'.

Severe fighting continued in many areas of Trieste throughout that day. The Germans and their Italian allies had prepared their final points of resistance with care. They were in no mood to give in to the Yugoslavs in any event, and their stubbornness was increased by the knowledge that the Western Allies were now within striking distance. An Allied prisoner of war camp was infinitely to be preferred to capture by the Yugoslavs. The Fourth Army met strong resistance at the two main barracks, around the railway station, in one of the chief factories, at the Sports Stadium, around the docks. On the hilltop areas also the battle continued with intensity. Basovizza fell during the day, but at Opicina, where bitter street fighting continued, the Germans mounted constant counter-attacks right through the day and into the night.

The next day, 2nd May, the German resistance was maintained in the most formidable strongpoints – the Castle, the Law Courts, the coastal batteries, the high ground of the Villa Revoltella, the suburb of Konkonelj, and Opicina itself It was against these, in a combination of attack and parley, that the Fourth Army forces were engaged when the foremost troops of the New Zealand Division entered the city from the north that afternoon.

General Drapsin had left the clearance of Monfalcone, Gorizia and the Isonzo Valley to the North Partisan Corps. They had attacked Gorizia at dawn, and chased the bulk of the Chetniks and Slovenian Home Guards and the scattered German and Italian troops across the Isonzo. Monfalcone had been captured at 1 p.m. and the Isonzo Bridge reached soon afterwards. Further north the Partisans had not only cleared the upper Isonzo Valley, but had moved into territory well within Italy proper, where there was a strong Slovenian element in the population – an area called by the Yugoslavs Beneska Slovenia The Yugoslav High Command was therefore able to claim that on this Tuesday, May 1st, 'the units of the Fourth Army achieved great successes. After pitched battles in Trieste they conquered the city, except for a number of isolated points of resistance, and also captured Monfalcone, Gorizia, the entire Isonzo Valley, and Beneska Slovenia'. If their title to these areas had rested on conquest, it would indeed have been a strong one.

CHAPTER FOURTEEN

Photofinish

We had no clear knowledge of these events when, at 8.30 on the morning of 2nd May, the New Zealand 9th Brigade resumed the advance from Monfalcone towards Trieste, with a squadron of 12th Lancers leading the way. There was a brisk early battle against one German strongpoint just east of the coastal town of Duino. Here the tanks of our 20th Armoured Regiment fought the division's only naval action of the war, when they fired on three German vessels five miles out to sea. They set one on fire, and forced the crew to abandon another.

Our advance continued along the two roads towards the city, one over the hills and the other carved from the rock alongside the sea. On the upper road there was some stubborn resistance by the Germans at Prosecco, where the Germans made use of one of our anti-tank guns. They had captured this in the dark the night before, as the crew of the gun, mounted on its lorry-like portee, had unwittingly over-run our frontline positions. The Germans made another haul during the morning, when they captured two Royal Navy officers in a jeep, who were heading for Trieste to begin opening up the port. The Naval officers were in due course recaptured by the advancing New Zealanders, but the khaki naval uniforms were unfamiliar to the Bren carrier patrol which gathered them in. The Navy men were told, along with the Germans, to line up in a courtyard for transport to the rear. The New Zealand sergeant giving the orders was understandably surprised when a voice, in ringing Dartmouth tones, demanded, 'Don't you bastards know a British Naval officer when you see one?'

By two thirty the column on the coast road had reached Miramare, a small peninsula with a fairy tale white castle on its promontory. Here they came up against 88 mm guns, but the New Zealand commander, Lieutenant-Colonel Donald, called down the cab-rank aircraft, and soon afterwards the German commander at Miramare surrendered. He had had command of all the German coastal artillery. He based his surrender on the order which had been broadcast by Admiral Dönitz, who had become chancellor of the Reich after Hitler's suicide on 30th April and in defiance of his immediate superior at Rijeka, where 97th Corps were still under orders to fight on. This was the first surrender within Trieste of any major German force. In all fifteen officers and 600 men were taken at and around Miramare. Beyond Miramare the Germans had established a road block, protected by pillboxes. The tanks silenced these with a burst from their Brownings, and at three o'clock were in the centre of the city, amidst the Yugoslav infantry and tanks. Their arrival marked the fact that the race for Trieste had ended in a virtual deadheat.

The tanks were followed by the main body of 22nd Battalion, in their trucks and Bren carriers. Their arrival brought the crowds into the streets in wildly excited, cheering lines. They were mostly Italians, waving the tricolour, and greeting us in Italian. Their relief at our arrival was manifest. This was an altogether different greeting from the half deserted streets of Monfalcone the previous afternoon, or from the organised demonstration which had been mounted earlier this same afternoon in the main square at Monfalcone. These were individuals ecstatically welcoming both the end of the war and the hope that they might have a say in their own future.

The 22nd Battalion moved towards the docks, the Castle and the Law Courts. The Castle, a heavy medieval structure, in good repair, was still under siege by Yugoslav troops and partisans. A lot of indiscriminate shooting was going on, and the tanks with 22nd Battalion were greeted by a shot from a German bazooka, which luckily missed. When the Germans realised that these were British troops, they opened the gate and, to the fury of the Yugoslavs, allowed the trucks carrying C company of 22nd Battalion to enter. The gates were then shut whilst the German garrison of 12 officers and 170 men surrendered.

The Yugoslavs claim that they had in fact arranged a surrender for five o'clock, but that the Germans, realising that the British were near, had held on until the 22nd Battalion force had arrived on the spot at 5.30 p.m. A topsy turvy situation then developed. Partisans started sniping from the surrounding houses at any movement in the Castle, whether made by Germans or New Zealanders. The New Zealanders took over the defence position the Germans had vacated, and prepared in turn to withstand a siege. The Germans indeed proposed that they be given back their arms and be allowed to join in, but the young New Zealand Company Commander refused. That evening the prisoners and the New Zealanders shared a meal of mixed New Zealand and German rations. In the morning the Germans were removed in the battalion trucks, under escort, through a crowd of angry partisans and Yugoslav troops. The Castle remained under our control, but with partisan forces on the alert all around.

At the Law Courts Colonel Donald found a strong force of Reichswehr troops and SS men surrounded by Yugoslavs. Here too the official Yugoslav War History claims that our arrival forestalled inevitable surrender. 'At 1600 hours just when the enemy had put out white flags to arrange a surrender seven or eight English tanks arrived,' it reports. These tanks were from two squadrons of the 19th Armoured Regiment, and Donald went forward to parley with the German Commander. But he had less success than at the citadel. The SS Commander could not be persuaded to give in. He was, Donald said, 'humbugging undecidedly, and was apparently under the influence of alcohol'.[1]

So Donald proposed to the Yugoslav Commander that they should mount a combined New Zealand – Yugoslav assault. This met with eager agreement. At 7 p.m. our tanks moved up to within pointblank range, and blasted holes in the walls. The Yugoslav infantry poured into the building, and though the Germans fought on in the cellars, by the end of the night the capture was complete, and 200 prisoners were taken. The Yugoslav official history tells the same story, with one omission. Though it records that their 10th Brigade assaulted the building 'with the support of strong tank and artillery fire', it does not detail whose tanks or guns they were. But the Yugoslavs had reason to be satisfied with the outcome, for the prisoners went to them.

General Freyberg and Brigadier Gentry had been well up with the foremost tanks and had entered the city shortly after Colonel Donald reached it. They went to the chief hotel, the Grande Albergo della Citta, where Brigadier Gentry set up his headquarters. That night he was nominated by Freyberg as Allied Commander of the city. The General established his own headquarters in Miramare Castle.

By six o'clock the Divisional Cavalry had broken through on the upper road, and were also in the city area. One of its squadrons, D squadron, had in its ranks two future Prime Ministers of New Zealand. One was Major John Marshall, the other Corporal Robert Muldoon.

Two main German strongholds remained unsubdued at dusk. On the northern edge of the city the Commander of Trieste and North Western coastal area, Lieutenant General Linkenbach, was holding out with some 700 men. During the night an Austrian civilian brought a message to Colonel Donald, who had established his headquarters in another hotel, the Regina, offering to surrender to the British. Linkenbach was brought to the Regina in a jeep, under Kiwi escort, who made their way through a series of Partisan roadblocks. At daybreak the German force was marched downhill under New Zealand escort and sent back to Monfalcone.

The other German force was that under siege at Villa Opicina. It was a powerful unit of over 2,500 men. They had now been under heavy attack for three days. On 2nd May the Germans had launched a series of counter-attacks which held off the Yugoslavs during daylight hours, but street fighting on the northern edge of the village continued throughout the night. At daybreak on 3rd May the German Commander got out a message offering to surrender to the British. Colonel Donald promptly sent out a company of infantry and three tanks. Two of the tanks, with infantry riding on top, got into the centre of Villa Opicina and started to negotiate with the Germans. But this time the Yugoslavs were not going to be denied the victory or the prisoners which they considered to be their due. They opened up with mortars and small arms, killing one New Zealander and wounding another. 'Here we were, among armed Germans who greatly outnumbered us, and subject to the same dangers in a private war which was being prosecuted after the official cessation of hostilities,' the Battalion was later to record.[2]

Whilst the New Zealand tank commander dashed up and down between Villa Opicina and the Yugoslav lines 'with my heart in my mouth' trying to stop the battle, a British liaison officer who had been with the Yugoslav 20th Division during their advance on the city appeared on the scene. He and the Commander of the 20th Yugoslav Division were persuaded to go into Trieste to meet Brigadier Gentry. The Brigadier decided that he was not going to risk any more casualties so he ordered the New Zealand troops and tanks to withdraw. As soon as this took place the Yugoslavs gave the Germans five minutes in which to surrender. They did so. This surrender was the end of the battle for Trieste, as both War Histories were in due course to record. 'With the capture of Villa Opicina, all resistance in the Trieste sector ceased,' states the Yugoslav volume. 'The Division had fired its last shot in the War,' says the New Zealand account.

For the Western Allies the surrender of most of the enemy strongpoints and the storming of the Law Courts on 2nd May, and the fall of Opicina on the 3rd, marked also the end of the war against the Germans in Venezia Giulia. But for the Yugoslavs the fighting was far from complete. Away to the south 97th Army Corps still held its lines around Rijeka, and still constituted a dangerous threat to the rear of the troops now spread out around Trieste. Several days of further bitter fighting lay ahead of the weary Yugoslav soldiers who had now been engaged, almost without break or even pause, for five weeks since their first onslaught in the half light of the early morning of 20th March.

Once the commander of the German 97th Corps realised that the Yugoslavs had swarmed around his position in order to get to Trieste, he decided that his best plan was to form an all-round defence, and prepare to stand a siege as long as he could. Such a 'hedgehog' position could also provide a starting point if he was ordered to break out to the north, and link up with the rest of Army Group 'E'. Against this stronghold the Yugoslavs had continued to launch attack after attack throughout the days of their advance on Trieste. They were keenly aware that if the 97th Corps broke out, either northwards across their lines of communication, or westwards to link up with the garrison of Trieste, it might have created havoc in the rear of the divisions attacking Trieste. But the shortsightedness of the commander of the German Army Corps Group 'E' saved them from this danger. He had told 97th Corps to hold out where they were, in the belief that this could protect his own position at Ljubljana.

Only when Trieste had fallen, and the Yugoslavs were free to concentrate the bulk of their forces once again against this Balkan position, did Army Group 'E' give permission for 97th Corps to attempt a break out. On 3rd May the Corps formed up in a series of mobile squares, and tried to cut their way northwards. They managed to get as far as the road junction of Iliriska Bistrica, in a series of battles which claimed still more lives on both sides. Finally the Germans were hemmed into an area only four kilometres across, every corner of which was subjected to Yugoslav artillery and tank fire.

On the evening of 7th May the Germans finally surrendered. Some sixteen thousand German troops and officers gave themselves up – a force which, had it been ordered back to defend Trieste, as might well have been the case if the Corps had been left under the Command of the German Army Group in Italy, would certainly have held the city intact until the Eighth Army reached it from the west. Pola had fallen the day before. For Venezia Giulia the Second World War had at last ended.

If the Yugoslavs were prepared to take such risks in their drive on Trieste, could – or should – the Western Allies have done likewise? Would it have been possible for us by a swifter or earlier move to have avoided the grave post-war dangers which resulted from the Eighth Army arriving too late to stake an undisputed claim to the city, yet in time enough to challenge the Yugoslav hold?

The answer lies in the fact that the Western Allies did not see the seizure of Trieste as a major objective throughout this final campaign, whereas the Yugoslavs did. For the British and Americans in Italy the objective was the destruction of the German armies in Italy, armies which formed the southern protection of the Reich, armies which had to be broken if the war was to be ended. This rightly dominated the thinking of the Combined Chiefs of Staff. The future of a few hundred thousand Italians in what had been in any event a long disputed fringe area of Italy and the Balkans appeared a minor issue. Only when the German armies had been clearly defeated south of the Po were the Allied military leaders prepared to switch their minds to the political advantages which Churchill had so long descried in this north east corner of the Adriatic, the gateway not only to Venezia Giulia, but to wider influence throughout the Northern Balkans. Indeed our concentration on securing a decisive victory in Italy helped Tito's advance, by tying down German reinforcements which might have been diverted to Yugoslavia.

It is possible that, when the time came, the switch of emphasis from finishing off the Germans in Italy to seizing Trieste might have been made more quickly. It was not until 24th April that Field Marshal Alexander sought his clear instructions about Trieste. It was not until 30th April, when Drapsin was already on the edge of Trieste, that they were issued. The German collapse south of the Po was more extensive than we at first realised. Our belief that they might hold the Venetian Line on the Adige proved unfounded. Had the Eighth Army been given Trieste as an objective earlier, and had been told to accept all the risk of an earlier narrow thrust across the Fruili, we might have reached Trieste one, two or even three days earlier. It would nevertheless have been a different task, for great rivers lay in our path which had to be bridged.

Moreover the question poses itself now, as then – would such risks have been merited? The Germans had demonstrated again and again in Italy their capacity for lingering, stubborn resistance. What proof was there that they would not, had they had the chance, have exacted a heavy toll in casualties on an Allied force stretched thin around the long curve of the Northern Adriatic shore? The dead New Zealanders, the burnt out vehicles of that last attack on the Piave in the early hours of 1st May were a reminder of this. The fighting in Italy, with its large numbers of tanks, its massed artillery, its fully equipped, highly organised formations on both sides was a different dimension – if no more deadly to the individuals concerned – from the battles in the mountains of Croatia and Slovenia.

More was at stake for the Western Allies had such a decision proved wrong. A mistake in Italy could have had momentous consequences. In particular Western commanders had to ask themselves whether, with the war nearly won, they were right to increase the risks on the lives of their troops for what seemed a marginal point on the post-war maps. For the Yugoslavs the capture of Trieste, the rounding out of their frontier up to the Isonzo, was an understandable and legitimate aim, to be accorded a high priority. For the Western Allies Trieste gained this priority only when the battle in Italy was decisively over. Only when the main job was done in Italy, and only then, did it seem proper to set Trieste as a goal – a goal which was indeed to be reached by the Eighth Army in the time it did only because hazard had placed on the road to Trieste, in the New Zealand Division, one of the few formations in Italy with training and the impetus to cover the ground swiftly.

These things, however, were not uppermost in our minds on that night of 3rd May, 1945, as we moved our trucks into the grounds of Miramare castle. What mattered then was that at last the end of the war had come. There, with the Adriatic lashing the rocks below us, we picked up on our radio the news that the German forces in Italy had surrendered unconditionally. The Italian campaign was over. We had carried out our orders and had got to Trieste. The German rations in Miramare yielded Danish butter and fresh ham for our supper. We ate abundantly of them, and in the darkness toasted victory in Rhenish wine. For us surely the war was finished.

We had a sounder night's sleep than that which had been possible the previous night for the British Liaison Officer with the Yugoslav Fourth Army. He had been roused from his bed at one thirty on the morning of 2nd May and summoned to meet General Arso Jovanovic, Marshal Tito's Chief of Staff. The Yugoslav General made plain his anger at the sudden appearance of the 2nd New Zealand Division across the Isonzo. The British officer was told that contact had been made by the Yugoslavs with Allied forces west of Monfalcone. Two Allied officers had stated at this meeting that a strong Allied contingent was heading for Trieste – presumably a reference to General Freyberg's talk in the square at Monfalcone. Jovanovic went on, 'We have already informed you that Monfalcone and Gorizia are liberated, and that the area up to the Isonzo is occupied by our troops. I have now a directive from GHQ in Belgrade which states clearly that since our Army has reached its planned objective, the River Isonzo, and since the area east of the Isonzo is already occupied by Yugoslav troops, there is no need for

Allied troops to enter this area. The Fourth Army cannot allow your forces to cross the River Isonzo. Please inform your forces of this, and have any units who have crossed the river return at once to the west, in order to avoid any unnecessary accumulation of troops in the area'.

The use of Trieste as a port for the Allies could be settled between Marshal Tito and Field Marshal Alexander, but the Isonzo River should be regarded as the demarcation line between the Allied and the Yugoslav forces.[1]

The terms and the tones of this statement confirmed General Freyberg's estimate earlier that evening that the speed of our advance had taken the Yugoslavs by surprise. Field Marshal Alexander had indeed dealt adroitly with the task of informing Tito of his plans to move into Venezia Giulia. On Monday, 30th April he had sent the Yugoslav leader a message in which be based himself on the ambiguity of the talks they had had in Belgrade in February, in which the exact nature of the control to be exercised over Venezia Giulia after a German defeat had not been agreed. His plans, the Field Marshal told Tito, were 'similar to those we discussed at Belgrade'. His forces were now approaching Venezia Giulia, and he wished to secure Trieste and the lines of communication to Austria. 'I presume that any of your forces which may be in the area affected by my operations will come under my command, as you suggested during our recent discussions in Belgrade, and that you will issue orders to that effect.'

Field Marshal Alexander then went to the nub of the matter – the question of control of the civil administration. This, he said, would be exercised by Allied Military Government, the organisation which, under the initials AMG, had set up interim administrations in each area of Italy as the Allies advanced. But in Venezia Giulia AMG, Alexander stated, would 'function through such local authorities as are found to be in effective control in areas occupied by my troops'.

He ended by asking Tito to advise him about his military operations Venezia Giulia.[2]

This message ignored Tito's caveat at Belgrade that Alexander's writ should not run widely in Venezia Giulia, but only along the narrow areas bordering the lines of communication. At the same time Alexander had stopped short of disclosing that his instructions from the Chiefs of Staff went much further than just securing the port of Trieste and the lines of communication to Austria, and required him to secure control of the whole of Venezia Giulia.

Tito replied at once in a message permeated with confidence – the confidence of a man whose commanders were reporting to him that their tanks and their troops were on the point of entering Trieste, and that the nearest Western soldiers were some eighty miles away, on the far side of the unbridged Piave. The situation had changed appreciably since the Belgrade talks, Tito asserted. In order to liberate Yugoslavia and round up all enemy troops as quickly as possible, a new Yugoslav plan was being carried out. This would liberate Istria, Trieste, Monfalcone and the rest of the territory up to the Isonzo river, and along the line of that river up to the Austrian border.

Tito agreed that the Allies could use the ports of Trieste and Pola, and the railway lines to Austria. As to the proposal that all Yugolsav troops in the area should come under Alexander's control, the Yugoslav leader replied blandly that any of his troops operating *west* of the Isonzo – that is in Italian territory outside Venezia Giulia – would do so.

This exchange made plain that the views of the Western Allies and of the Yugoslavs were widely divergent. The British Ambassador in Belgrade, Mr Ralph Stevenson, cabled the Foreign Office at once to point out that Tito's intentions 'cut clear across' those of Field Marshal Alexander. 'The Yugoslav High Command do not want us to cross the Isonzo, and would not accept Allied Military Government east of that river. Though he may order his local commanders to avoid clashes with Allied troops Tito's declared plan of campaign makes such clashes likely.'

The Ambassador urged that we should immediately make plain to Tito that we were going to go through with our plan to occupy and rule the area, whatever Tito might think. That plan could be realistic, however, only if it were narrowed down to securing control of Trieste and the western area of Venezia Giulia, instead of aiming at control of the whole province, the bulk of which was already in Tito's hands. The Head of the Foreign Office, Sir Orme Sargent, set himself therefore to getting Alexander's task reduced to these manageable limits – and indeed to considering what we should do if we had already lost the race to Trieste.

On 30th April he sent a memorandum to the Prime Minister saying that if Alexander did not succeed in capturing Trieste before 'Tito's forces, who are sitting on the outskirts, can get it' we would face quite a different problem, that of taking the city from the Yugoslavs. 'We ought, before using force, to try to persuade Tito to evacuate it.'

This was likely to prove difficult enough. To go further and try to persuade the Russians to join with us in levering Tito's grip off the whole of Venezia Giulia was impracticable. It would be far better to authorise Field Marshal Alexander to limit himself to occupying only Trieste and the western half of the province.

Alexander himself was busy trying to get his masters to cut his task down to size. On 1st May, as the New Zealand Division began its sweep eastwards from the Piave, the Field Marshal put his views direct to Churchill. The Prime Minister had on that day sent a personal message to Alexander. It was in cordial terms, those of old friends and old comrades in arms.

'Let me know your plans about Trieste – how and when you plan to take it', the Prime Minister cabled. He had no doubt about what Allied policy should be.

> There is of course going to be a frightful row between the Italians and the Yugoslavs for these territories. I am in favour of backing up the Italians because that will split their Communist forces and will also fit in with the very friendly interest the Americans have in Italy, and which I should like also to share. . . . I doubt very much whether Tito will agree, if he got there, to your turning him out. He is claiming all sorts of territories.[5].

Alexander seized on this chance to stress the unreality of the idea of securing the whole of Venezia Giulia.

> Tito's regular forces are now fighting in Trieste and have already occupied most of Istria. I am quite certain he will not withdraw his troops if ordered to do so unless the Russians tell him to.
>
> If I am ordered by the Combined Chiefs of Staff to occupy the whole of Venezia Giulia by force if necessary, we shall certainly be committeed to a fight with the Yugoslav Army, who will have the moral backing at least of the Russians.

The Field Marshal then raised a further major factor – that of the practicality of getting British and American troops, weary after a harsh battle in Italy, and with the prospect of peace at hand, to undertake a new war against a power who was at present one of our allies. Before we committed ourselves to a policy of securing Venezia Giulia by force, Alexander wrote,

> I think it is as well to consider the feelings of our own troops in this matter. They have a profound admiration for Tito's Partisan

Army and a great sympathy for them in their struggle for freedom. We must be very careful therefore before we ask them to turn away from the common enemy and fight an ally.

He concluded with a hint that such an action might also prove unpopular within Britain, though he worded this point with great care. 'Of course I would not presume to gauge the reaction of our people at home whom you know so well.'[6]

Events in the field were in fact already making clear that any question of the Western Allies asserting control over the whole of Venezia Giulia was out of the question.

Indeed it began to look highly unlikely that we would be able to establish a grasp even on Trieste and the lines of communication to Austria. We might find ourselves having either to bargain or to force our way into these areas, which seemed to be falling rapidly and completely into the hands of Tito. By the evening of Tuesday, 1st May, despite the speed of the New Zealand thrust eastwards, our troops were still some ten miles west of the outskirts of Trieste, halted on the edge of Monfalcone, whilst inside Trieste the Yugoslav Fourth Army was established in strength. The bulk of the city was in their hands, and they had the remaining enemy strongholds under siege. It looked as if the race for Trieste had been lost.

That was certainly the deduction drawn by Sir Orme Sargent. The next day he had a memorandum on the Prime Minister's desk, setting out, as a good adviser should, the harsh facts, as he saw them, and the even harsher options they opened up. 'Having lost the race for Trieste, we must make the best compromise we can.' That was not going to be easy. 'The only bargaining counter we could have in any negotiations to get Tito out of Trieste was that the Americans were in occupation of a large part of the Russian zone of Germany.'

Winston Churchill himself seemed to share this view. Not only were the despatches from Italy indicating that Tito had got to Trieste first, but the Prime Minister had now in front of him President Truman's cable that he wished 'to avoid having American forces used to fight Yugoslavs or being used in combat in the Balkan area'.

Without firm American backing, a tough line towards Tito had no hope of success. Churchill's reply to Alexander was, as a consequence, restrained, and avoided any discussion about getting Tito out of the area. He confined himself to endorsing the instructions which had been issued to the Field Marshal by the Chiefs of Staff that, since the 'dangers of a clash between your forces and those of Marshal Tito are very real' he was to 'avoid hostilities with the Yugoslav forces at all costs, except in self-defence'.

The Prime Minister stressed that

should unco-operative contact be made, no violence should occur, except in self-defence. There should be a pause and a halt. The matter can only be settled by the three major Governments. If obstructed, you should parley and report to the Combined Chiefs of Staff. A quarrel with the Yugoslavs would be a matter for the Peace Table, not for the field.

The tone of this message was that of a man seeking to save at the negotiating table what he believed had already been lost in the field. It was not that of a leader who believed that he had the bargaining counter of a foothold in Trieste.

Yet within a further twelve hours that counter was in fact to be in the Allied hands. For it was the Yugoslavs and not the Foreign Office in London, nor the staff at Mediterranean headquarters at Caserta, who had read the situation correctly. The anger and concern which lead General Jovanovic to summon the British Liaison Officer in the middle of the night of 1st/2nd May sprang from a knowledge that not only had the 2nd New Zealand Division appeared at Monfalcone out of the blue, but that we were still in time, if we pressed hard, to secure the surrender of the main German forces in Trieste.

The Yugoslav message handed over at 1.30 in the early morning of Wednesday, 2nd May, was a bid to get us to halt at least until the Yugoslavs had overcome the enemy in the Castle, the Law Courts, at Villa Opicina, and their other strongholds. But it was a bid that failed.

Before the message had been read in Caserta or London or in the British Embassy in Belgrade, the 9th New Zealand Brigade was on its way along the twin roads to Trieste, with the Sherman tanks well to the fore, to stake a very real claim to the city.

By mid-afternoon the diplomatic situation had been transformed by the military fact that we were in Trieste, in force, and that it was to us that the bulk of the German garrison had surrendered. At the last moment we had, as Churchill was later to comment, 'got a foot in the door'.

Inside Trieste on 3rd May we woke to find that, if war had gone, it had left behind a very strange type of peace. Within a few hours incident after incident was being reported from Trieste which showed that we were up against a situation containing the seeds of widespread trouble. The fighting at Opicina was the most serious of these, but there were many others. At one stride we were in amongst the whole tangled, troublesome situation of the present and future of Venezia Giulia.

That first night, 2nd/3rd May, General Freyberg had appointed Brigadier Gentry as commander of all British troops in Trieste. Gentry from his headquarters in the Grande Albergo on the waterfront had garrisoned the main strongpoints in the city, including the castle. He contacted the Yugoslavs, told them of his plans, and found that they had set up their own headquarters and their own civil administration in the Piazza del Unita, just around the corner from the Grande Albergo. On the morning of 3rd May, when I drove in by jeep, the streets were empty of all but occasional civilians and the troops of the two armies, already eyeing each other warily. There was little traffic. Occasionally another jeep or an army truck or a yellowish ochre-coloured motor-cycle with a partisan rider and a partisan officer in the sidecar would go through.

The Yugoslavs had, I found, set up as the head of their local administration General Josip Cerni, with General Kveder, an ex-officer of the International Brigade, and now one of Tito's senior commanders, as military commander of the area. Posters on the walls carried their first orders. There was to be a curfew between three in the afternoon and ten the next morning. All civilian vehicles had to be declared within five days and could move only with special permits. The clocks were put back one hour to conform to Yugoslav time. All arms had to be surrendered. Employees of all public concerns such as gas, electricity and tramways were to report for work at once. Widespread arrests began.

This led to a flood of delegations through the doors of the Grande Albergo. Frantic Italian business men wanted to get protection for their property. The Bishop of Trieste was concerned about the extent of the arrests. Italians who had belonged to the Italian Committee of National Liberation protested that not only were ex-Fascists being run in by the Yugoslavs and marched away into the interior, but that also anti-Fascist Italians who were opposed to the city going to Yugoslavia were being held. Over the whole city fear spread like a miasma.

With this highly inflammable situation, diplomatic and not military in character, Freyberg had now to deal. We had been joined by a diplomatic adviser on Yugoslavia, and by a Scots Guards officer, Colonel Clarke, who had been a liaison officer with the Yugoslav National Army. A number of critical decisions had to be taken at once. The first con-

cerned the civil administration. Were we to accept the Yugoslav administration which was already functioning, or were we to advise Caserta
that Allied Military Government be installed here as in the other areas
we had liberated? The Yugoslav civilian administration was clearly in
being – though we did not realise how slight was the margin of time
by which it had taken office on the evening of 2nd May. Freyberg
decided that it was better to allow it to function until further orders
reached us from Caserta. When a delegation from the Italian CLN
leaders came to the Grande Albergo that evening, seeking an interview
with him, he decided not to see them. The AMG officers were told to
wait at Monfalcone, and a bus-load of Italian Carabinieri, who had
been sent forward to police Trieste, was stopped on the outskirts of the
city and hurried back to Monfalcone. We duly notified the Yugoslavs
that, without prejudicing the future discussions at a high level, we
accepted the Yugoslav civilian administration. Brigadier Gentry conveyed the message himself to the Yugoslav commander, and the matter
was affably discussed as between soldiers. The only reservation was a
statement that we could not stand by if summary arrest were carried
out or people removed from the city without trial.

By now, however, the centre of the struggle had moved from the
streets of Trieste to the Chancelleries and to the Supreme Headquarters.
Field Marshal Alexander had lost no time in pressing home the advantage he had suddenly gained by the arrival of the 2nd New Zealand
Division in Trieste. He ordered the other formations of the Eighth
Army to move forward to line the Isonzo, and at the same time sent
off on 3rd May a message to Marshal Tito. It reflected the new strength
which the British commander felt. In it Alexander agreed with Tito
that events had moved fast since their Belgrade meeting 'due to the
great victories won by the gallant soldiers of our respective armies'.

He then went on, urbanely, to inform Tito, 'you will have heard that
my New Zealand troops entered Trieste on 2nd May, and that the
German garrison, some 7000 strong, surrendered to General Freyberg's
forces.' He saw no reason why the overlapping of the operational areas
of the two armies 'should create serious difficulties, as I have confidence
in your co-operation, and the good sense of your subordinate commanders and their troops'. The Field Marshal then went on to make
plain his intention not only to use Trieste as a supply base, but to occupy
the city and set up 'there and elsewhere the necessary organisation to
ensure that the lines of communications to Austria are brought into
operation rapidly'.[1]

Though this was a tough note, Tito was in a position to negotiate

from the strength which he too possessed on the ground. But he had
weakened that position by a message he had already sent off to
Alexander, and which was to cross Alexander's cable to him. This
message reflected the shock and anger which the Yugoslav leader felt
at our sudden arrival across the Isonzo, at his realisation that at the
last moment the prize of exclusive possession of Trieste had been
snatched from him.

> This moment I have received a signal from my Fourth Army saying
> tanks and infantry units of the Allied forces under your command
> have, without any prior notice entered Trieste, Gorizia and Monfal-
> cone, cities which have been liberated by the Yugoslav Army. Since
> I do not know what was meant by this I wish you would give me
> your immediate explanation of the matter with expedience.

Alexander's reply was swift, and steely. 'I am astonished at your
apparent failure to honour the agreement we made in Belgrade.' That
agreement, the Field Marshal asserted, had provided for full control
of Trieste and of the lines of communication to Austria, and that any
Yugoslav forces in the area would come under Allied command.

> To enable you to clear the enemy from the surrounding country
> I have provided you, and am still doing so, with great quantities of
> different munitions of war, medical supplies and food. I have thus
> fully kept my promise to you and I still believe you will keep yours
> to me. So far however you have taken unilateral action by ordering
> your troops to occupy territory as far west as the Isonzo river.[2]

The best way forward, the Field Marshal suggested, was for Tito's
Chief of Staff to meet Lieutenant-General Morgan, the Allied Chief
of Staff. Meanwhile, Alexander stated adamantly, 'I have ordered my
troops to maintain their present positions in the Trieste, Monfalcone
and Gorizia areas'.
The lines for the confrontation had been drawn.

Field Marshal Alexander kept General Freyberg, now installed in his
new headquarters at Miramare Castle, advised of this serious turn of
events, and agreed that Freyberg should try to establish direct contact
on the ground with the commander of the Yugoslav Fourth Army. The
General decided to send Colonel Clarke to find General Drapsin to ask
him to come and meet General Harding, the commander of 13th Corps,

who had now set up his headquarters at Duino, just outside Monfalcone. I grabbed at this chance to go with him and see something of the Yugoslav Army.

Colonel Clarke was at first sight the typical Guardee of the romantic novelists; tall, with a tiny scrap of sandy moustache, a vivid Scots Guards flash on his shoulder, and a Military Cross ribbon alongside his Africa Star. They formed a strange group, these liaison officers who were parachuted into Tito's forces, a mixture of tall young men from the best families and the best regiments, dons, tough guys, and a few pro-Communists. The Yugoslavs must have been as puzzled by their appearance as were our own orderlies and guards when Clarke and his radio operators moved in to join us at Miramare. Yet he was, despite his languid appearance, possessed not only of efficiency but of judgement, a fact which Freyberg realised rapidly, and used to the full.

We drove now through Trieste, where the cold, cloud-shadowed streets seemed to reflect the mood of the people who hurried by. Outside the town we began to climb the steep hills to the east by winding lanes, as the main roads were still mined. Almost at once we found ourselves amid the Fourth Army troops, moving back from the city to new positions. They were, though we could not know it at the time, on their way to take part in the battle against the encircled 97th Corps, which was then striking northwards in its endeavour to break out to Ljubljana. Avidly I studied these troops which had found their way to fame, these mountain bands who had grown to a national army. They marched slowly, wearily, mile upon mile of them, in a multitudinous variety of uniforms.

Khaki battledress was predominant, but some were in German and Italian greys, greens and blues. One man wore the uniform of a captured Italian aviator. They all carried rifles or automatic weapons and wore bandoliers or cartridge belts. A surprising number of them had automatics – Tommy-guns, Stens, Birettas, Brens. Their transport, apart from a rare truck, consisted of narrow army wooden carts, with sloping sides like mangers. They were heaped with boxes of ammunition, cooking gear, bundles, old suitcases. Over some were tarpaulin covers making them look like the covered wagons of American history. The horses and oxen which hauled them strained at the heavy load. One pair of oxen were almost turning over on their hooves to get a grip. The drivers walked alongside, or led the horses. There was, too, a column of small neat mules carrying 75 mm. British mountain mortars and ammunition. At the head rode three officers, one on a troublesome horse which leapt about as our jeep passed. At a corner farther on an NCO kept looking down at his watch and shouting dramatically to his column to hurry. Then we caught up with more infantry, carrying Spandaus over their shoulders.

Over the whole column hung an air, if not of war weariness, certainly of ordinary weariness. They were all heavily laden and they marched with their grubby, unshaven faces set and silent. At every resting place bodies of men sleeping were spread out like the dead, their faces pressed against their calf-skin knapsacks, booty from the Germans. The officers on the whole were neatly dressed with Sam Brownes and German map cases.

Here and there on the way we passed groups of villagers riding on carts or waving red and white banners, and shouting and singing. The tired soldiers looked up at them without interest. In the villages the walls were already painted with black slogans *'Zivio Tito. Zivio Stalin'*. All ages were represented in these marching columns. Men with beards and grey hair, boys in their teens. Most were, however, young men in their twenties and thirties.

There were plenty, too, of the girl soldiers who figure so prominently in the photographed records of partisans. They were mostly squat peasant girls, distinguishable as we drove past the columns from the rear only by their wide hips in their battledress trousers and by their hair falling on to their shoulders. They wore the same caps with the red star on the front, carried the same arms and ammunition and packs. Only when we drew level, did we see that the face was not that of a man but of someone who might well have been a beardless, long-haired boy, who stared back with a set expression and little interest. None wore make-up of any kind. All looked utterly weary. A few rode on the wagons, but in no greater proportion than did the men.

The liaison officers who had been with the Yugoslavs agreed that the position of these women was exactly the same as that of the men. They were for a time mobilised for general service, just as were the men – for Yugoslavia's manpower was low – and they were put into the ranks to fight alongside the men. This was very hard on them, and they stood the long marches and the fighting only with difficulty. Now they were used mostly for medical and cooking work. They were usually very brave. Their position was safeguarded by a rigid puritanism which was dictated by the hard fact that there was no possibility of coping with pregnancy in a constantly moving army. If a girl became pregnant she and the man were punished with death. One French prisoner who had escaped from Austria and served with the partisans for the rest of the war was emphatic about this. 'I know women, but believe me I would not have risked making a pass at any of those girls,' was his comment.

Once we got onto the tableland behind the city we were in country made for partisan warfare, the harsh mountains of the Balkans. It was an undulating, rocky, hard countryside, with beeches and oaks alongside the roads, and dark pinewoods covering low, rocky hills. In the background rose stark, bare ranges from which the snow had just gone. On the outskirts of the village of Basovizza were the marks of the battles fought here. There were wrecked lorries, an overturned German 50-millimetre gun, and a broken-down Stuart tank. Further along was a Russian-built tank, immobilised on the grassy road edge.

We called at a divisional headquarters, in a farm house. In the yard stood Stuart tanks, and a car or two, mostly requisitioned civilian vehicles. One or two troops stood guard, and in the corner of the yard a miserable German soldier, his face as grey as his uniform, stood waiting. Waiting for what? Undoubtedly to be shot, said Clarke. They almost always shot stragglers, as they had no means of evacuating them. In a village street nearby we passed another, a fat German standing helplessly watching the traffic pass, a typical quartermaster-sergeant. He looked bewildered. I was not sure that he might not be a partisan, in captured German uniform. But our escort clinched it. 'German swine' he shouted, as we passed.

We had gathered in the escort at Divisional Headquarters – a boy who could not have been more than fifteen. He squatted on the back of the jeep, rifle in hand, delighted with this ride, to guide us through the control posts. We continued on to St Peter, passing on the way the Yugoslav Armoured Brigade. The passing consisted of our pulling rapidly off onto the verge as the column of Stuart tanks came roaring along the winding white road at thirty-five miles an hour. Here and there was a German 50 mm gun mounted on a Stuart chassis, the work of a British ordnance officer attached to the brigade. They had trucks, some buses, and civilian cars as transport. This Brigade too, though we were not to know it, was certainly bound for the final battle with the 97th Corps.

We had driven now into a lovely valley, with fruit trees, many still in blossom, thick alongside the road, and with grassy, rolling slopes running down to a river. When we stopped the car the sound of running water came clearly to our ears; in the distance we could hear a cuckoo.

St Peter was a tiny timber-milling town. The streets were full of soldiers sleeping on their packs on the pavement, or standing around. Fir branches had been built into an arch of welcome, a trifle askew where a tank had hit one support. The Army headquarters were in a neat villa in a timber-yard. A girl in blue partisan uniform, revolver on hip, stood by a truck with a tall wireless aerial. In the hall of the house we came face to face with a tall man in a well-fitting olive grey uniform, with a Sam Browne belt and leather revolver holster. He had a square, severe face and his skin was taut over his wide jaw and cheek-bones. His uniform was buttoned up tightly under his chin in the German and Russian manner. Clarke saluted and introduced me as liaison officer from the New Zealand troops in Trieste. 'This is General Jovanovic, Marshal Tito's chief of staff.'

The General saluted, shook hands, and then said in French in severe tones: 'I have a protest to make to your commander, in the name of Marshal Tito, a protest against your troops in crossing into our operational zone.' That said he led us into the sitting-room of the house. It was a room like an English country drawing-room, with chintz-covered furniture, sun coming through the windows, and only a fourteen-pointer stag's head to give an exotic note. On the table was a book, in German, on stag hunting, and a plate of sliced brown bread. We sat down. Through an interpreter Jovanovic developed his point. 'I must ask your commander to withdraw his troops at once behind the Isonzo. You are getting in the way of operations we are undertaking to the north, and in Gorizia your tanks have broken up a partisan demonstration and protected local Fascists. You are interfering, too, with our civilian administration.'

Each sentence of this he said sharply, closing his mouth tightly while the interpreter translated. But when it was finished he relaxed suddenly and said: *'Et bien, comment ça va?'* to Clarke, as if to say: 'We are officially angry but personally let us remain friends' – an attitude which was intensified by a sudden alarm outside. Three or four shots sounded in quick succession, as if from a bofors or some other quick firing cannon. General Jovanovic at once looked concerned, listened intently for more shots, and it was clear that he was no longer concentrating on the conversation. He was unmistakeably nervous and worried, and left the room with some words about telephoning. We went out into the yard, where a tall Russian officer in a dark green uniform joined us. Jovanovic reappeared. 'Only exercising, only exercising' he said with a smile. The firing had come from a tank commander trying out some captured ammunition. Everyone laughed, and we went back to our talk.

This nervousness puzzled me. It seemed out of character for men like this. I put it down to the years of strain which had worn their nerves thin, a strain no doubt the greater now that peace was so near. But there was a simpler explanation. When the Yugoslav accounts of the war were published, it was clear that St Peter was only ten miles to the north of the area into which, on that morning, the German 97th Corps was being pinned. A sudden German thrust towards the Fourth Army Headquarters was a possibility at any moment.

Arso Jovanovic was a Montenegrin, and had been Captain in the Royal Yugoslav Army when the war broke out. He had been one of a small group of officers who had secretly joined the Communist Party before the war. He had taken to the hills in Montenegro after the Axis victory in 1941, and had formed his own partisan band before linking up with Tito. Colonel Deakin, the first British liaison officer with Tito, described him a 'an obstinate, impulsive man, conscious of his military training, but as far as we could perceive, a frustrated adviser on tactical matters, transmitting Tito's orders to visiting commanders, not entrusted with decisions.'[1] Arso Jovanovic was to survive the war, but was not to know many years of peace. He was a determined Stalinist, and when Tito broke with Stalin in 1948 he was shot trying, it was stated, to escape to Bulgaria.

Back in the sitting room of the villa, General Drapsin, the Fourth Army commander, joined us. He was a small, intelligent man in his early thirties, with a cheerful, easy manner. Before the war he had been a schoolmaster, and had later served with the International Brigade in Spain. He too had only a short span of life ahead of him. He was to be assassinated in a Belgrade Street a year later. But on this day his manner was sure and confident, the manner of someone right in Tito's inner councils. He emphasised to Clarke that in his view the Allies had not captured Trieste but had merely wiped out the remaining points of resistance. He could not therefore see why we needed such a big force in the city. Though we were entitled to use the port, ourt troops should not have come east of the Isonzo. But he agreed to come and meet the Corps commander the next day. We drove back reasonably satisfied with our journey. Surely everything would be smooth from now on.

CHAPTER FIFTEEN

Confrontation

It was soon clear our hopes were misplaced. When Clarke and I got back to Miramare, we found that a message had come in from the permanent British liaison officer with the Fourth Army, containing a formal protest from Tito in much the same words as the one we had had from Jovanovic. To it, however, General Jacsic, chief of staff of the Fourth Army, had added a warning that from now on the Fourth Army would not be responsible for anything that might happen if their request was not met. This was described as 'categorical'. A demand was also made for the immediate withdrawal of all Allied liaison officers and military missions with the Yugoslavs.

The same evening the Yugoslav News Agency, Tanjug, put out a communique from the supreme headquarters of the Yugoslav Army stating:

1. Trieste and Gorizia could not be occupied by the New Zealand Division as both these towns were liberated after hard and bloody struggles by the Yugoslav Army.
2. There is also no question of any German garrison being found in these two towns, as both towns were completely cleared of enemy by our forces as far back as April 30th.
3. It is, however, true that some Allied forces have without our permission entered into the above mentioned towns, a fact which might have undesirable consequences unless the matter is promptly settled by mutual agreement.

Freyberg had not received this communique when we returned but he had the earlier signal. His reaction was immediate. The statement that the Yugoslav Fourth Army 'would not be responsible for anything that might happen' was the core of the message. It might be bluff, aimed at scaring us back from the Isonzo. Yet again it might not be. It might be a genuine threat.

The only thing possible, for the security of our own forces, was to take it seriously. Counter measures would have to be set on foot. Clarke was sent back at once to Drapsin with orders to inform him that Freyberg understood that the whole question of the garrisoning of Trieste was being discussed between Field Marshal Alexander and Marshal Tito; that we ourselves would ensure that no trouble broke out meanwhile from our side; but that we should certainly defend ourselves with great effect should the forces under his command dare to dispute our presence by force. 'We would meet force by force if necessary.'

The General then summoned a divisional conference to draw up defence plans should we be attacked. The brigadiers gathered in the red and gilt salon of Miramare, sitting on high-backed oak chairs. The troops were to be put on the alert, but we were to show restraint. 'You must keep your people well in hand,' he told the brigadiers.

I did not go back with Clarke to the mountains. After the conference I was once again at work in my truck, preparing an estimate of where this new potential enemy would strike, and with what force, if they decided to make this more than a bluff. The troops, tired, anxious for a rest and for some relaxation of duty now that the war in Italy was over, were deployed once more into defensive positions. The artillery prepared a fire plan, the reconnaissances started, and security measures were instituted on our telephones, which the signallers informed us were being tapped.

Late that night Clarke was back with his report. Drapsin had responded unhesitatingly that no threat was meant. There must be an error in translation. In a thousand years the Yugoslavs had never turned on an ally, and there was no reason why they should now. Clarke asked for a guarantee that he would not attack our troops. If he did we would resist most violently. Drapsin answered that there was no question of their ever attacking us. The blood of Yugoslavia and England had flowed in a common cause. He would certainly agree to discuss it all with General Harding the next day.

General Drapsin drove across to Monfalcone the next afternoon. If he had any doubts about our intentions, they should have been removed by what he saw en route. We deliberately displayed the very real preparations we were making should it come to fighting. By the roadside New Zealand troops, shirtless in the sunshine, dug slit trenches and piled ammunition. The gunners were out surveying their positions and digging in their 25 pounders, facing noticeably towards the Yugoslav lines. Our tanks were on guard throughout the centre of the city and at the crossroads outside. Overhead the RAF maintained a constant, low level and very noisy cabrank of fighter bombers. Offshore the minesweepers were busy clearing a way into the harbour.

It was a convincing display, and it seemed to convince Drapsin. He and General Harding talked in friendly fashion. Both agreed to do everything to avoid incidents on the spot while the talks were continuing between Tito and Alexander. Football matches and other sports events were to be arranged between the two armies. The Gorizia incident of which the Yugoslavs had complained was inquired into. Our tanks, it appears, had moved through the square at the same time as the partisans were holding a demonstration. As demonstrations were being held incessantly these days, and as the squares were usually the only places where tanks could form up in these towns, such incidents were inevitable. Exactly the same thing had happened in Monfalcone on the afternoon of our final thrust to Trieste. Our tanks had been summoned forward to deal with road blocks outside Trieste, and had swung impatiently through the demonstrators in the Monfalcone square in a way which anyone could have interpreted as a deliberate attempt to break up the meeting. The tension between the two armies, it was agreed, should be reduced wherever possible.

Had it come to a battle it would in fact have been impossible for us to have held the city of Trieste. The roads and the railway linking it to Italy were too narrow and too vulnerable. The Yugoslav partisans could have cut them at a dozen points. The city would have had to be supplied by sea, and at this stage the minefields were not yet cleared. Nor could we have dominated its streets against the mass of partisans who would have poured in from the surrounding countryside. Had the Yugoslavs attacked, we would have had to withdraw towards Monfalcone, and hold a bridgehead there on the eastern side of the Isonzo until the full weight of the Fifteenth Army Group could be brought to bear from within Italy and Austria. An attack on us in Trieste could not have been confined within the dimensions of even a major frontier incident. It would have signalled outright war between Yugoslavia and the Western Allies.

Reinforcements were brought forward to support us in the city. 56th Division moved up to the Isonzo, and the 91st United States Division took over Gorizia and Palmanova. To make clear to the Yugoslavs that they were up against the combined weight of the Western Allies, an American infantry battalion and a battalion of the Scots Guards moved up to join the New Zealanders in Trieste itself. We settled down to endure what was in fact a mutual siege between the two armies, Yugoslav and Allied, as each kept watch over the other within the narrow confines of western Venezia Giulia.

Throughout the five weeks during which the negotiations were conducted between Washington, London, Belgrade and Moscow about the future of the territory, the strain within Trieste never slackened. You only had to drive through the area to see this tension at every turn. At each crossroads, on each bridge the local Partisans and the Yugoslav troops stood in irritated silence alongside the British and American sentries. On the great cornice road which is cut into the rock above the sea between Monfalcone and Trieste, our supply trucks wound in and out of the columns of marching Tito troops, some of them Mohammedans with faces as dark as Moors. In the fields, on all the strategically important hills and slopes our troops and the Yugoslavs found themselves side by side. 'It was not unusual to find opposing weapon pits so close together that, in the event of trouble, the occupants would scarcely have needed weapons – they could have punched each other on the nose.'[1] The wonder is not that there was tension, but that there was not more of it. Apart from the political strain there were the inevitable disputes between two armies occupying the same region. This would have arisen even if it had been American, French or British troops all jammed into the one zone without a clear arrangement as to where each unit should live. We would have had hard things to say then about Yanks or Tommies or Frogs. As it was, we said them about the 'Jugs', who tried to get the best billets or occupy the best camping area.

The situation was not without comedy. At our own headquarters a mysterious party of Yugoslav officers drove in a car on three successive mornings through the front gateway of Miramare castle, raced through the grounds, and out by the back gates. Clearly they must be spies. We sent out the Defence Platoon the next morning and stopped them. What did they want? In German they explained that they came from Slovene Army headquarters. Their general wanted Miramare castle as his own headquarters, and he was keeping constant watch on it so that if we moved he could race any other unit to possession of it. It was a story so typical of any army in the world that I for one certainly believed it. We gave him and his companions a cup of strong tea, which they drank with a grimace, and parted with a promise that if we moved out they could, so far as we were concerned, have first refusal.

When I visited 13th Corps in their headquarters in Monfalcone I found the Intelligence Office grappling, partly in amusement and partly in annoyance, with a request, followed by a demand, from the local Committee of Liberation for the removal of the General's latrine. The latrine, its Elsan discreetly hidden by a screen of sacking, had been set up on the grass verge of the suburban street in which the command caravans had been parked. This, the Committee complained, 'did not fit in with the city's sanitary arrangements'. The complaint had been conveyed by a stern woman partisan.

It was an odd experience, this visit to corps headquarters just after my trip into the mountains with Colonel Clarke. The headquarters' vehicles were set up in the main square in Monfalcone, as had been done in countless other towns and villages as we moved up the Italian peninsula – indeed as ours had been in the square at Matelica. But now, with the war ended, they seemed out of place in the midst of these office buildings and houses, with the big mess tents and other caravans spreading down the side streets. The military police in their white gloves and red caps seemed suddenly over-dressed. In the mess the extravagant, unorthodox garb which in the days of battle had added a dashing, cavalier touch to these officers – men, many with wound stripes and decorations for gallantry, as daring and cheerful as any Prince Rupert in his day – now seemed affected if not effete. One officer wore a neck scarf of vivid carnation and gold; another had a coat with a white fur collar. His black hair was, by military standards very long; a great white hound lay at his feet. Their easy bantering manner, so valuable as a counter to tension in hard fighting times, now seemed out of touch with the world beyond their caravans.

The Camp Commandant was told in jesting tones about the lavatory. 'I have had a beautiful partisan girl looking for you,' said the Intelligence Officer. 'She wants an explanation from you'.

The Camp Commandant grinned The Intelligence Officer continued. 'Don't you want to know what she wants?'

'No, I'd sooner know what see looks like.'

'Very beautiful.'

'Did she have a Tommy gun and all?'

'Yes, a nice Biretta.'

Their tone was that of two men at a cafe table in Cannes, watching the passing crowds. It was friendly at heart, not patronising, but it seemed a world away from those tired, drab brown-faced girls I had watched trudging behind the bullock carts. War indeed produces strange conjunctions and strange contrasts.

The day after General Drapsin's visit I drove from Miramare into Trieste, into the scene which changed little throughout the next month. In front of Gentry's headquarters stood two New Zealand sentries, their bayonets fixed, their posture slack and yet alert. At the corner two Shermans stood facing a Yugoslav Stuart tank. Opposite, some sort of Tito headquarters had been set up in a bistro whoch proclaimed itself to be, inappropriately enough, the 'Bar Nationale'. On the pavement outside a Yugoslav platoon was parading. Some had khaki uniforms, others German grey, while one tall man in the centre wore a bluish grey. They carried their Tommy-guns and rifles slung across the body, Russian fashion, and their peaked caps with the red star in the front completed the Soviet appearance. They looked for the most part to be big, strong, somewhat sluggish, heavy-booted peasant boys.

Outside the hotel door a few civilians were gathered. One or two were white-faced, with red-rimmed eyes, and they gazed towards the doorway as if it led to the promised land. Others were just part of a normal, unconcerned Saturday afternoon crowd. The front of the hotel was marked with fresh bullet holes where the Yugoslavs had fired when a crowd had demonstrated for Italy the day before. Several hundred people had marched along the waterfront carrying an American flag, a New Zealand flag, and many Italian tricolours. They had chanted, '*Italia, Italia*'. The Yugoslav sentries had opened fire. The Italians claimed that at least five demonstrators had been killed, and ten wounded, but these reports were difficult to check, as the city morgue and hospitals were crowded with dead and wounded from the earlier fighting. Certainly little sign now remained of the event. One pretty blonde talked eagerly to the provost sentry, probably in quest for food or a lift to Italy. On the tanks the crews sat in the sun, eating their supper, while below their Benghazi burners sent up a plume of black smoke and red flame.

In the square around the corner – the Piazza del Unita – partisan sentries in khaki greatcoats, with cartridge boxes and bandoliers slung across their chests, paced to and fro, or lay at corners behind Bren guns. Along the docks things were quiet enough. Tito patrols paced in front of the wharf gates, and two sections of our own infantry, in steel helmets, and looking exceptionally purposeful and apart, moved up the other side of the street. Out to sea two mines blew up, shaking the ground as if with an earthquake and sending two great spouts of water cascading up against the sun.

In the wide, yellow-walled streets of the town – a normal enough mid-European commercial city – there were crowds in the streets again. Only a few wore the red Tito star. They waited around the paper booths till the evening paper came out, and then struggled for it to see what new decisions had been made about their fate. There was practically no traffic. Occasionally a jeep or an army truck, or an ochre-coloured motor-cycle with a partisan rider and an officer sitting in the sidecar would go past. The paper, in Italian, contained an article date-lined Paris, and bearing all the marks of being officially inspired, stating that the British admitted that the greater part of Trieste had been freed before the New Zealanders got in. There was also a new decree putting the curfew back to 1800 hours.

We drove up to the castle, groping our way in the jeep through streets of old houses as grimy as those which lay around Edinburgh castle. People stared at us curiously but unemotionally. The castle was a medieval building, restored, with crenellated ramparts and sheer walls of great blocks of stone. Beyond the portcullis the Div. Cav. cooks were preparing supper, their pressure cookers and dixies and cans of food stacked alongside an old cannon that poked out of an aperture The troops in their dark blue berets were lining up for tea.

Up on the ramparts the troop on duty watched through glasses the city below. The wharves, the great sweep of the bay, with Miramare castle white on its promontory, the hills rising sheer behind the town, were all clear in the evening sunshine. Away in the distance, by Villa Opicina, we picked out the red-and-white flags of a Slovene procession coming into the city. Immediately below us were the ruins of old Roman buildings, like the Forum in Rome. Shermans were parked on the edge of them, the crews of some talking to civilians, but of most keeping apart, to themselves. Civilians sat in the sun in a little park below. On the castle terrace here mortar bombs, packets of cartridges and stick grenades showed that the Germans had material had they chosen to fight it out. By the waterside I could see our patrols and the Yugoslavs pacing slowly up, each watching the other constantly, cautiously. It must have been as wearying to their nerves as to ours.

*   *   *

In the midst of all this we had had to deal with a further problem – the Chetniks. Opposite Gorizia on May 2nd the bulk of Mihailovic's armed forces, numbering some 9,000 troops, had arrived in our lines, pursued by the Yugoslav 9th Corps. With them were 3,000 dependents, mostly women and children. The force had retreated from Slovenia across the Isonzo opposite Gorizia, as Tito's forces advanced. On the Isonzo they faced Tito's Army, forming a localised war of their own right astride the supply lines of the troops we had put into Gorizia.

The Chetniks had first swum into our ken on the morning after we reached Monfalcone. A message had come through from a signals officer, who had been contacted by some Yugoslavs wanting to surrender. 'They aren't very clear about what they are, but they are certain that they're not on Tito's side,' he said. I told him to send them on to us.

At lunch-time an ancient green bus drove up filled with grey-bearded and moustachioed soldiers in a uniform we had not seen before, grey with eagle badges. One introduced himself as a brigadier in the Royal Yugoslav

Army. With an insistent cheerfulness he explained in French the situation along the Isonzo. They would be willing to be interned if they could keep their arms. All they wanted was a chance to use these arms in the coming war of Britain and America against Communism.

I explained to him that there wasn't going to be any war between Britain and America and Russia, but that we would accept his surrender as prisoners All arms would have to be dumped. This shocked him. He made it clear he had no authority to agree to such a step. Yet something had to be done, as 6th Brigade were reporting that there was a battle about to break out right astride 26th Battalion's line of communication, and that they had sent out an officer to arrange a truce.

I tried to persuade the Ops people that this was really their responsibility, but they were adamant. 'Prisoners. Over to the Intelligence blokes.' There was nothing for it then but for someone who spoke French – the only medium of communication we had with these envoys – to go along and see what could be done. Cursing, I started off in a jeep, with the Chetnik brigadier and his band of moustachioed guards in their charabanc behind.

We had not gone ten yards before I saw that this was going to be no picnic. The Tito demonstration in the Monfalcone square was in full swing. The crowds and the marching columns were still moving through the streets. To get my bus load of Chetniks out of town there was no alternative but to drive through these streets filled with demonstrators. I put a New Zealand private in the front seat of the bus with the driver, with his Tommy-gun slung ready, and set off. So we drove off, through the streets of Monfalcone, through the crowds of ecstatic Tito partisans, with immediately behind us a bus filled with troops wearing the emblems and uniforms the partisans hated most in the world. We went at speed, which was just as well, for all along the roads I could see people start to cheer and clap us, then stare first in curiosity, then in amazement, and finally in fury at the Chetniks. I must give the bus passengers credit for courage. They took that ride through those hostile streets without turning one of the copious hairs on their moustaches.

It was late afternoon before we got near the area which the Chetniks had occupied. Sandy Thomas of 23rd Battalion had joined me, for his battalion was to take over the party when they surrendered. We raced across the flat, uninteresting Italian countryside, with its vines and rows of trees and tiny villages, where the population cheered us ecstatically, running into the streets from their tiny houses. We were clearly the first British troops to come into this area. Then, suddenly, at a turn of the wheel we were out of Italy and into the depths of Serbia.

I had the Chetnik brigadier riding with me in the jeep as a guide, and also as some protection, should the Chetniks open fire. Suddenly he pointed to a knoll in a field set back from the roadside: '*Voilà – les Chetniks,*' he said. Under poplars on the knoll stood a group of troops. An officer was watching us through field-glasses. The rifles of the others were outlined against the evening sky At the next corner were grey-uniformed patrols standing by the roadside. The drive leading to a large villa was lined with carts such as the German Army uses, well packed, neatly parked, efficient in appearance. Now there were troops in grey uniforms everywhere. As soon as they saw the officers with us they drew themselves up with Prussian stiffness and saluted with abrupt movements, their hands held palm downwards to their caps They crowded the villages through which we drove, leaning out of windows, drawing water at the wells, strolling with girls who may have been their wives or followers, or may have been peasant girls. At the crossroads was an old truck filled with more men, then a column of carts and then, to our surprise and relief, a British armoured car. It was negotiating a road-block into the small town of Cormons.

'Are you 12th Lancers?' I asked the driver.

'No, we are from 6th Armoured Division. We've come up to take charge of these Chetnik chaps. It seems that they have moved into our area, not yours.'

Never again would I say a hard word about the way divisional boundaries were drawn. This one had clearly been drawn by a genius. He had put the Chetniks into someone else's area, had made them 6th British Armoured Division's responsibility. They could have all the bother of disarming them, shepherding them back in their thousands with their women and children and everything else. It was going to be hell of a job, anyway. The size of their force, seen on the ground in this way, had staggered both Thomas and myself. Over to 6th Armoured Division, we said with delight.

But we still had to see that the battle did not develop between the Chetniks and the partisans. We drove on into the small town of Cormons. Its streets were jammed with men in Chetnik uniforms, tall, moustachioed, abrupt. Here our brigadier brought out his general. Yes, everything was arranged. They were to draw back tomorrow morning behind a line of British troops who were this minute deploying. But perhaps we should see General Damjanovic, the Chetnik commander. He was in Mosse, the next village.

We drove on to Mosse in the fading light. Just short of the village itself a company of the Rifle Brigade was getting into position to hold a

'No Man's Land' through which the Chetniks would withdraw to-morrow, to be disarmed and interned. Farther along we passed two columns of Chetnik troops, marching in fours. I must record that they looked excellent soldiers, tall, marching with disciplined ease. They were fully equipped with automatic weapons – including some Bren guns and Spandaus. They were mostly young men, some only boys. They looked fresh, well fed, well equipped – in short like an army which has received ample help, not like a partisan band.

Mosse village was crammed to the outskirts with more Chetniks. A brass band played in the square. Wildly excited, bearded men rushed at us and tried to embrace us as we got out of the jeep. The walls were marked with black slogans in English, Italian and Serbian 'Against Germany and Communism' – 'Long live England, America and King Peter.'

Damjanovic led us into the room of a white-washed house. On a wall hung a portrait of King Peter. The General himself was a tall, pale, bespectacled man. It was later that I learnt he was classed by the Tito forces as a war criminal. His wife, short, with greying hair, and a group of others joined us. Some were tall young officers, confident and jubilant. Some were civilians, with the hard, shrewd faces of men who had been – as indeed they had – bankers, politicians and diplomats and newspaper editors in the old Belgrade. The General showed us his map. He had retreated over the river three days ago, through a bridgehead he had had across the Isonzo. Now his men, here, here and here faced the Tito men. He had given a promise that his troops would not fight tonight, and tomorrow they would withdraw. An officer from the British forces in Gorizia had been over that afternoon, and spoken with him. Now the officer had gone back to ask the Tito forces to keep the truce tonight too.

Where was Mihailovic, I asked him? Still in the mountains, he said, in Serbia.

'We want only one thing – that you let us fight on your side against Communism,' he said. 'We want only to fight the Russians.'

'But we are not going to fight the Russians. They are our Allies.' The whole room was full of heads that shook sceptically, jeeringly. 'You will see, you will see,' they said.

Many of the men had hair falling on their shoulders like women and flowing beards. 'They swore not to shave or cut their hair until King Peter is back in Belgrade,' the General explained. A newcomer came in, with even longer hair than most. He must have been a straggler whom they had given up for lost, for the other men rushed towards him kissing him, full on the lips. Outside the upper windows of the village houses

were crowded with men roaring some lusty chorus with the full strength
of their voices. There were few villagers to be seen. It was not surprising.
When the Field Security officers came to arrange the final surrender
the next day, they found that in this village at least two Garibaldi
partisans had been killed, and others locked up. And that in their own
country.

The next day I found that the officer who had visited Mosse that
afternoon from 26th Battalion had been my own brother. The Battalion
had been sent up that morning from Route 14 to occupy Gorizia, at
the same time as 9th Brigade continued the advance on Trieste. In
Gorizia the fighting for the town had only just ended. Wounded and
dead lay in the streets, the houses were bristling with Partisan machine
guns, and the Chetniks could be seen in the hills a few hundred yards
away on the western side of the Isonzo. The partisans brought in two
young Chetniks whom they had captured, and whom they intended to
shoot. My brother persuaded the partisans to hand them over, but it
became clear that the battle was not over. The partisans were gathering
for a new assault, and the towns-people suddenly disappeared from the
streets to take shelter in their homes. Ken decided to contact the Chetniks
and try to arrange a truce. So he took the two Chetniks in his jeep, to
act as his passport to their lines, and with one other New Zealand jeep
as escort set out through the deserted streets on the edge of the town
and into the hills. They were soon aware that weapons were trained on
them from the hillsides, but the Chetnik uniforms of the youths provided
protection.

In the village of Lucenico they found the Chetniks preparing new
frontline positions. The brigadier in command agreed, after a lot of
arguing, that he would accept an overnight truce if the Yugoslav partisans
did the same. Ken then went on to Mosse, and saw General Damjanovic, who confirmed this agreement.

This truce between the Chetniks and the Yugoslavs held, and the next
day the withdrawal of the Chetniks began. Yet Ken later that evening
found his own troops under fire from them. A column of 26th Battalion
supply vehicles moving along the Isonzo were fired on by machine gun
and rifle fire. It had all the signs of a final pocket of Germans, and in the
dusk there was no opportunity for parleying. The only thing was to
take action. Ken halted the column, told the drivers to get their rifles,
and deployed them to deal with this sudden attack which was ripping
holes in the bodywork of the trucks and in the canopy canvas. The drivers
thought this a hell of a business: 'I'm due to go home with the next
leave draft. That's why I'm a driver. I'm too bloody old to start fighting

now. To hell with all these Balkan bastards,' was their view. But they went to it readily enough, for they saw that it was the only way to clear up an ugly situation, which was getting all the more ugly as it got all the darker. It took them half an hour of fire and movement to get to the area from which the enemy fire came. Then they found themselves suddenly staring down a vineyard filled with Chetniks crouching behind a row of vines. Ken shouted on them to stop firing. This they did, crowded around, and argued that they had taken his column for Tito's men. The action had cost one driver's life. The column went on cursing the Balkans in general and the Chetniks in particular.

That was the end of these Chetniks as an armed force. They were taken gradually to the rear, disarmed, and sent to camps near Forli.

They were more fortunate than many of their fellow Home Guards in the north from both Croatia and Slovenia. As Tito's forces advanced to the Austrian border, many of these troops tried to cross into the British zone. One large force, at Bleiburg, was persuaded to surrender to the pursuing Partisans by the British commander in the area, Brigadier T. P. Scott, who already had a massive problem on his hands from the force of Cossacks who had been fighting with the Germans and who, under the Yalta Agreement, had to be handed over to the Soviet authorities. Scott persuaded the mainly Croatian force to surrender, on a firm undertaking that they would be treated by Tito as prisoners of war, and that any accused of war crimes would be tried by Allied, and not just Yugoslav tribunals.

These undertakings were not kept. The leaders were tried by the Yugoslavs alone, and many of them executed. Their troops were, it is claimed, often brutally treated, and many were executed.[1] Ten thousand Slovenian Home Guards, constituting what was called the Slovenian National Army, were at first interned by the British Army, near Klagenfurt, and then handed over to Tito. Most of these, so sources sympathetic to them claim, were machine gunned down in the Kocevje forest.[2] Other Croatian leaders were among the hard core of opponents of the Tito regime who formed part of the last group of Soviet and Yugoslav prisoners sent back behind the Iron Curtain in the forcible transfer of May 1946, under the macabre codename of 'Operation Highjump'. They were despatched on a train which, because so many prisoners in previous such transfers had attempted suicide rather than fall into Soviet hands, had a mortuary van attached to its line of carriages.

CHAPTER SIXTEEN

An Integral Part of Yugoslavia

As the days of that first long post war week wore on, it became clear that the Yugoslavs did not intend to use their immediate superiority on the ground to try to thrust us out of Trieste. Their first threatening words could now be read as part anger, part bluff. When the bluff did not work, and these threats did not produce an Allied withdrawal, Marshal Tito reverted to an attitude of pained reason. He sent off to Alexander a telegram expressing surprise that there should have been any doubts about his honouring the Belgrade Agreement. Instead, he argued, the German capitulation had produced a situation in which our advance into Austria would be unopposed. We had therefore by implication no longer any need to garrison Trieste or to station troops in Venezia Giulia to protect our lines of communication. And he expressed himself ready to meet General Morgan, Field Marshal Alexander's Chief of Staff, in Belgrade.[1]

Though the Yugoslavs had seriously damaged their cause by this early display of hostility, and of veiled threats, they were still in a position to stake a formidable claim to Trieste. For they had in their hands one very powerful instrument – control of the civil administration. Our decision, on that first evening of 2nd May, to leave them to rule the city placed them in a position to carry out a de facto merger of Trieste, Gorizia and Monfalcone into the Republic of Yugoslavia. If they could accomplish this, the peace conference would have to prise the area out of a Yugoslav state of which it had become a part. Without delay the Yugoslavs set about achieving this.

From their first evening in the city they proceeded to administer Trieste as an integral part of Yugoslavia. They followed the same technique as they had evolved during the war years for the swift establishment of their rule in regions from which they drove the Germans. This was to recognise the local underground leadership as an interim administration, until a more formal one could be established. In Trieste, of the two underground movements, one pro-Italian, one pro-Yugoslav, they turned of course to the one which stood for association with Yugoslavia.

This was the CEAIS – the Italo-Slovene Council of Liberation. Its thirteen members were summoned to the Prefecture on the night of 2nd May, and informed by General Josip Cerni, who had been appointed Military Governor of the city, that they would be recognised in a few days as the new administration. In the meantime Cerni, who was flanked by a Communist Trieste trade unionist, Franc Stoka, as Political Commissar, ruled the city under martial law. Shortly afterward Cerni was replaced by General Kveder, a Slovenian Communist of long standing who had served with the International Brigade in Spain.

The first decrees of the Military Government were posted on the walls the next morning. A translation of their Order No 1 was brought to me during the day at Miramare, written out in pencil on a sheet of rough blue paper.

'Within the city of Trieste control has been taken over by the Military Command of the City of Trieste, which proclaims martial law,' it read. 'The civilian population has permission to walk in the streets of the city from 10.00 hours to 15.00 hours.' Any Germans remaining in the territory were to surrender immediately; anyone with knowledge of the whereabouts of former enemy groups was to inform the Authorities. Five days later the CEAIS were constituted as the administrative body of the city. This was enlarged to nineteen members, and renamed the CLT – the Council of Liberation of Trieste. It had as its President, Dr Umberto Zoratti, an Italian Democrat.

On 12th May posters went up in the streets of Trieste preparing the ground for Trieste to be incorporated into Federal Yugoslavia, with the status of an autonomous city. Any other solution, the poster declared, 'is simply the open or concealed plan of those who are really Fascists'. The proclamation hailed 'autonomous Trieste inside Federal and Democratic Yugoslavia, and the Yugoslav Army which has, under the genial guidance of Marshal Tito, liberated Yugoslavia, the Littoral and Trieste, and created conditions under which all the remnants of Fascism will be destroyed'.

The next day General Kveder formally handed over the administration of the city to the CLT, at a ceremony in the Town Hall. British, American and Russian representatives were present. Kveder acknowledged in his speech that the majority of the population of Trieste were of Italian origin, but promised them 'the most ample autonomy'.

The CLT reinforced its position at a meeting four days later of a Constituent Assembly of some 1350 delegates elected at factory and shipyard meetings by trades unions and various pro-Slovene and pro-Communist organisations. The Assembly confirmed the 19 members of the CLT in office, and elected 120 members of a new City Council to support them.[2]

Similar Committees of Liberation were brought into being in Gorizia and the other towns and villages of the region. By mid-May the whole western part of Venezia Giulia, roughly up to the line proposed by Eden at Yalta, had been organised as a Region of the State of Slovenia, and placed under the Slovenian Government in Ljubljana. The Region comprised two provinces, Trieste and Gorizia, and the autonomous City of Trieste. The remainder of the Giulian Peninsula had been even more thoroughly absorbed into the Yugoslav State, though the Italianate port of Pola had been given an ostensible measure of autonomy. So swiftly had this process of absorption been carried out that something akin to political surgery was going to be necessary if any part of Venezia Giulia was to be severed from Yugoslavia.

The Liberation Council of Trieste, with a Communist as its Secretary and a Communist as its Vice-Chairman wasted no time in asserting their authority. They organised the former Partisan units into a People's Militia – the *Guardia del Popolo* – which constituted a police force some 2,500 strong. Flanked by the Yugoslav Secret Police, the OZNA, the Militia not only maintained law and order, but set in train a hunt for former Fascists – and for anyone who opposed the transfer of Trieste to Yugoslavia. The proclamation of 12th May had classified anyone who opposed the Yugoslav solution as a Fascist, which gave a further ideological backing to the suppression of any pro-Italian elements, however sincere these may have been in their anti-Fascism.

These twin objects – the crushing of Fascism and the securing of the Yugoslav grip on the city – characterise the main decrees issued by the Liberation Committee. A commission was set up to direct the main branches of the economy – a tentative step towards socialism which sent a shudder through the business community. All banks were closed. When they re-opened the most any depositor could draw out was 3,000 lire – later raised to 5,000 lire. Each bank was controlled by a commissar.

The property of the German Government and of German subjects – unless they had fought with the Partisans – and of collaborators was confiscated. All industry was listed, and though property rights were left untouched, future sales or transfers of property were forbidden. All newspapers were closed down, and the radio station was taken over. Four new daily papers were established, all to a greater or lesser degree under Communist control. These were flanked by periodicals preaching the same party line. No paper which advocated union with Italy had a chance of securing a licence to publish.

The new authorities moved equally swiftly to change the legal system. All laws 'enacted by the Nazi regime, which established radical, national and social inequality for members of the Semitic or other non-Aryan races' were abolished. The Italian Penal and Civil Codes were swept away. Six Popular Tribunals, each with three judges, were set up to try lesser offences. These Tribunals were on the Soviet pattern, with a lawyer as Chairman flanked by two laymen – or laywomen. The only requirement for the lay judges was that they should be eighteen years old, and sane.

Over the tribunals, as an Appeal Court for their decision, and as a superior court to deal with more serious crimes, a Central Court was established. It had eight lawyers on its panel of judges, as well as twenty laymen. To deal with the problem of housing, which became urgent as refugees streamed back into the city from hiding places in the country, a special Housing Court was set up.

But the most formidable instrument was the so-called People's Court. Its job was to judge Fascist crimes, to try 'persons who are stained by collaboration with Fascism and are directly or indirectly guilty of the wrong which the Fascist regime has caused to the national community'. The first list of Popular Judges included seven manual workers, five white collar workers, a fisherman, a butcher, a storekeeper, a housewife and a woman school teacher. The Tribunal sat only twice before it was disbanded after the Yugoslavs withdrew. It condemned one Slovene to death, and acquitted one Italian Fascist.

But it was not through the courts that the new regime made its strength felt. More direct action was employed for that. The pro-Italian underground forces, the CLN partisans, were rapidly disarmed. From the first hours of the entry of the Yugoslav Army any window which displayed the red, white and green Italian tricolour – unless it had a red star in the midst of the white band – was liable to be fired on. The CLN partisans had quickly removed their arm bands and hidden or surrendered their weapons. The pro-Italian CLN committee, which had established themselves in the Prefecture after their rising on 30th April, and were acting as interim rulers of the city, were ousted from the Prefecture on the evening of 2nd May by Yugoslav troops. Six of their leaders were arrested.

Though a decree of 6th May ostensibly forbade all demonstrations of national sentiment, whatever their origin, and all gatherings in streets or public places, this was inevitably one-sided. It meant that no pro-Italian claims could be publicly asserted, no Italian flags shown. But the Yugoslav flag was everywhere. The streets were placarded with pro-Tito signs. Every Yugoslav soldier in the street, every member of the *Guardia del Popolo* with a red star on his cap, was a demonstration in favour of Yugoslavia. And the fact that the city was being ruled as an autonomous area within Yugoslavia meant that any opposition to the Yugoslavs amounted virtually to treason.

It was not these administrative measures, however, which aroused, and then steadily but deeply angered the New Zealand, English and American troops on the spot, and which brought about remarkably quickly a complete turn around in opinion from the early warm recognition of the Yugoslavs as gallant fellow fighters. What bit deep was the policy of ruthless oppression of all opposition which went hand in hand with this administrative policy. This oppression was in fact as much a part of the policy of Tito's regime in the areas it liberated as was the establishment of a new machinery of government.

Yugoslavia was in the midst not only of a war of liberation, but of a civil war. Though the Government in Belgrade was still ostensibly a coalition, in which six Ministers representing the former royal government sat alongside twenty-one Ministers representing the Liberation Front, the effective power was in the hands of Tito's Communist Party. Nowhere were they more determined to assert this authority than in Trieste and the other parts of western Venezia Giulia, where opposition to their political attitude could be all the more dangerous if it was rooted in an Italian minority which could look for support across the border. They proceeded therefore to move against both types of opposition – those who might be against them because they wished the city to remain Italian, and those who might be against them because they opposed the communism which was the long-term Titoist aim.

Swiftly widespread arrests became common. The Italian Carabinieri were amongst the first to be rounded up and marched off into the interior of Yugoslavia. Our patrols reported groups of men and women being marched off night after night through the darkened, deserted streets to the railway station under Yugoslav or Partisan guard. Many of these were no doubt ex-Fascists, or those genuinely suspected of Fascism. Others may have been Slovenes being drafted for service with the Yugoslav Army. But day after day reports reached Allied headquarters of people disappearing from their homes, taken off not because of pro-Fascism, but because of pro-Italian sympathies. When the Allies took over control of the city in mid-June the names of two thousand people were notified as missing from Trieste itself. Many others were taken from Gorizia and the country districts. The Italians were later to claim that in all 6,000 people were arrested from the Trieste and

Gorizia areas. Others were deported from Pola and Fiume. Of these 1,850 were deported into Yugoslavia, of whom 1,150 never returned, and were presumed dead. Others were later released, but Bogdan Novak estimates that about 2,100 people never returned to their families. The great majority of those perished without a trial.[3]

These arrests, coupled with the seizure of property and some looting – though Trieste never suffered one tenth of the looting of many towns in Germany, and though rape and sexual crimes were slight – aroused an unmistakeable atmosphere of fear. Italian civilians hovered around our headquarters and around the billets of our troops, seeking protection, seeking lifts to Venice, seeking help, seeking food. Many of these suppliants, with their drawn pale faces and reddened eyes, were no doubt relatives or friends of former Fascists. But many were not.

These events in Venezia Giulia were far from being unique. Much of Europe in those May days was in a social turmoil. In France the Maquis continued to take vengeance on the men of Vichy. In Milan Mussolini's body, and that of his mistress, were dangling from a filling station wall. Around Bologna landlords were being attacked on their estates by peasant bands. The Yugoslavs had just emerged from one of the bloodiest wars in their history. They remembered how the Italian Fascists and the Ustachis had treated them, and they struck back hard.

Events in Trieste constituted therefore a tangled skein. Indeed at the time the Yugoslav arrests often seemed to us to follow no coherent plan, or, if they followed such a plan, to follow it inefficiently. A good proportion of Gestapo agents and Fascists of some seniority came unscathed through the Yugoslav clutches to fall into our hands later. Other people who were taken were not Fascists by any means, and some may even have been cases of mistaken identity, or were people arrested for personal or trivial reasons.

But to the troops on the ground the one thing which emerged clearly was that Yugoslavs were giving the Italians a very rough time, that one nation was riding rough shod over another. Certainly not all the people who came weeping into our camping areas to tell of husbands arrested, of fathers marched off, of sons imprisoned, were Fascists or felt they were being dealt with as Fascists. Many were, or felt themselves to be, Italians, under attack because they were Italians, because they wanted their Italianate city to remain part of Italy. Their experiences affected directly the attitude of the ordinary soldiers in the British, American and New Zealand armies, and made them in a remarkably short time antagonistic to the Yugoslavs.

'Maybe these are only Eyeties' our troops for one would argue. 'But that's no reason for the Jugs to push them around. After all the city is more Jug than Eyetie. No one can deny that.' It may have been a simplistic argument, but it struck deep.

CHAPTER SEVENTEEN

The Mutual Siege

This swift assertion of power by the Yugoslavs within Trieste was soon noted by the Western allies, and gave added urgency to General Morgan's mission to Belgrade. The General arrived in the Yugoslav capital on Monday, 7th May, and arrangements were made for him to see Marshal Tito without delay. The previous day Field Marshal Alexander had reported that the Yugoslavs were arresting prominent Italians, and sending others to labour camps. They had reinforced their troops in the province, up to the line of the Isonzo, and were now estimated to have some 60,000 men in western Venezia Giulia. They were establishing full civilian control, and any question of introducing Allied Military Government was out of the question.

This led Churchill to resume his direct contact with Alexander. He cabled him on 7th May: 'I am very much concerned about all this. Pray let me know whether any lack of authority is hampering you.' He urged Alexander to reinforce the area, as being 'most likely to maintain peace and most convenient if unpleasantness arises. Let me know what you are doing in massing forces against this Moscow tentacle of which Tito is the crook'.[1]

General Morgan had a meeting with Tito within hours of his arrival in Belgrade. Field Marshal Alexander had proposed to London and Washington that he should seek a deal which gave the Allies control of Trieste and of the lines of communication to Austria. Allied Military Government would operate in this area, but would 'make full use of any Yugoslav civil administration already set up and working satisfactorily'. But in a separate message to Churchill the Field Marshal did venture onto this ground of long term policy. He reported that Tito

now finds himself in a much stronger military position than he foresaw when I was in Belgrade and wants to cash in on it . . . Then he hoped to step into Trieste when I finally stepped out. Now he wants to be installed there, and only allow me user's rights . . . We must bear in mind that since our meeting he has been to Moscow. I believe that he will hold to our original agreement if he can be assured that when I no longer require Trieste as a base for my forces in Austria he will be allowed to incorporate it in Yugoslavia.[1]

This last sentence, from a less stalwart figure than Alexander, would have smacked of appeasement. Churchill was quick to reject it, and reject it with force. But the Field Marshal was an old friend, and the Prime Minister was careful with his phrasing :

I am very glad you got into Trieste, Gorizia and Monfalcone in time to put your foot in the door. Tito, backed by Russia, will push hard, but I do not think they will dare to attack you in your present position. Unless you can make a satisfactory working arrangement with Tito the argument must be taken up by the Governments. There is no question of your making any agreement with him about incorporating Istria, or any part of pre-war Italy, in his 'New Yugoslavia'. The destiny of this part of the world is reserved for the peace table, and you should certainly make him aware of this. In order to avoid leading Tito or the Yugoslav commanders into any temptation, it would be wise to have a solid mass of troops in this area with a great superiority of modern weapons and frequent demonstrations of the Air Force.[2]

General Morgan's remit was therefore confined to the immediate present. He was instructed to put forward a proposal for a line of demarcation – later to be called the Morgan Line – which would have given Alexander control of Trieste, Gorizia and Monfalcone, and of the territory up to and including the railway line to Villach. It was a modified version of the line put forward by Anthony Eden at Yalta, and amounted to a division of Venezia Giulia into a western segment, to be held by the Western Allies, and a much larger eastern segment to remain under Yugoslavia. British and American troops were already in much, but not all of the western area, their positions interwoven with those of the Yugoslav forces also in the region.

Tito refused on the spot. He sought no time to think over the proposition, or to consult his colleagues. He told General Morgan that the Yugoslavs had conquered this territory, and that he intended to claim it at the Peace Conference. What is more he intended to claim some areas west of the Isonzo as well. He was prepared to allow the Western Allies unrestricted use of the port of Trieste, and the railways to Austria. But he considered that he should be allowed to occupy the territory.

General Morgan tried to gain some elbow room for the Allies by probing what Tito meant by 'unrestricted use'. The Yugoslav leader was prepared to go as far as accepting a joint military command, with joint commanders of equal rank each of whom would be responsible for the troops of his own nationality. But the civilian administration, he insisted, must stay in his hands. Control of the civilian, as well as of the military power, was now the nub of the matter.

This was deadlock. Though the meeting ended 'on a friendly note with drinks all round' the Yugoslav attitude made clear that there was no hope of this soldier-to-soldier approach succeeding. Ambassador Stevenson immediately pointed out to the Foreign Office that the problem was simply one of sovereignty over the area. 'It is thus removed from the military to the political plane.' The British and American Governments were 'therefore faced with the necessity of taking a decision on whether they are ready to acquiesce an immediate and necessary assumption by Yugoslavia of sovereignty over Venezia Giulia up to the Isonzo'.

The Ambassador had no doubt of what that decision should be. He gave his estimate that Tito was not sure of Soviet support in the event of a show-down with Britain and America, and urged that we should seek a show-down. He recommended that we should send Tito what amounted to an ultimatum, informing him that we intended to assert our control over the administration of Trieste, Gorizia and Monfalcone, and over the hinterland as far as the Morgan Line. Within this area we would require Yugoslav troops to recognise our authority or get out. The American Ambassador in Belgrade, he said, was of the same mind, and was recommending this policy to the State Department. This advice Mr Stevenson reinforced the next day. 'If we let Tito get away with Trieste he would lay claim to Southern Austria, onto which his troops were now advancing, and would help the Communists in the Macedonian provinces of Greece to rebel against Athens. I do not think it too fanciful to say that the interests of future peace in South East Europe are now at stake.'

Tito was indeed weakening his claims to Venezia Giulia by overplaying his hand in Southern Austria. The Yugoslav Army, hot in pursuit of the retreating Slovenian anti-Communist forces, had moved across the border into Carinthia, even though this formed part of the British zone of Austria, and proceeded there too to try to establish an administration of their own. In Klagenfurt the Yugoslavs managed to seize the only newspaper presses, though the British got hold of the radio station. The local Yugoslav Commander announced that 'Free Carinthia' had been established, under his control. This caused Mr

Harold Macmillan, the Resident Minister in the Central Mediterranean, to cable from Caserta : 'In addition to trouble over Venezia Giulia Tito is engaged in a scamper into Austria'. The Yugoslavs were very annoyed when they found the British forces had got to Klagenfurt three hours ahead of them, and, in Macmillan's words, 'started to beat up the Austrian police'.[3] No doubt in moving into Austria, and in crossing the upper Isonzo into territory which was overwhelmingly Italian, Tito felt that he was gaining bargaining counters to support his position in Trieste. But Southern Austria was in quite a different category. It was territory whose occupation had already been agreed between the Soviet Union and the West, and in seeking to slice off a piece of Southern Austria the Yugoslavs were running counter to an agreement the Russians had signed. This proved to be an unwise move.

The British Ambassador reinforced his advice by arguing that in his opinion Marshal Tito was 'not sure of Soviet support on Trieste, particularly in the event of a show-down with the United States'. The same view came from Field Marshal Alexander. 'Personally', he wrote to Churchill, 'I am not too sure that Tito has the full backing of Moscow, and I think he will agree to my proposals in the end'.

Neither the Ambassador nor the Field Marshal gave any hint as to the origins of this estimate. It opens up an intriguing question. Was this an instance where the British Secret Service was particularly well informed, or was this just an instinctive judgement, based on many months of dealing with Tito? I incline to this second interpretation, certainly as far as the British Ambassador in Belgrade, Mr Ralph Stevenson (in due course, Sir Ralph Stevenson) was concerned.

Certainly the despatches which Ralph Stevenson sent from Belgrade during the Trieste crisis are models of diplomatic advice – clear, reasoned, and courageous, now advising firmness, now advising caution. He was a man well shaped by experience for the task. Like Anthony Eden, he had served in the trenches in the First World War, in the Rifle Brigade, starting as a nineteen year old subaltern in 1914. He had a good deal of direct dealing with the Communists, and with a Communist dominated Government, when he served as British Charge d'Affaires to the Spanish Republican Government in Barcelona in the closing stages of the Spanish Civil War. From 1943 onwards he had been accredited to the Yugoslav Government in exile, and had returned to Belgrade, as Ambassador to Tito's Government, once the city was liberated in 1944.

The reports of this deadlock in Belgrade, and of the harsh options which it posed, coincided with the final German surrender and the formal ending of the war in Europe. The messages from Belgrade and Caserta reached Winston Churchill on 9th May, within hours after hostilities against Germany had ceased at midnight the night before. He studied them in Downing Street against a background of cheering, rejoicing crowds, on the day on which he sent off messages of greetings and thanks to Truman and Stalin for the achievement of their common purpose, greetings none the less sincere for the realisation of these new problems to come.

When the Prime Minister came to deliver his Victory broadcast, he added to his thankfulness a note of caution. 'On the continent of Europe we have yet to make sure that the simple and honourable purposes for which we have entered the war are not brushed aside or overlooked in the months following our success, and that the words 'freedom, democracy and liberation' are not distorted from their true meaning as we have understood them.'

Yet the options were harsh indeed. Orme Sargent pointed out that we had either to authorise Alexander to make the best deal he could with Tito, even if this meant militarily our using the railways from Venice through Udine to supply our forces in Austria, and politically our having allowed Tito to secure, in advance of the Peace Conference, control of the whole of Venezia Giulia, or we had to face the need to use force against the Yugoslavs. 'If we use force to push Tito out this will constitute a direct challenge to the Russians. . . . If we want to force Tito from his present positions, it is essential that we should carry the Americans with us, not only politically, but militarily.'[4]

But could the British carry the Americans with them? This problem the Prime Minister pondered over – and hesitated over. He knew that only the threat of force, based upon a readiness to use force, would shift Tito. This was the only way ahead. Yet across it lay the barrier of the words of the President's telegram of 30th April : 'I wish to avoid having American forces used to fight Yugoslavs or being used in combat in the Balkan area.' This was a virtual veto on any threat of military force against Tito.

Winston Churchill had at that time only a cursory acquaintainceship with Harry Truman He had no knowledge of how bold, or how cautious the new President was likely to be. But he did know the magnitude of the problems queuing up on the desk of the newcomer to the White House. Foremost was the huge preoccupation of the war against Japan. This was moving towards the moment when a landing must be attempted on the Japanese mainlands, a landing which would result in hundreds of thousands of American casualties. Russian help in the

Far East could shorten that war, and save some of these lives. The atom bomb was as yet untested. There was no certainty that it could be available in time to avoid the carnage of these further battles, no knowledge of the extent of its destructiveness. The war against Japan could still be a long war.

To urge President Truman at this moment, when the relief over the ending of the European war was sweeping the Allied countries, to contemplate the risk of a new war with two of those Allies, Yugoslavia and Russia, could well meet an immediate rebuff. Churchill knew that there were plenty of advisers in the State Department and in the White House ready to argue that, on matters in the Balkans, the British Prime Minister was inclined to be trigger-happy. A premature move could merely harden the American attitude against a strong line in Trieste.

Winston Churchill therefore bided his time, dangerously short though he knew that time to be. The most he agreed to at this stage was that Field Marshal Alexander be ordered to draw up an appreciation of the forces he would need if it came to a military showdown around Trieste and Gorizia. But in his messages to the White House the Prime Minister did not broach the question of whether such a show-down should be precipitated. Wednesday, 9th May and Thursday, 10th May went by without him making any move. And when he came to cable Truman on 11th May, the most Winston Churchill thought wise to suggest was an early Three Power meeting with the Russians. No word of early action in Trieste, or indeed of any action at all in Trieste, found expression in this message. Even to this proposal Truman's reply was wary. The meeting was a good idea, but he suggested that Stalin be induced to call it, and that Truman and Churchill should go to it separately, so as to avoid any suspicion of ganging up.

At one point the Prime Minister toyed with the idea of a personal message to Tito which would be part warning, part evocation of the days when Britain had come to the help of the partisans. He cabled a possible draft for Field Marshal Alexander's comments. It began toughly, telling Tito that Alexander had been instructed 'to make a heavy concentration of all arms upon the British front facing your men in Venezia Giulia' and adding 'it would be a great mistake I am sure for you to make an attack on him. In such circumstances he has already the fullest authority to reply'. The tone then changed.

As I gave you all support at our disposal in the days of your weakness and tribulation, I greatly hope that you will not try to anticipate the decision of the Great Powers at the Peace Conference by violent action, for which we are nonetheless fully prepared both in willpower and in arms.[5]

It was eloquent prose, but it was not an ultimatum, and had it been sent it might merely have underlined the weakness of our stance so long as Truman's attitude was unsure. Alexander advised against the idea.

The Prime Minister therefore determined upon a more fundamental approach. He decided to set out to the President his deep forebodings about the whole future of relations with the Soviet Union in Europe, forebodings aroused not merely by events in Trieste, but by the Soviet disregard of the Yalta undertakings about Poland, and about their growing intransigence along the whole line from the Baltic to the Mediterranean. He settled down to draft what has come to be called the Iron Curtain Telegram, that five paragraph message of which Churchill was later to write 'of all the public documents I have written on this issue I would rather be judged by this'.[6] The message contained no new proposals, other than the Three Power meeting 'to come to an understanding with Russia, or to see where we are with her, before we weaken our armies mortally or retire to their zones of occupation'. Its force lay in its analysis of the Russian position.

An iron curtain is drawn down on their front. We do not know what is going on behind. There seems little doubt that the whole of the regions east of the line Lubeck-Trieste-Corfu will soon be completely in their hands. To this must be added the further enormous area conquered by the American armies between Eisenach and the Elbe which will, I suppose, in a few weeks be occupied, when the Americans retreat, by the Russian power. All kinds of arrangements will have to be made by General Eisenhower to prevent another immense flight of the German population westward as this enormous Muscovite advance into the centre of Europe takes place. And then the curtain will descend again to a very large extent, if not entirely. Thus a broad band of many hundreds of miles of Russian-occupied territory will isolate us from Poland.

This sombre assessment went off to Washington on Friday 12th May, as Churchill prepared to travel to Chequers for the first week-end of peace in Europe for over five and a half years. In Trieste the proclamations were going up declaring the city to be an autonomous territory within the Republic of Yugoslavia. Along every major road, at each key point the two armies, British and Yugoslav, both khaki-clad, both carrying for the most part the same weapons, watched each other, shadowed each other, drew up their plans against each other, the embodiment of this confrontation going on in the political stratosphere above them.

One man's decision was suddenly to change this deadlock. At the very moment that Winston Churchill's Iron Curtain Telegram was on its way to Washington, another message, marked 'Priority: Personal and Top Secret. Number 34 to the Prime Minister, from the President' was on its way to London. Typed out on a machine with a stiff, un-attractive typeface, bound now within neat, sky blue covering of the Public Records Office volumes, it stands in the files today, much less important in appearance than the bulk of the top-level papers of the period. It has been formally and none too clearly marked with a rubber stamp 'PRIME MINISTER'S PERSONAL TELEGRAM'. But its contents are formidable.

It made clear that President Truman had decided to stand up to Tito and tell him to withdraw from Trieste and the other areas which Field Marshal Alexander had demanded. Balkans or no Balkans, Harry S. Truman had had enough of being pushed around, and he determined to act. A fortnight before, when Mr Molotov had called on him on way to San Francisco, the President had demanded that the Russians honour their agreements about Poland.

'I have never been talked to in my life like that,' Molotov had said.

'Carry out your agreements, and you won't get talked to like that,' had been Truman's response.[7]

Now he was prepared to use even tougher words to Marshal Tito, and use them in a context which implied that they might well be backed up by the use of force.

On Friday 11th May the President summoned the Chiefs of Staff and the heads of the State Department to the White House to discuss Trieste. After listening to these advisers the President made the first of those firm, clear, swift interventions into foreign policy which were to charac-terise his presidency. Tito was to be told to hand over control of Trieste and its immediate hinterland to Alexander immediately. This decision was embodied in Truman's telegram to Churchill – telegram No 34 in the series of their interchange of views. It is a cardinal document both in the President's personal development, in the evolution of American foreign policy, and in the history of the Trieste conflict, and merits quoting at length:

Since sending you my telegram of 30th April I have become

increasingly concerned over the implication of Tito's actions in Venezia Giulia. You are no doubt receiving the same reports which indicate that he has no intention of abandoning the territory or of permitting a peaceful solution of this century old problem as part of a general Pacific post-war settlement. I have come to the conclusion that we must decide now whether we should uphold the fundamental principles of territorial settlement by orderly process against force, intimidation or blackmail. It seems that Tito has an identical claim ready for South Austria, in Carinthia and Styria and may have similar designs on parts of Hungary and Greece if his methods in Venezia Giulia succeed. Although the stability of Italy and the future orientation of that country with respect to Russia may well be at stake the present issue, as I see it, is not a question of taking sides in a dispute between Italy and Yugoslavia or of becoming involved in internal Balkan politics. The problem is essentially one of deciding whether our two countries are going to permit our Allies to engage in uncontrolled land grabbing or tactics which are all too reminiscent of those of Hitler and Japan. Yugoslav occupation of Trieste, the key to that area and a vital outlet for large areas of Central Europe, would, as I know you will agree, have more far-reaching consequences than the immediate territory involved. In these circumstances I believe the minimum we should insist upon is that Field Marshal Alexander should obtain complete and exclusive control of Trieste and Pola, the line of communication through Gorizia and Monfalcone, and an area sufficiently to the east of this line to permit proper administrative control. The line suggested by Alexander at Allied Force Headquarters in March extended to include Pola would, I believe, be adequate. Tito seems unsure of himself and might not put up more than a show of resistance, although we should be prepared to consider if necessary further steps to effect his withdrawal. I note that Alexander, who has lost patience with Tito's latest moves, is prepared to go ahead if we agree.

The President concluded by proposing that both Britain and the United States should inform the Yugoslav Government that they expected it immediately to agree to control by Alexander of a region which must include Trieste, Gorizia, Monfalcone and Pola. Yugoslav forces should be instructed to co-operate in establishing Allied Military Government in the area. An immediate reply was required. At the same time Stalin would be informed of this move.[8]

This was indeed a decisive step. The President's telegram was not only to commit the Americans to securing Trieste, but was to form the first step in the policy of resisting further Soviet expansion in this period which was to earn the name of the Cold War. It was wrong to describe it as the beginning of that War. If a starting point has to be put onto what was a complex and remorseless historical process, it must surely be the arrest by the Russians of the non-Communist Polish Underground leaders on 28th March, leaders whom they had induced to go to Moscow under a written guarantee of their safety. But 11th May marks a great watershed in American thinking, when the softer line of the ailing President Roosevelt was changed into the hardened approach of Harry S. Truman. On that day the new President discovered, and revealed, his stature on the world stage.

Winston Churchill's relief, indeed his delight at the contents of Telegram No 34, was great and immediate. He had had a hint from the British Embassy in Washington that American policy on Trieste was hardening,[9] but the Washington message had been offset by one from Caserta, where the American Deputy Commander, General McNainy, had informed Field Marshal Alexander that he had categorical orders from Washington that no American trops were to be involved in the Yugoslav affair. This message therefore must have exceeded Churchill's wildest hopes.

He cabled back to Truman immediately : 'I agree with every word you say, and will work with all my strength along the lines you propose'. He hastened to pass the news onto Alexander. 'You will have seen the most robust and encouraging telegram I have just received from the President about Tito.' He assured Alexander that he could count on using all the eighteen divisions under his command and concluded 'you must indeed rejoice at the prospects of so much help being given by our great ally and by the new President. This action if pursued with firmness may well prevent a renewal of the World War.'

What had happened to make President Truman change his mind in the eleven days which had passed since his statement that he did not wish American troops to be used in combat in the Balkan area – a possibility which, if this new note to Belgrade was to have any meaning, must now be regarded as very real? One answer may lie in a sequence of events which had begun earlier in the week, on Monday 7th May, at the bridge over the Isonzo, where the highway from Trieste crosses into northern Italy. This was the bridge which the Lancers had first sighted six days earlier, at the forefront of our move to Trieste. Approaches to the bridge were guarded by patrols of both sides, British and Yugoslav.

The Yugoslav patrols were strong, and active, for they were determined to prevent anyone from Venezia Giulia travelling to Italy without a permit from the new pro-Yugoslav administration of Venezia Giulia. They were well aware that this was the main escape route for the Triestini.

On that Monday a cumbersome black vehicle, escorted by a British jeep, approached the Yugoslav cordon. It was a hearse. In the jeep was a British army chaplain, who explained that he was taking to Italy the body of a British soldier. The kit and blankets and gear of the dead man were heaped alongside the coffin. The guards waved the hearse through. Only when it was well into Italy, and out of sight of the guards, did it stop. From under the blankets emerged three men. They were leaders of the Trieste Committee of National Liberation, the pro-Italian underground organisation of the city, the regional branch of the organisation which had led the partisan struggle throughout Northern Italy. By the afternoon they were in Venice, in contact with the CLN leadership in Rome and Milan – and through them with the Italian Government which all three Allies – Russia as well as America and Britain – recognised. To their colleagues the escapers told in detail the story of the harsh and arbitrary actions of the Yugoslavs in Trieste, providing clear evidence that despite the presence of Allied troops the territory was being swiftly incorporated into Yugoslavia, and all opposition crushed.

The Trieste CLN had gone underground when the Yugoslav army entered the city in strength on 2nd May. They established secret meeting places, first in the public library, and then in the vestry of a church. When our troops reached the city that afternoon the CLN had sent a delegation to our headquarters, seeking our support and help. General Freyberg, following his decision not to intervene in an already complicated situation, refused to see them. The CLN then realised they would have to fight their own battle. They defied the Yugoslav ban and put out a manifesto calling on the Triestini to 'have faith in the future, have faith in the wisdom of the Allies'. Two days later they organised the ill-fated demonstration in the centre of the city on which Yugoslavs fired.

When this brought no intervention from the Allied troops, the CLN realised that they would have to operate clandestinely within Trieste, and to seek help from their comrades in Italy. They established a steady flow of underground pamphlets and newspapers, printed in Italy and smuggled across the Isonzo. They also set about finding a means of getting out a delegation of their leaders to put their case in Rome. The sympathetic Allied chaplain provided an answer, and within a couple of days of their crossing into Italy the three CLN leaders were being received by Government Ministers in the Italian capital.

The detailed information which the delegation brought of the Yugoslav actions in Trieste strengthened the hands of those within Italy who were determined that, even if Fiume and perhaps Pola were lost, Trieste should remain Italian. The historian Benedetto Croce, and the former Cabinet Minister Carlo Sforza had been campaigning in the Italian press for Trieste to remain Italian. Their voices had been echoed by virtually all the non-Communist newspapers throughout liberated Italy in the early months of 1945. But even more eloquent than the pleas of the CLN delegates from Trieste were the blunt facts of the Trieste situation. If Tito could get away with his defiance of the might of America and Britain, then the position of the Left in Italy itself would be greatly strengthened. In the north partisan bands of different political beliefs were still under arms. On 3rd May Reuter reported that every night in Milan some twenty or thirty murdered people were found by dawn patrols. In Rome there had been a street fight between Communists and students demonstrating for an Italian Trieste. Though a deadline of 13th May had been set for handing in of all partisan arms, it was clear that many would be hidden for future use.

Both the American and British Ambassadors in Rome cabled grave warnings to their governments. The despatch sent by the British Ambassador, Sir Noel Charles, on 9th May was marked as 'of particular secrecy, and should be retained by the authorised recipient and not passed on'. In it Sir Charles reported that negotiations to reconstitute the Italian Government were taking a 'baddish turn'. 'It is now known that the Allies have not set up a Military Government in Trieste. Togliatti (the Communist leader in Italy) has told Signor de Gasperi (the Christian Democrat who was Foreign Minister) that the British and the Americans do not dare stand up to the Russians.'[1]

On the strength of this the Communist leader was demanding that the Premiership and the Ministry of the Interior should be given to Signor Nenni, a left-wing Socialist who could be counted on to work closely with the Communists. Indeed Nenni was considered to be so much a fellow-traveller that he became the centre, soon after the war, of a celebrated row in the British Labour Party. In 1948 a group of Labour back-benchers sent him a telegram of support during an Italian election, much to the wrath of the official Italian Socialists, and to the fury of Ernest Bevin, the British Foreign Secretary. In May 1945 Sir Noel Charles certainly had no doubts about Nenni's attitude, nor the reasons why the Communists were backing him. It was to give a man of the far Left control of the police and the Carabinieri. Securing the Ministry of the Interior, with its grip on the police, had been a key tactic by which the Communists and their allies had won power in the various interim coalition governments which had taken over in Rumania, Hungary and Poland. If they could get it in Italy their position would be dangerously powerful.

The Italian Premier, Ivanoe Bonomi and de Gasperi, were emphatic about the dangers. On 10th May they told Sir Noel Charles that if the Allies did not insist that Allied Military Government be installed in Trieste, and the administration taken out of Yugoslav hands, the Italian Government might have to resign. Togliatti was arguing that Italy must yield over Trieste as Tito would not have set up his administration unless the British and Americans had given him their approval.

The Italian press was by now full of reports from Trieste of acts of violence on the part of the Yugoslavs. 'Arrests, executions and mass deportations are apparently being carried out,' Sir Charles reported. The object was apparently to eliminate all Italian influence and resistance in anticipation of a plebescite which 'in such circumstances could hardly fail to be favourable to the Yugoslavs. The fact that this is being done almost under the noses of Allied troops inevitably saddles us with a certain responsibility'.

It was against this background that President Truman decided to act. He saw the issue as straightforward.

> The American Government never for a moment considered that Trieste should go to Yugoslavia. That was Roosevelt's position, and it was mine. Tito was plainly determined to use force to gain his territorial objective, instead of waiting for a peace conference to settle all boundary claims. I therefore called the Chiefs of Staff and representatives of the State Department to a special conference at the White House.[2]

The President's bold stand came almost immediately under pressure from within his own Administration. 'It seems probable,' Churchill was to comment 'that a somewhat violent internal reaction at Washington followed'.[3] The Prime Minister attributed this to a combination of those who had, in isolationist vein, long argued 'Don't let us get tied up in Europe', and those who wanted to concentrate all forces on defeating Japan. It is however probable that many in the State Department were imbued with the views of the late President that 'Uncle Joe' was someone with whom the Americans could yet do a reasonable deal, that

America's role was to arbitrate between Communist Russia and the stub-bornness of Winston Churchill – who was in any event liable to be depicted as being obsessed with the Balkans, and probably hankering to restore the monarchies there.

Churchill, in his delight and relief at the decision which Truman had taken, was himself to supply these critics with ammunition. In his tele-gram giving his strong and instant support to the President, he had urged that a standstill order be given on the movements of the American armies and Air Forces from Europe, at any rate for a few weeks. This was within the logic of the situation, but it was spelled out all too plainly for some of the President's advisers. 'My suggestion of a "standstill" or "standfast" order seems to have raised this issue abruptly in the President's circle,' the Prime Minister noted.[4]

Truman cabled back to once that he preferred to await further developments before 'giving serious consideration to a continued occupa-tion of the agreed Soviet zone in Germany'. As for Yugoslavia, we should see how Tito reacted to our messages before deciding what forces to commit there. 'Unless Tito's forces should attack, it is impossible for me to involve this country in another war.'[5]

This last sentence alarmed Churchill. It looked like a return to the President's earlier position of not allowing American troops to get involved in the Balkans. Relentlessly, indeed rashly, the Prime Minister continued to thrust the hard logic of the situation onto the President. What exactly did the President mean by his sentence beginning 'Unless Tito should attack'?

> I thought from your telegram No 34 that if he were recalcitrant, we should have to push his infiltrations east of the line you have prescribed. I presume his prolonged intrusion into these regions would, if persisted in, constitute an attack. I believe myself he will give in and conform to our wishes, especially when he realises we are in deadly earnest.[6]

This brought a brisk and curt reply from the President. His words meant, he said,

> that I am unable and unwilling to involve this country in a war with the Yugoslavs unless they attack us, in which case we would be justified in using our Allied forces to throw them back to a distance that would preclude further attack on our troops.

President Truman's attitude may well have been influenced by reports from the Mediterranean Headquarters at Caserta. Into Washington had come on 12th May, the day after the President had reached his decision at the White House, Field Marshal Alexander's appreciation on the military tasks posed if we were to use force to get Tito out of Trieste. Eleven divisions would be required – four in Venezia Giulia itself, three to hold the British zone in southern Austria, into which Yugoslav troops had also infiltrated, and three to guard the Austro-Yugoslav border. He could make available only ten of these from those already under this command, and the use of many of these – the New Zealand, South African, Indian, Polish and Brazilian divisions – would have to be cleared with the Governments concerned.

But most significant of all were the Field Marshal's comments about the morale of his troops. His estimate, he said, was

> based on the assumption that my forces would display the same fighting spirit and high endeavour in battle as hitherto. In view of the announcement of VE Day and the long publicity given to Tito's operations in aid of the Allied cause I am doubtful whether in fact this would be the case. In my view both the United States and British troops would be very reluctant to engage at this stage of the war in a fresh conflict against Yugoslavia.[7]

Had this estimate reached Washington before the meeting of 11th May the President's initiative might well have been blocked at the outset. Even now Alexander's words could endanger the next stage of the policy. Churchill saw this at once, and cabled to Alexander that the wide circulation of this paragraph had done much harm.

> I hope that in the changed circumstances of the President's telegram No 34, you will find it possible to give me the assurance that the Army you command will obey your orders with its customary sense of duty and discipline.[8]

This was a powerful thrust, for implicit in it was the ex-soldier reminding the serving officer that it was part of his duty to ensure that his troops were ready to fight. The worry nagged at Churchill's mind even more when Anthony Eden reported on a talk he had had with Truman in the White House on his way back from the San Francisco conference. The Field Marshal's appreciation had come up in these discussions, and seemed to be raising doubts in the President's mind. Churchill sent off a further, stronger cable to Alexander, amounting to something close to a formal reprimand.

You will I am sure be grieved to see how much the reference to your doubts about the reluctance of your troops to do their duty when ordered by the Governments and their Commander has counted against the pursuance of a firm policy.

I supported you, as I always have, in the very strong line you took with Tito from the outset. I was angry at the rebuffs you received from him.

I was surprised that you did not welcome more ardently the all-powerful backing I have been gathering for you. . . .

At the present moment the President and the State Department are waiting to see what Tito will say. If the slightest want of confidence appears in our attitude or movements, the answer will be negative.[9]

It was a crushing rebuke to an old friend and an old colleague in arms. There could not have been a plainer indication of Winston Churchill's belief that the Allied policy, though tougher than he had dared hope, might not yet prove durable in the face of continued resistance by a Yugoslavia backed by the massive weight of the Red Army. Though the American and British notes had gone off to Tito, demanding his withdrawal from all areas to the west of the Morgan Line, it was still unclear what would happen if his answer was, for a second time, 'No'. It was with many deep anxieties that Winston Churchill called a War Cabinet for the afternoon of Sunday 12th May 'for the nearest quarter hour after we return from the Thanksgiving Service at St Pauls'. It endorsed fully the support which the Prime Minister had given to the President's initiative, but it knew that, if a further crunch came, all would again depend on how firm would prove to be the resolution of the American President.

Within Trieste the two armies continued their mutual siege. For the staff of the New Zealand Division Headquarters an air of unreality was interwoven with the continuing tension. We worked against a Ruritanian background more appropriate to a comic opera than a crisis which could at any moment become a war.

Miramare Castle was a white, wedding-cake structure on a promontory overlooking the wide sweep of the bay. It had been built by the Archduke Maximilian of Austria, and it had been his home for five brief years before he and his Archduchess Charlotte went off to their deaths as Emperor and Empress of Mexico. History must have had its tongue in its cheek when it led this New Zealand force from our remote homes in the South Pacific, to end our war in this lovely and haunted spot. The travel-worn Intelligence truck, still marked by the bullet holes where it had been hit during the break out from Minquar Quaim in the desert in 1942, was now parked under a great olive tree on the edge of the Castle terrace. Here we listened to the broadcast of Churchill's VE Day speech, and to the cheers of the crowds outside Buckingham Palace. Here we now worked on the plans for action – should the need arise – against the Yugoslavs.

Behind us was the park which Maximilian had had planted, with cedars from North Africa and cypresses from California, mingled with olive trees, poplars silvery now with foliage, date palms and magnolias, myrtle, cacti and arbutus. Sixty feet below us stretched the sea, blue, calm and shining, where jelly fish could be seen in shoals in the clear water, where the minesweepers were busy, and where innumerable small motor boats came and went, piloted by resourceful Kiwis on bathing expeditions.

Miramare has no doubt seen many strange sights, but it can have known few so strange as this 1945 occupation. Crowds of New Zealand troops, wearing old underpants or torn bathing costumes or no clothes at all, dived frim the jetty or splashed about in the waters of the little harbour from which Maximilian and his Duchess had set sail. To get to the jetty we had to move cautiously along a marked path across lawns which the Germans had sown with mines. Farther east, on the beaches where James Joyce had walked in his day, men cleaned their equipment or brewed up tea on blackened, tubular Benghazi boilers. Inside the castle the knights in armour with pennants on their lances looked down the wide marble staircase on Kiwis in grey jerseys climbing up with billies of hot water. At night the smell of frying oysters – there was usually a tin of them in every New Zealand Patriotic Fund parcel – permeated the upper floors. The cipher staff occupied the lovely nursery, with frescoes on the wall which would have delighted any children – fishes, galleons in full sail, the Italian transatlantic liner Rex (which now lay, beached, just around the bay). There was too a city scene, with trams, buses, fire engines, and a Wild West scene with Indians and cowboys. These were decorations put up for the Duke of Aosta's children, who had played here before their father went off to lose the Ethiopian Empire for Mussolini.

On the ground floor one room reproduced the quarter deck of the Archduke's frigate, the *Novera*. There was too a huge library, with marble busts of Shakespeare and Dante, and a chapel which was a copy of the Church of the Holy Sepulchre in Jerusalem. In the red and gilt

salon on the first floor we now held our planning conferences. It was
into this salon that Maximilan had come, with tear-stained face,
accompanied by his brother the Emperor Francis Joseph, to announce
that he had agreed to the Emperor's wish to go off to rule Mexico. Here
now, watched from the walls by portraits of Frederick the Great, looking
slyly over one shoulder, of Catherine the Great, portrayed as matronly
and domesticated, and of Cesare Borgia, we held the meetings at which
the past campaigns were wound up, a present conflict with Yugoslavia
prepared for, and our future role against Japan – for we were due to
be part of that war too – was studied.

There was no deterioration, but no improvement in our relationships
with Yugoslavia. The underlying political tension was intensified by the
strangeness of these troops with whom we found ourselves sharing an
area, men speaking a tongue which was not only strange but difficult
to learn, men whose attitude was difficult to estimate, let alone judge.
The Yugoslav soldiers who paced the streets, the officers who sat at bare
wooden tables in their hastily prepared headquarters were men whose
very facial expressions were often baffling, so that you could not tell
when you spoke with them whether they were puzzled or thoughtful
or sad. Moreover it was extremely difficult to speak to them. There was
hardly a soldier in the Allied armies who spoke a word of a Slav tongue,
and interpreters were rare indeed. This language barrier was immense.
It might, however, have been overcome had the Yugoslav Army and the
local Slovenes been prepared to mix, as individuals, with us. The New
Zealand soldier had become an expert at getting to know strangers, and
at picking up that smattering of a foreign tongue which makes social
contact possible. He had learnt a rough Arabic which had led him into
homes all over Egypt and Syria. In Italy he had acquired enough
Italian to get a better insight into life, high and low, then most peace-
time vistors to that country get in a lifetime. I believe he could have
done the same with the Yugoslavs had they been prepared to meet us.
Certainly as an army we had a deep respect for the Tito forces, a
respect which could have quickly grown into friendship, had it met
with any response.

But we came up against a barrage of reserve which discouraged any
individual mixing in Venezia Giulia. We and the Yugoslavs met on
the football field or at other sporting events. We got drunk together at
formal dinners. We saluted each other's officers. But when the matches
were over or the dinner done you realised that, though you might know
Yugoslavs better, you did not know any one individual Yugoslav better.
There was fraternisation but no friendship, mingling but no meeting.

The Tito troops may have had orders to avoid us except on official occasions, or they may have genuinely disliked us as intruders into what they felt was their country. The civilians were either unwilling to mingle with Western troops, and so be singled out as being pro-British or pro-American, or they disliked us too. As a result it was only towards the end of the first month of Yugoslav administration that any real contact developed at all, and then mostly in the villages and outlying areas. In Trieste itself there was never any really close association comparable to that which rapidly grew up between the Italians and the British, American and New Zealand troops.

The one group of troops who, strangely enough, did overcome the language barrier was the Maoris. Some of them had Dalmatian blood in their veins, derived from settlers from the Dalmatian coast who had emigrated to New Zealand and inter-married with Maoris. These Maoris could speak a smattering of Dalmatian dialect. The peasants and the partisans in the Iamiano area, where the Maori battalion was stationed, were delighted to find these strangers speaking a tongue at least resembling their own. The Maoris are also superb singers, as are the Slovene peasants, and music rapidly provided one more common bond between these two strange groups.

Colonel Peter Awatere, the commander of the Maori battalion, had handled the situation with common sense from the start. He was at this stage in his early thirties, possessed of a good education (he was an accountant) with a thorough knowledge of his own people and of the pakeha – the white man among whom the Maoris lot had been cast. Indeed he understood both so well that I often wondered if he did not deliberately overstress his Maori characteristics in a sardonic belief that that was what the pakeha liked, and so he would give it to them in good measure. He could smother his normal English with a rolling Maori-ised accent, and could retreat behind that screen of incomprehensibility which, for all their intermingling, still hides the true Maori from the casual pakeha.

His big, brown face, with its very white teeth and very brown eyes, his heavy yet athletic figure girded with weapons like a sheriff from a Wild West film, and his peculiar dignity and picturesqueness were all typical of his people. I learnt of his dignity first one day in the desert. Awatere was then Intelligence officer of 5th Brigade. A British liaison officer arrived to make contact. He asked for the IO's name.

'You just call me Peter,' was the reply.

The officer was not satisfied. He ought, he thought, to know the surname as well.

But Peter refused. When pressed he finally explained, with some annoyance : 'My surname is Awatere. You won't be able to pronounce that properly, I know. Now I don't mind so much hearing my own name mispronounced, but it is my father's name as well, and he's not here to defend himself. So you just stick to "Peter" '.

He was a superb fighter, like all his race. 'After all my father's generation was the first in Maori history which had not spent most of its life under arms,' he commented to me once. He knew, too, how to get the best out of his Maori 'boys'. One afternoon in January we had been training on the Lamone river at assault crossings. Brigadier Parkinson watched the Maoris go across, and then pointed to one sheer bit of bank. 'What are you going to do if your men strike a bit like that in the dark?' he queried.

The colonel's reply was imediate. 'I'll say to my boys, look here, you're the best damn infantry in this army, you get up that bank there.'

Now in this mountain village of Slovenia the Maoris had a new role to play. From fighters they had to turn diplomats. Their friendliness with the villagers had started with an incident which, foolishly handled, could have caused trouble. Awatere gave me the details of it himself, his eyes glinting with mockery at a pakeha world which got itself into such ridiculous situations.

'We had an international incident of our own yesterday,' he said. 'One of these partisans – not a Tito soldier, just one of the local boys with a cap on – said something unpleasant about one of my boys, in Italian. Called him a bastard and a few other things thinking he didn't speak Italian. Now that boy is a clever student, and he speaks first class Eyetie, so he goes up to the partisan and asks him what he meant. The partisan just gets more abusive still. So I get hold of the local partisan commander and say, now look here, we are here to fight the Tedeschi, not each other, and we don't want this sort of trouble. You tell your fellow not to do this sort of thing, and we'll forget all about it. The captain bloke was quite agreeable, but not the partisan. He says now that he's been insulted and he wants satisfaction. He wants to fight our boy. So I say to this Maori boy 'Sammy' – he used to be the padre's driver, and he's only a little fellow – "Sammy this fellow wants to fight you. What do you say?" He says : "I'll fight him." So they strip off, and we form a ring, with all the partisans, and I say to my chaps : "Now then no barracking. This is not just a fight. This is an international incident!" Then they go to it. Then the padre tells me that Sammy has been a boxer for years, and knows all about it. Anyway he beats hell out of the partisan, and after that everyone is very friendly in our village.'

Unfortunately not all the difficulties could be settled in this way. The Maoris, and a few of the outlying companies in the country districts from other battalions, made friends with the Slovenes and kept them. But for most of the troops the barrier remained, as hard and harsh as the Slovene mountains to the east. The Italians, on the other hand, came more than halfway to meet us. Desire for protection, desire for bully beef and the chance to buy a pair of army boots or an old blanket, friendliness for the troops whose arrival had prevented the city passing completely to Yugoslavs, natural friendliness (there is more than a touch of the Viennese about the Triestini) and calculated designs to influence our opinions may all have entered into this. As a result, before many days were past, our relations with the local Italians were much closer than with the Slovenes. It would have taken a soldier either of puritanical habits or rigid political discipline to resist these approaches, particularly if they were made by a Trieste blonde in a two-piece bathing suit – the daring costume of those pre-bikini days.

The British and American soldiers had by this time come to regard the Italians as full allies, not – as did the Yugoslavs – as enemies who had invaded their land, and committed terrible acts of repression only four years earlier. The New Zealander saw simply that there was an Italian majority in Trieste itself, and that there were Italians elsewhere throughout the area. He argued that the Yugoslavs had therefore no right to run the place, and his sense of justice was constantly affronted by the arbitrary arrests and the continuing atmosphere of fear. 'Many incidents of beating up and looting were reported, but our troops were not in a position to interfere as Tito's Government was administering the city,' noted the 6th New Zealand Infantry Brigade in its War Diary. It was an entry typical of many.

The Allied troops in Trieste were tired, and resented deeply this continuing tension. They disliked having to stand to arms and to be ready for incidents, or perhaps even for action. They found themselves called upon to observe greater care and to show more restraint than had ever been the case, out of the front line, during the Italian campaign. They could not even have a few drinks without the risk of getting into a row which might precipitate an international incident. Never before in the whole war had they gone on leave armed. Now they had to carry their Tommy guns or rifles to the movies or to the bathing beach. There could be no celebrations, even on VE night, for fear of trouble. These personal irritations, coupled with their resentment at seeing the Italians roughly and arbitrarily treated, gave a hard edge to their feelings against the Yugoslavs. Field Marshal Alexander's first estimate of the morale of his troops may have applied to the formations in rear areas in Italy, or in Austria. The divisions there may well have relaxed, and felt that the war was over and done with, and have taken badly to the idea of having to gird themselves for a battle against a former ally. But that was not the feeling of the New Zealanders, nor I believe of those American and British troops who were in this strange new front line of Venezia Giulia. Had they been called upon to fight they would have done so readily enough – if only to put an end to this continuing tension – and to the continuing persecution of the civilians around them. So the ordinary New Zealand soldier cursed the Yugoslavs, wrote '*Zivio Brigadier Parky*' or '*Zivio New Zealand*' derisively on the much placarded walls, and draped the statue of Diana at the entrance to Miramare with a steel helmet and a suitcase marked, 'When do we go home?'. This, it was agreed, was a hell of a way to end a war.

CHAPTER EIGHTEEN

'Reminiscent of Hitler, Mussolini and Japan'

Marshal Tito's reply to the British and American notes came on Friday, 18th May, one week after Truman's conference in the White House. It was a forthright 'No'. Tito refused to accede in any way to the Allied demands. The resolute Mr Stevenson in Belgrade did not delay either his response to the Yugoslavs, or his advice to London. 'When the Yugoslav Under-Secretary of State for Foreign Affairs handed me Marshal Tito's note,' he reported to the Foreign Office,

> I told him it seemed to me merely a repetition of Tito's counter-proposal which Field Marshal Alexander had already rejected. He confirmed this was so. I left him in no doubt that I considered Tito's reply highly unsatisfactory. I told him bluntly that His Majesty's Government and the United States Government had taken their stand on a matter of principle on which they could not and would not yield. He had nothing further to say and he was obviously acutely nervous and unhappy.[1]

In these corcumstances, the Ambassador recommended 'our rejoinder should be swift and decisive'. Tito should be told that unless he was prepared to accept in full within a given time limit the Allied proposals, Field Marshal Alexander should be instructed to occupy in force the whole region up to the Morgan Line.

In London the Prime Minister was quick to urge such action on to the Americans. He was helped by two further messages from Alexander. In one the Field Marshal revised his estimate of the morale of his troops. Their feeling against the Yugoslavs, he repeated, 'is now strong, and is getting stronger daily'. In the other he said he was no longer prepared to accept – as he had been earlier – that the Yugoslav administration in Trieste might continue to function, so long as it was answerable to him. Now Alexander wanted his own AMG – Allied Military Government. Moreover, if any Yugoslav forces remained, they too must come under his command. 'It is now certain that any solution by which we shared an area with the Yugoslav troops or Partisans or permitted Yugo-slav administration to function would not work.'²

Churchill was now fully convinced that we must be prepared to use force if necessary to assert our authority up to the Morgan Line. But how was such a policy to be reconciled with Truman's insistence, so clearly spelled out only a few days before, that he was not prepared to involve America in war with the Yugoslavs 'unless they attack us'? As soon as Tito's rejection of the Allied notes was to hand, the Prime Minister set himself to shifting the President from this rigid position. 'I hope you will not mind my putting to you with great respect the need for some further consideration of the words "a war with the Yugoslavs" and "attack us" ', he cabled.

The Prime Minister stressed that he did not envisage war with the Yugoslavs, but that immediate action was necessary 'otherwise we shall merely appear to have been bluffing and will in fact be bluffed out'. He reminded the President that Alexander had pointed out that if Tito refused either to put his troops and administration under Alexander's command, or refused to withdraw from the area, 'it will inevitably lead to armed conflict, since I must very soon insist on the proper functioning of my AMG. For example, I must remove Tito's proclamations and replace them with my own. I cannot allow my movements to be restricted by Yugoslav posts or sentries'.

The Prime Minister went on to argue that in these circumstances the line the President had drawn as to when American troops could or could not be used was too rigid.

> For instance, (Churchill argued) supposing they (the Yugoslavs) take up positions all around a British or American unit until they have it at their mercy, are we to wait till they open fire before asking them to move back beyond the lines you have indicated as desirable? I am sure this is not what you mean, but it is just the sort of incident I think may arise.
>
> In these conditions I should not consider action by Alexander to ensure the proper functioning of his military government as con-stituting 'a war with the Yugoslavs'. But I certainly think pressure should be put upon them to quit Trieste and Pola and return to the lines marked out, and that this pressure should be regarded as in the nature of frontier incidents rather than as principal diplomatic decisions. I cannot allow your own troops to be knocked about and mishandled inside the zone we both occupy on the basis that they are in no circumstances to open fire. A great many of the Yugoslavs

have been filtering back today over the Isonzo and their truculent attitude is already somewhat abated. I rest myself on your No 34.

The crunch had clearly come. But President Truman was not going to be hustled by his allies, any more than he had been deterred by the critics in Washington of his decision on 11th May. He still saw no reason why the conflict should decline into a shooting war. One key figure in this conflict had not yet shown his hand – Joseph Stalin. The Soviet leader had been kept fully informed of the British and American notes to Tito, but he had not responded. But equally he had not given any overt sign of his support for Tito.

Truman therefore decided that we might still get our way if pressure was intensified on the Yugoslav leader, though we should still move with caution. He sent off a shrewd and thoughtful reply to Churchill's request that he redefine what he meant by the Yugoslavs 'attacking first'. Tito's answer, Truman said, should be rejected as unsatisfactory, and he should be called on to reconsider his decision. At the same time we should mount a show of force in and around Venezia Giulia of such overpowering strength that 'the firmness of our intentions will be clearly apparent to the Yugoslavs'. This was to be carefully timed so that our troop movements would be evident to Tito at the moment when we presented, in Belgrade, a renewed demand that the Yugoslavs reconsider their stand.

The President had used the intervening days, whilst Tito considered the first message, to ensure that this display of force would be massive and convincing. He began, with some relish, to flex the formidable muscles of a fully mobilised United States.

> I asked General Eisenhower if he could send three divisions to the Brenner Pass, or above Trieste. I asked Admiral King whether he could send some units of the Mediterranean Fleet to the Adriatic, and how long it would take to get them there. I told him to alert the necessary ships. I asked General Arnold what air squadrons he could move, and I asked him to alert them.[3]

The response of the commanders was indeed dramatic. Eisenhower reported that he was prepared to dispatch General Patton with up to five armoured divisions to the Brenner Pass and if necessary into Italy. Admiral King reported that units of the Mediterranean Fleet had been alerted to steam into the Adriatic. General Arnold had several air force squadrons ready to move at a moment's notice. An area around Rimini was designated as an operational base. It was then, as now, the main holiday area for the industrial north and had many hotels which could be used as barracks and hospitals. In Rimini itself and in the surrounding countryside, 25,000 Italian civilians were notified that they must evacuate their homes to make way for the incoming reinforcements. On 16th May a British naval force arrived at Trieste, through a channel swept through the mine-fields. The American infantry battalion stationed in Trieste was regrouped with its parent formation near Gorizia in readiness for battle. In Belgrade British and American citizens were warned to be ready to leave and the Embassy staffs of both countries prepared for evacuation.

These military operations were, even in normal circumstances, likely to attract the attention of the Soviet observers and Soviet agents. Made as they were, with considerable openness, word of them must have been in Moscow and Belgrade within hours.

To this array of hard facts Field Marshal Alexander now added some hard words. On 19th May he issued an Order of the Day to the troops under his command intended in part to prepare them for possible battles ahead, in part as a blow in the war of nerves with Yugoslavia.

> Our policy, publicly proclaimed is that territorial changes should be made only after thorough study and after full consultation and deliberation between the various Governments concerned.
>
> It is however Marshal Tito's apparent intention to establish his claims to Venezia Giulia and territory around Villach and Kelgenfurt by force of arms and by military occupation. Action of this kind would be all too reminiscent of Hitler, Mussolini and Japan. It is to prevent such actions that we have been fighting this war . . . it is our duty to hold these territories as trustees until their ultimate disposal is settled at the Peace Conference.

Those in the inner circle of command noted that the words 'reminiscent of Hitler, Mussolini and Japan' were virtually identical with those used by the President in his message of 12th May.

This pressure President Truman now supported by a personal cable to Stalin. On Sunday, 20th May, he told the Soviet leader that Tito's reply had been entirely unsatisfactory, and that the Americans could not accept any compromise upon the principles of an orderly and just settlement, and 'are so informing Tito'. He gave a long detailed argument of the American case, one which the Russian leader could take on two levels. It was both a plea for his intervention against Tito, and a detailed justification, in advance, of any military actions on which the Western Allies might embark. Churchill sent a similar message to Stalin.

This powerful pressure worked. On 20th May, the day after Alexander had issued his proclamation to the troops, the Yugoslav Foreign Minister, Edvard Kardelj, called the British Ambassador to the Foreign Ministry in Belgrade, and announced that the Yugoslavs would make a major move towards acceptance of the Western demands. They were prepared to agree to Field Marshal Alexander having control of the region up to the Morgan Line, provided that the Yugoslav military representatives could participate in any Allied Military Government we would establish, and provided this AMG worked through the civil authorities which the Yugoslavs had already set up. At the same time Tito issued a pained rebuttal of the charges in Alexander's message to his troops. The Yugoslav leader said :

> I cannot but express my resentment and surprise at the impossible comparison that the presence of Yugoslav troops in Istria and the Slovene Littoral is similar to Hitler's, Mussolini's and Japanese methods of conquest. Such an accusation can be thrown in the face of an enemy. It cannot be thrown at a tortured Ally who has been bled white and who has until now been recognised by all freedom-loving people as an example of heroism and self-sacrifice in this great war of liberation. The Yugoslav Army expelled the enemy by the might of their arms from the area up to the River Soca (the Isonzo) and beyond, and no character of conquest can be attributed to its presence in this territory.

These too were strong public words, but the private indication by Kardelj that the Yugoslavs were prepared to accept the principle of Alexander's control of the territory was an even stronger fact – and a fact which marked a significant withdrawal by the Yugoslavs. The astute Stevenson in Belgrade at once saw this. He therefore advocated that we should begin negotiations which would enable the Yugoslavs to save face, now that they had yielded. The degree of their yielding was confirmed in Stalin's reply to Truman. After insisting that 'it would not be fair, and would be an undeserved insult for the Yugoslav Army and the Yugoslav people to refuse Yugoslavia the right to occupy the territory retaken from the enemy' Stalin went on to propose the same solution as the Yugoslav Government had already put forward – a solution tantamount to at least a partial retreat. At the same time

Pravda, on 21st May, gave the Russian public the first news of the dispute publishing both Field Marshal Alexander's note to Tito and Tito's reply.

Tito and Stalin no doubt both hoped that Yugoslavia could, under this formula, still retain de facto control through the pro-Yugoslavian administration in Trieste, even if military control was ceded to Alexander. But Anthony Eden and Churchill would have none of this. Eden advised the Prime Minister that if Tito's civil administration remained, it would seek to communise the country and prepare for its transference to Yugoslavia. 'Time is working on our side, and I do not attach any importance to saving Tito's face,' he minuted.

Field Marshal Alexander was even more adamant that his full demands must be met. All traces of his former willingness to compromise had now gone. He was not prepared to have Yugoslav officers as participants in his military Government, though he was prepared to accept a small mission as observers, and to allow a Yugoslav military detachment to serve under him. Nor would he agree to the Yugoslav civil administration continuing in any way. AMG must have power to use whatever civil authorities they wished. Alexander added, too, a new demand. The Yugoslavs must return all non-Yugoslavs whom they had arrested or deported, and restore all property they had seized. Alexander had not been impressed by reports of a parade the Yugoslavs had held in Trieste, designed to show how many Italians had fought alongside them in the city. Some 1200 pro-Yugoslav Italian partisans paraded, but all but 250 of these wore the red Garibaldi scarves which indicated that they had been brought in from across the Isonzo.

The Field Marshal's determination to have the matter settled once and for all, along the lines he wished, was almost certainly strengthened by the complete success of an astute military move he had carried out within Venezia Giulia on the day before, 22nd May. He had instructed the Allied forces in the area to move forward at a number of key points so as to improve their tactical positions, occupying commanding heights in some places, key crossroads in others, better lines of communication in yet others. This move had a triple objective. It would strengthen our position should we resort to military action – and was indeed the first stage of a planned move up to the Morgan Line; it would remind the Yugoslavs in a very practical way that we meant business; and it would test out the Yugoslav reaction, without a shot being fired. Coming at the same time as the widely observed preparations for the massive build up by General Eisenhower, Admiral King and General Arnold, it was a localised but shrewd way of increasing Allied pressure. The Field

Marshal himself went forward to Trieste to observe its execution, flanked by an impressive array of his leading generals – General Mark Clark, commander of Fifteenth Army Group; Major-General Alfred Gruenther, his Chief of Staff (who was later to command the NATO forces in Western Europe); Lieutenant-General Sir Richard McCreery, commander of the Eighth Army; Lieutenant-General John Harding, commander of 13th Corps; Lieutenant-General Geoffrey Keyes, commander of the US Second Corps, the formation which had come up to strengthen the Eighth Army.

It was a plan not without its dangers. It could have precipitated many 'frontier incidents', could indeed have led to the Yugoslavs taking the significant step of firing first. General Mark Clark, Commander of the Allied Fifteenth Army Group, who was responsible to Alexander for both Venezia Giulia and Southern Austria, decided in particular that a powerful force of American infantry and tanks should move through Gorizia and take up the higher and defensible ground to the east, regardless of the fact that this ground was already held by Yugoslav troops.

General Clark, never a man to shun the limelight, went forward himself with the foremost column. He has given his own account of what happened :

> The order for the advance was given, and a short time later I drove a jeep along the road followed by the main column in order to see how things were going. Approaching Gorizia, the road led under a railway bridge, and there the Yugoslavs had set up a road-block. . . . I motioned my driver to proceed under the bridge, where there was a gap in the road-block wide enough to allow one vehicle to pass. We buzzed past the Yugoslav guards, and the column followed us with no difficulty, although I must admit that I held my breath for several minutes for fear that some reckless guard might fire a shot. Everyone else felt the same way; nobody wanted the distinction of being the last killed in the Second World War.

The Allies had not undertaken this venture lightly. General Freyberg had advised the New Zealand Government on 20th May that the New Zealand troops were 'sitting at the point of greatest tension, and that fighting may break out. If it does, we must expect a number of casualties'. On 22nd May the New Zealand Division was given the right hand flank role, with 56th Division in the centre, and 10th Indian Division on the left. Our orders were to apprehend, disarm and evacuate through prisoner of war channels any Yugoslavs who offered resistance.

If it became necessary to 'mop up', the Yugoslav troops were to be surrounded quickly and unobtrusively, and called on to surrender, whilst the strongest possible demonstration of strength was made. Leaflets printed in Slovene, Serbo-Croat and Italian were distributed. If the Yugoslavs resisted in strength we were to employ naval and artillery bombardment, air support, tanks and other heavy weapons to achieve our object quickly and with as few casualties as possible.

It was not just a display of force but a display of very real and very ready force. It worked with hardly a hitch. The Allied forces had reached a much more effective defence line. We were still not up to the Morgan Line at all points but we had made a significant move towards it. The Allied communique spoke of the Eighth Army having completed 'a further stage in their forward concentration in Venezia Giulia' and of our having carried out a peaceful taking-over of certain positions that were part of the territory agreed for occupation by the Western Allies. Nowhere did the Yugoslavs resist – even though the day before it looked as if they were preparing to do so. On the evening of 21st May they sent a force of 25 powerful Russian-built T34 tanks – quite a match for our Shermans – into Trieste. They moved ostentatiously along the waterfront, and then split into two groups. One stayed in the city; the other disappeared into the countryside. But they were never brought into action, and a couple of days later the remaining tanks withdrew towards Opicina. In several places hard words were exchanged between the Yugoslavs and ourselves, but no fire. At the village of Comena the Yugoslav commander asked the British to withdraw, and threatened to set up road blocks behind our forward positions, but in the end both sides settled into this key communications centre without a fight. The Yugoslavs did put up some new road blocks around Trieste, but when a New Zealand Sherman tank pushed over the most troublesome of these there was no response. Indeed the only firing occurred when a Maori sentry shot up the rear tyres of a Yugoslav staff car which had refused to halt. But in the end the staff car hobbled on its way, despite its punctures, and no more was heard of the matter. Indeed three days later the Yugoslavs entertained Allied officers in Trieste to a full-scale banquet in honour of Tito's birthday, and lit up the skyline with a fireworks display.

The final Allied demands were agreed upon in Washington on 26th May. They had been delayed by a last minute argument between the military authorities in Caserta and the Governments in Washington and London about the port of Pola, to the south of Trieste. This had a largely Italian population, and had indeed not been captured from the Germans by the Yugoslavs until several days after Trieste had fallen. It was completely under Yugoslav rule, and surrounded by Slovene territory. To administer it would be difficult. To capture and hold it, if we still had to use force to secure a settlement, would be militarily difficult and expensive. As a soldier Alexander resisted any commitment here even though Italian newspapers and Italian politicians were clamouring for its return to Italy, and even though the Americans thought it should come under Allied control.

This led the Field Marshal into one more dispute with Churchill. It was a dispute conducted by the Prime Minister in surprisingly acerbic terms. No doubt he could see a settlement so near, a success so close at hand, that he was doubly irritated at this last minute snag. Churchill was also coming under great pressure from another source. The General Election campaign in Britain was about to begin, constituting a formidable strain on the energies of the Prime Minister, now in his seventieth year. He cabled to Alexander on 29th May:

> We do not seem to be looking at the situation from the same angle. I regard it as of the first importance not to back down before Tito's encroachments or to give the impression to the Balkans or to Russia that we are unable in the last resort to use force . . . President Truman evidently attached great importance to Pola, and if it were omitted the United States might lose interest in the main operations which you have now prepared.[1]

Three days later Churchill prepared an even stronger rebuke.

> Almost everything you have said (his message to the Field Marshal began) whether about the reluctance of your troops to engage the Yugoslavs or about Pola has had a very bad effect in the United States, and but for the fact that the President stands firm, would have left us in hopeless deadlock. I have not asked you at any time to take violent or unauthorized action, but I do ask you not to put obstacles in the way of concerted United States and British action'.

It was a crushing mesage, too crushing, in the event, for Churchill to despatch to his old friend. He marked it 'Hold', and it remained in his files, undespatched, until it ultimately made its way into the official archives.

The Field Marshal's attitude is, however, a reminder that a military operation remained in contemplation, and was indeed in an advanced state of preparation in case Tito continued to resist. It was the military difficulty of capturing and holding Pola, rather than any problems of administering it, which ranked high in Alexander's mind. As the negotiations wound on in Belgrade, so did the military planning on the spot. The British Scots Guard Battalion, and the Battalion from the American 363 Regiment which had come into Trieste to manifest an all-Allied presence had gone back to their parent units, to be ready for action. The 2nd United States Corps had moved up fully on the left of 13th Corps, along the Isonzo.

The negotiations dragged on into June. Then, on June 9th, just over five weeks after the fall of Trieste, Tito finally yielded. Agreement was signed in Belgrade along the lines demanded by the Allies. It covered all Venezia Giulia, not just the Trieste-Gorizia-Monfalcone area, for the Western Allies had not abandoned their claim that the future of the whole region was a matter for the peace conference. Venezia Giulia was to be divided into two zones, along the Morgan Line. Trieste, Gorizia, Monfalcone and the countryside up to and including the lines of communication to Austria became Zone A, under direct Allied Military Administration. So too did Pola. The rest of the province remained under Yugoslav military and civilian control. The Yugoslav Army would have to retreat to the east of the Morgan Line. Any Partisans would have either to go with them, or remain and be disarmed. The Yugoslavs could keep a token force of 2,000 men in Zone A, but they would be confined to one district, and under Allied command. The Allies agreed to a face saving formula under which they agreed to use the Yugoslav civilian administration if, in the view of the new Allied Military Government, it was working satisfactorily. This was, so far as areas of Italian population were concerned, virtually meaningless – and soon proved to be so. For it was followed by a further sentence empowering the Allies 'to use whatever civil authorities they deem best in any particular place, and to change administrative personnel at discretion'. AMG rapidly deemed their own administrators best in all but the purely Slovene villages and countryside.

The Yugoslavs undertook to return all residents they had arrested and deported with the exception of 'those possessing Yugoslav nationality in 1939', and to make restitution of all property confiscated or removed. Finally they recognised formally that this agreement in no way prejudiced the ultimate disposal of any part of Venezia Giulia.

So ended the struggle for Trieste, the last battleground in the Mediterranean of World War II, and the first battleground of the cold

War. It had ended in a victory for the Western Allies. Everything which Field Marshal Alexander had demanded of Marshal Tito when Trieste had fallen on 2nd May had been conceded.

CHAPTER NINETEEN

A Victory—and a Precedent

Marshall Tito took his defeat with dignity. When the Belgrade Agreement was announced he issued this statement :

> The denying of our rights (to Venezia Giulia) tempered the joy of our peoples during the first days of our great victory over the enemy. Such injustices root themselves deeply in the soul of our peoples and are forgotten with difficulty. But, loyal to the ideas of peace and aware of the burden of responsibility for the preservation and strengthening of a peace so arduously gained, the Government of Democratic Federal Yugoslavia is exerting itself, even at the cost of great sacrifices, to avoid differences and conflicts, even where right is on our side. Our country wishes to live in peace in friendly relations not only with our neighbours but with our allies in this great struggle for liberation.

On the face of it the statement was addressed primarily at the Western powers and at Italy, and seemed to be a warning that in this decision were planted the seeds of future trouble between Yugoslavia and Italy. But in the light of later events it can be seen as designed also for the eyes of the Russian leaders. For the fundamental reason why Tito had yielded after such a stubborn early stand must have been the refusal of the Russians to back him. To the Soviet Union the future of Trieste was a detail in a long and complicated pattern of relationships with the Western Allies across the breadth of Europe. The city had little strategic value. Its loss represented no dangerous dent in the new frontier between East and West. The Americans still held formidable cards – not least the fact that they occupied huge tracts of Germany which were due to come under Soviet rule. To jeopardise these for the sake of a corner of Slovenia must have seemed to Stalin a very bad bargain. His intelligence service may well have picked up word that the American atom bomb was very close to being tested. He too wanted to get his forces into the war with Japan in time to secure frontier advantages there. These must have added up to a solid list of reason why the Soviet Union should not risk backing Tito further once it was plain that

Americans meant business. And Truman had succeeded in making plain that that is what he did mean.

Yet to the Yugoslavs the decision was an injustice, and one which Tito and the Yugoslav Communists were indeed to forget with difficulty. The Soviet refusal to support them over Trieste undoubtedly rankled, and must have formed a major contribution towards their decision, three years later, to break with Stalin.

For Winston Churchill agreement in Belgrade had come just in time to remove this dangerous issue before he was plunged into the midst of the British General Election. On 23rd May the wartime Coalition had been dissolved, and a new predominantly Conservative caretaker Government had been formed. Four days after the signing of the Belgrade Agreement Parliament was dissolved and the Election campaign began. Trieste disappeared from the news pages of the British press, to reappear only in brief stories telling of the Yugoslav withdrawal and the establishment of Allied Military Government.

Not that the Trieste crisis had attracted much public attention. It is one of the quirks of history that President Truman and Winston Churchill conducted this first major confrontation with the Soviet Union with remarkably little publicity. Little if any sense of crisis reached the capitals of the West. One reason was that wartime controls over the press continued in Trieste, and wartime habits and restraint of the press continued in London and Washington. Civilian correspondents, and in particular Italian political commentators, had been kept out of the Trieste area during the five critical weeks. Other reporters worked under military censorship. Celia Sprigge, of the *Manchester Guardian*, wrote two vivid articles which, under the pooling system of wartime coverage, appeared also in *The Times*. In these she set out the issue clearly, describing the life of the Italians in Trieste as being 'life in a captured city'. But in the Slovene villages 'faith in Marshal Tito burns like a furnace'.

The newspapers had however other matters on their minds and in their headlines. The outcome of the race for Trieste was merely one item in the huge story of the end of the war in Europe. On 1st May, as we moved across the Isonzo, the news of Hitler's death reached the outside world. A week later came the final German surrender. The photographs on the news pages were of cheering crowds in the streets of London and Washington, of the ruins of Berlin, of Thanksgiving Services – and of the American Marines in terrible fighting on Okinawa. Trieste was an item which rated little close attention.

British newspaper opinion, such as it was, was largely on the side of the official British and American policy. The *Manchester Guardian*, in one of the two leaders it was to devote to Trieste during the five weeks, said on 2nd May that 'to permit Tito to seize Trieste without any pretence of justice would be both weak and dishonest'. These were brave words, but they were written at a time when it looked as if the city had already fallen completely into Yugoslav hands, and it was not clear how the policy they advocated should be implemented.

When the crisis reached its peak later in May the *Manchester Guardian's* tone changed closer to that of a nurse dealing with a troublesome child.

> In these days of emotion it is important that we at least should try to keep our tempers and our heads. There are unfortunately signs that we are losing both over Trieste. Marshal Tito's claim to take Istria and Trieste is not a matter of great importance . . . Clearly we must stick to our point (for we are right, and Tito is wrong) but let us keep a sense of proportion.

The Times offered even less advice. In a long editorial on 2nd May about the Balkans as a whole, its view was merely that British and Russian policy in the area should be brought into line. It was equally unemphatic when it returned to the issue on 21st May. The publication of Field Marshal Alexander's message comparing Tito's actions to those of Hitler, Mussolini and Japan had brought the crisis back into the headlines. The facts of the case would, *The Times* suggested, 'indicate to Marshal Tito the need for a compromise acceptable to the British commanders.'

The *New Statesman* had opened its pages on 19th May to the Italian writer Gaetano Salvemini. He had said, 'this is a small problem, but it is the test case of the method by which larger analagous difficulties will be calmed – or envenomed, and World War Three made unavoidable within the next few years.' He advocated intenationalisation of the port of Trieste, even though he was 'pretty sure arbitration would give Trieste and Western Istria to Italy'. In its editorials the *New Statesman* saw no contradiction between speaking censoriously on 19th May of 'de facto settlements with no sanction behind them save that of armed force, and no justification even in inter-Allied agreement', and on 26th May declaring indignantly that it was 'neither wise nor fair of Field Marshal Alexander to accuse the Yugoslavs of aping the totalitarian tactics of Hitler. The real and sufficiently damaging comparison is with the Italians at Fiume and the Poles at Vilna after the last war'. But there was no real heat in the controversy. With the war against Japan to wage, with the General Election campaign already under way in Britain, Trieste was an issue which clearly did not engage the passions of editors or leader writers.

Only in *The Times* letter column did real emotion intrude into this skimpy debate. On 23rd May a letter appeared, tucked away at the very bottom of the page, signed by 'A British soldier lately in Yugoslavia'. It contained a forcible denunciation of Tito.

> If when the truth is published, it is revealed that the regime of Marshal Tito has all the characteristics of Nazism – a secret political police, unscrupulous propaganda bureaux, judicial murder of political opponents, the regimentation of children into fanatical, hero-worshipping gangs, the arrests and disappearance of civilians for no other reason than that they spoke English . . . if these things are true, the nation will see where its duty lies towards people threatened with an extension of this regime.

This, the key sentence of the letter, ran in all to 274 words. The author, as he was himself to reveal later, was Evelyn Waugh, who had been a British liaison officer with the partisans in Croatia in 1944. This brought a riposte three days later from 'Another British Officer from Yugoslavia' – whom Waugh identified as Brigadier Fitzroy Maclean, who had played a decisive part, as head of the British Mission to the partisans, in swinging British support to Tito. He castigated the earlier letter as a 'disturbing example of the way prejudice is formed, when half knowledge is disguised as expert knowledge.' It was true that 'political opponents' have been executed, but 'it would be interesting to know on what evidence these are described as "judicial murders. That those who have intrigued with the enemy should be punished has long been a recognised principle of the United Nations'.

This brought 'A British soldier' back into the controversy a week later. 'I made no claim to expert knowledge of the Balkans,' Waugh's second letter said.

> What I said was that Marshal Tito's record in Croatia – the only area where he had ruled any considerable number of Catholics for any considerable time – was beastly.
>
> I wish I could share 'Another Officer's' hope that the federal autonomy promised to Slovenia will preserve the Church there. I believe those federal units will have as much autonomy as the States

of the USSR; that the OZNA and the Communist Party will continue to transcend these frontiers; that in whatever territory the forces of the Marshal emerge the future of the Church is precarious and, humanly speaking, hopeless.

This debate was, however, too late to affect policy either way. Six days after Evelyn Waugh's second letter the agreement in Belgrade was signed.

The Belgrade Agreement provided that the Yugoslav troops should retire to the Morgan Line by 12th June. The New Zealand War History noted that the Yugoslavs

> did not go empty handed. They stripped machinery and accessories from garages, and emptied some barracks, hotels and houses of their contents; the amount of loot seemed to be limited only by the paucity of transport. By the morning of 11th June 16,000 troops on foot, 400 vehicles, 28 guns and over 1,000 horses were seen straggling along the roads from Trieste to Fiume; the roads eastwards from the Isonza also carried much horse-drawn, motor and foot traffic. The retreating Yugoslavs seemed to be angry and humiliated.[1]

By 12th June the exodus was virtually complete, and the Yugoslav control of Trieste and Western Venezia Giulia was at an end. The crowds surged into the streets, shouting '*Viva Italia*'. The Allied Military Government moved in and established its administration. There was a period of trouble with the pro-Yugoslav People's Militia, the *Guardia del Popolo*, who still retained arms. They continued to make arrests, to intimidate people going to the new AMG offices, and to tear down Italian flags. But this ceased when the Militia were paraded, ordered to hand over their arms, and disbanded. By the end of June Allied control over the whole area up to the Morgan Line was complete, and strong forces were now in position all along the line itself.

The Belgrade Agreement, like so many other temporary agreements for the administration of post-war Europe, was to prove durable. It settled the long term fate of Trieste, Gorizia and Monfalcone. Though nine more years of pressure and argument and wrangling, of border incidents and of internal strife lay ahead, these three cities, the heartlands of Western Venezia Giulia, were ultimately to go to Italy. Pola was to go to Yugoslavia, and to be marked on the post-war maps and the tourist brochures by its Yugoslav spelling of Pula.

The settlement of the final frontiers of Venezia Giulia went through two main stages. Under the 1947 Treaty of Peace with Italy, Gorizia and Monfalcone went to Italy. Trieste city and the coastal strip between it and the Isonzo, and the area for some twenty miles to the south towards Pola, became an independent Free Territory under the aegis of the United Nations. This remained for eight years an area of contention, with the Western Allies and Italy ranged against the Soviet Union and Yugoslavia. The United Nations were not even able to agree upon the appointment of a Governor. It was clear that the Free Territory idea was not going to work. In 1954 Marshal Tito, no longer having Soviet support and eager to establish friendlier ties with the West, agreed to a new frontier. Trieste city, and the coastal strip westwards to the Isonzo, became Italian soil. The coastal and hill areas to the south went to Yugoslavia. Trieste at long last slipped out of the headlines and off the conference agenda.

The new frontier, drawn after so much hard negotiation, and after the seismic international pressures applied by the opposing Great Powers, conformed very closely to the forward lines on which the 2nd New Zealand Division had halted on 2nd and 3rd May 1945. The border line of today was by and large drawn by the infantry and the tanks of the 9th New Zealand Brigade and British 12th Lancers.

In all the lives of no more than a quarter of million Italians, and some tens of thousands of Slovenes had been directly affected by this fact; no more than a crinkle in the European post-war frontiers had been involved. Yet the long term effects of that eleventh hour dash of the 2nd New Zealand Division from the Piave to Trieste have been considerable. Our arrival in the city at effectively the same time as Tito's troops had not only precipitated the first crisis of the post-war period, but had provided the first great test in office of the new President, Harry S. Truman. Inexperienced in foreign affairs, having had little contact with Churchill and none at all with Stalin, he had met that test head on – and with success. He had discovered within himself, and displayed to the world, a capacity for swift courageous decision at the highest level of power, where the options were formidable and perilous.

When Truman had come to office three weeks earlier the other great immediate problem – the virtual seizure of Poland for the Communists by the Russians – had gone beyond recall. It was too big and too intractable for any other outcome than a Soviet victory. But Trieste was more manageable, and the President had managed it with both nerve and skill. His initial decision, at the White House on 11th May, had run counter to powerful trends within the American body politic; against

the Pacific Firsters; against those who distrusted Churchill as being liable
to involve America in new commitments in Europe, and in perhaps
unnecessary conflicts with 'Uncle Joe'; against those who were positively
pro-Soviet.

The President had indeed shown himself firm, not only against the
Russians, but against the more risky urgings of Churchill. He had played
his hand coolly, and had won. This experience must have not only
reinforced his personal confidence, but also have left him with the firm
belief that it was possible to stand up to the Russians and their allies
without precipitating war. The lesson of Trieste would surely have
reinforced his will when he took in 1946 the further, even greater, risk
of insisting that the Russians evacuate northern Persia. It was part of
the experience he brought to bear when, late in the same year, he
assumed the burden of supporting the anti-Communist Government in
Greece when Britain could no longer sustain the role – the first step
in the Truman doctrine of resisting Soviet expansion. It was experience
he could draw on during the Berlin blockade. It was available to prompt
him to his swift decision to send troops to support South Korea in 1950.
Trieste had indeed proved a testing ground for many crises to come.

In his swift, laconic way Harry S. Truman had dealt with the Trieste
crisis as if it was just one more irritating problem to be assessed quickly,
decided quickly, and set aside as one turned to the next issue. His success
had shown him, however, that this was a manner and method of
diplomacy which fitted his role, and his nation's role, at this new stage
in its history. In this battle of wills, and of nerves, Truman had tested
himself against the giants of the day. He had found he could match, and
indeed master them. Other crises, other confrontations would no doubt
have provided him with this experience in due course, had Trieste not
been cast for the first battleground of the Cold War. But chance had
selected it for that role, even though we had had little inkling of
anything of the kind as our armoured cars raced forward on that grey
spring afternoon towards the bridge over the Isonzo.

Acknowledgements

Acknowledgements

I wish to thank the authorities of the Public Record Office in London for access to their excellently catalogued records; to the New Zealand Government for permission to quote from their official War History; and to the Department of Printed Books at the Imperial War Museum.

Mr Mark Wheeler of the Department of Central and South-Eastern European Studies at the University of Lancaster gave me valuable help not only by guiding me through the first phases of the official Yugoslav War Records, but by the stimulus of his own lively and perceptive interest in the period. Mr Ian Leeke of the same Department provided an admirable translation of the Yugoslav War History, a translation typed with impressive clarity by his mother, despite the complications of Serbo-Croat accentuation. The relevant volume of the work of the Vojno-istoriski Institut in Belgrade – Zavrsne Operacije za Oslobodjenje Jugoslavije 1944-45 – provided an excellently clear and detailed record of events from the Yugoslav point of view. My thanks also to Malcolm Beatson and Peter Atkinson, whose design of the maps reflects the high quality of their television work for ITN.

Among others to whom I owe particular thanks are Count Alvise Savorgnan di Brazzà, for helping me to set our common experiences in 1945 against the perspective of the Italian Partisan Movement in general; to Lieut-Colonel P. Pavasovic, of the Royal Yugoslav Combatants Association, for information about the fate of the Chetnik forces who surrendered in Northern Italy; and to Sara Ricketts, who once again demonstrated her skill and patience in turning my handwriting into typescript.

Source Notes

Source Notes

Transcripts of Crown-copyright records in the Public Record Office appear by permission of the Controller of H.M. Stationery Office. The prefix 'Prem' indicates records of the Prime Minister's office.

I have used the Italian names and spelling for those places which, since the 1954 settlement, have been incorporated into Italy, and the Yugoslav names and spellings for those which have become part of Yugoslavia. I have taken the liberty of slightly anglicising Yugoslav names by omitting accentuation marks in both the text and on the maps.

Chapter I – The Goal

1. Official History of New Zealand in the Second World War. Italy. Vol II, Wellington 1967, p 537.
2. Churchill – Second World War. Vol VI. Cassell and Comp. pp 88-91.
3. Alexander's notes, quoted by Nigel Nicholson in Alex, Weidenfeld and Nicholson 1973, p 279.
4. Prem 3; 495/5.
5. Prem 3; 495/5.
6. NAF 872 (Prem 3/513/9).
7. Prem 3; 495/5.
8. Prem 3; 495/5.

Chapter III – Planning for Battle

1. Report by Field Marshal the Viscount Alexander of Tunis to Combined Chiefs of Staff (HMSO 1951).
2. Churchill, op. cit. p 461.

Chapter VII – Breakthrough

1. New Zealand War History, op. cit. passim.

Chapter VIII – Partisans

1. War Diary, German Fourteenth Army.

Chapter XI – 'Avoid Conflict in the Balkan Area'

1. Prem 3/495/6 – Minute PM/05/45/36.
2. Prem 3/495/6.
3. Prem 3/495/6 – Tel 662/5.
4. Prem 3/495/6. T.685/5.
5. Harry S. Truman. Year of Decisions, Hodder and Stoughton 1955, p 164.
6. Prem 3/495/6. T.703/5.

Chapter XII – To the Isonzo

1. Trieste 1941-54. Bogdan C. Novah, University of Chicago 1970.

Chapter XIII – The Other Side of the Hill

1. Zavrsne Operacije za Oslobodjenje Jugoslavije 1944-45 (The Trial Operations for the Liberation of Yugoslavia, 1944-45) Belgrade 1957.
2. Djilas. Conversations with Stalin, 1972.

Chapter XIV – Photofinish

1. New Zealand War History, op. cit. p 543.
2. New Zealand War History, op. cit. p 545.
3. Prem 3/495/6.
4. Prem 3/495/6.
5. Prem 3/495/6 NAF 946.
6. Prem 3/495/6.
7. Prem 3/495/6 Tel Guard 2765.
8. Prem 3/495/6 Tel MA 1091.
9. Prem 3/495/6.
10. Prem 3/495/6.
11. Deakin. The Embattled Mountain, Oxford University Press.

Chapter XV – Confrontation

1. Bullen. History of 2/7 Bn Queen's Royal Regt.
2. Information from Lieut-Colonel P. Pavasovic.
3. Nicholas Bethell. The Last Secret, p 85, Andre Deutsch.
4. Novah, op. cit. p 151.

Chapter XVI – An Integral Part of Yugoslavia

1. Prem 3/495/6.
2. Novak. op. cit. pp 168-194.
3. Novak. op. cit. p 180.

Chapter XVII – Mutual Siege

1. Prem 3/495/6.
2. Prem 3/495/6.
3. Prem 3/495/7.
4. Prem 3/495/6.
5. Prem 3/495/7.
6. Churchill. op. cit. p 498.
7. Truman. op. cit.
8. Prem 3/495/7.
9. Alex by Nigel Nicholson, Weidenfeld and Nicholson 1973, p 279.
10. Prem 3/495/6.
11. Prem 3/495/7.
12. Truman. op. cit. p 165.
13. Churchill. op. cit. p 485.
14. Churchill. op. cit. p 458.
15. Prem 3/495/9.
16. Prem 3/495/9.
17. Prem 3/495/7 – NAF 960.
18. Prem 3/495/9. Tel Guard 15 May.
19. Prem 3/495/9. T.940/5.

Chapter XVIII – Reminiscent of Hitler, Mussolini and Japan

1. Prem 3/495/9.
2. Prem 3/495/9.
3. Truman. op. cit. p 168.
4. Calculated Risk – General Mark Clark p 419, Harrap.
5. Prem 3/495/9.

Chapter XIX – A Victory and a Precedent

1. New Zealand War History. op. cit. p 565.

Index

Index

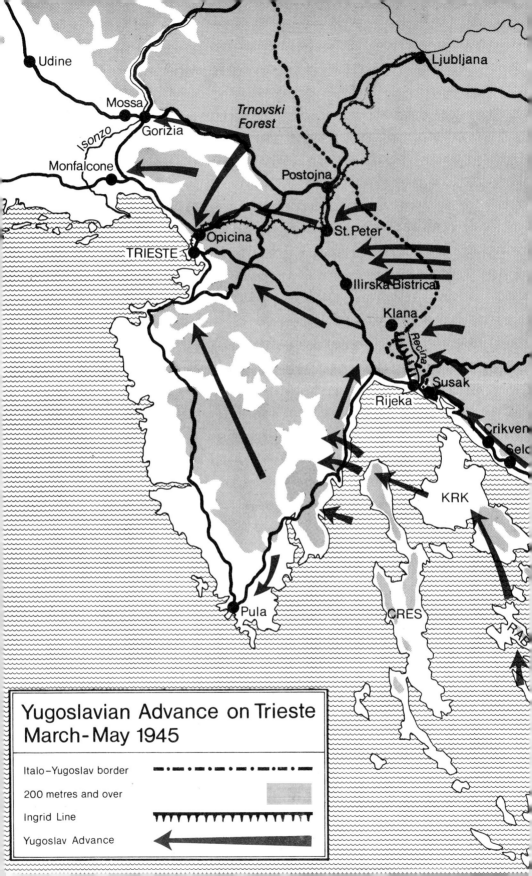

Udine

Mossa
Isonzo
Gorizia
Monfalcone

*Trnovski
Forest*

Postojna

Ljubljana

Opicina

St. Peter

TRIESTE

Ilirska Bistrica

Klana

Rečina

Susak

Rijeka

Crikven
Selo

KRK

Pula

CRES

RAB

Yugoslavian Advance on Trieste
March–May 1945

Italo–Yugoslav border	—·—·—·—·—·—
200 metres and over	
Ingrid Line	⊥⊥⊥⊥⊥⊥⊥⊥⊥
Yugoslav Advance	⬅